1916

WHAT THE PEOPLE SAW

1916

WHAT THE PEOPLE SAW

SELECTED AND EDITED BY
MICK O'FARRELL

MERCIER PRESS

IRISH PUBLISHER – IRISH STORY

*Dedicated to the civilians who lost their lives during
Ireland's Easter Rising, 1916*

MERCIER PRESS
Cork
www.mercierpress.ie

© Mick O'Farrell, 2013

ISBN: 978 1 78117 150 9

10 9 8 7 6 5 4 3 2 1

A CIP record for this title is available from the British Library

Printed and bound in the EU.

CONTENTS

ACKNOWLEDGEMENTS

Many thanks to the following for helping with material, allowing reproduction, or offering suggestions: Sandra McDermott (NLI); Sigrid Pohl Perry and Scott Krafft (Northwestern University Library); Miriam Walton and Mike MacCarthy Morrogh (Shrewsbury School); Jo Evans (The Institute of Telecommunications Professionals); Dessie Blackadder (*Ballymena Times* and *Observer*); Ursula Byrne (UCD Library); Brendan Delany (ESB); Virginia Brownlow and Josephine Slater; Angela Moore-Swafford (Southern Illinois University Press); Dr Máire Kennedy (Dublin City Public Libraries); Samantha Holman (Irish Copyright Licensing Agency); Helen Wright (Blackstaff Press); Sarah McMahon (Random House).

Thanks also to Derek Jones, and to Mary Feehan and the team at Mercier Press.

Special thanks to Ursula O'Farrell and Denis O'Farrell.

And most especially, thanks and more to my family – L & L to Amanda, Eve and Conor, for early mornings and late nights.

Note:

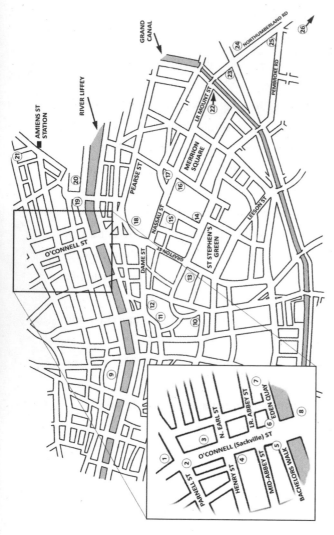

GRAND CANAL

RIVER LIFFEY

AMIENS ST STATION

O'CONNELL ST

NORTHUMBERLAND RD

PEMBROKE RD

LR. MOUNT ST

PEARSE ST

MERRION SQUARE

NASSAU ST

LEESON ST

ST STEPHEN'S GREEN

GRAFTON ST

DAME ST

O'CONNELL (Sackville) ST

PARNELL ST

N. EARL ST

LR. ABBEY ST

EDEN QUAY

HENRY ST

MID-ABBEY ST

BACHELORS WALK

1. 5 CAVENDISH ROW - JOSEPH HOLLOWAY

2. PARNELL MONUMENT

3. GRANVILLE HOTEL - BAB M'KEEN

4. GENERAL POST OFFICE - GPO

5. KELLY'S GUNPOWDER OFFICE

6. HOPKINS & HOPKINS

7. EDEN QUAY - EUSTACE MALCOLM

8. BURGH QUAY CORNER - IRISH LIFE CIVILIAN

9. FOUR COURTS

10. JACOB'S FACTORY

11. DUBLIN CASTLE

12. CITY HALL

13. ROYAL COLLEGE OF SURGEONS

14. SHELBOURNE HOTEL

15. KILWORTH HOUSE HOTEL - ROBERT LE CREN

16. 90 MERRION SQUARE - LADY CHANCE

17. CLARE STREET - MICHAEL O'BEIRNE

18. TRINITY COLLEGE DUBLIN

19. LIBERTY HALL

20. CUSTOM HOUSE

21. 8 KILLARNEY AVENUE - BELLA GLOECHLER

22. MOUNT STREET BRIDGE

23. 25 NORTHUMBERLAND RD

24. 32 NORTHUMBERLAND RD - ISABEL FLEMING

25. LANE-JOYNT HOUSE

25. HERBERT PARK ROAD - MARGARET MITCHELL

(GUIDE ONLY - MAP NOT TO SCALE)

8

THE EASTER RISING, DAY BY DAY

Apart from some small actions, the 1916 Rising lasted seven days, from Easter Monday to the following Sunday.

Easter Monday, 24 April 1916:
Beginning of rebellion. Main body of rebels muster outside Liberty Hall – conflicting orders result in a turnout much smaller than hoped for. From about midday on, the following locations are occupied by rebels:

- GPO and other buildings in O'Connell Street area;
- Four Courts, Mendicity Institution;
- St Stephen's Green, College of Surgeons;
- Boland's Mills and surrounding area, including Mount Street Bridge and nearby houses;
- City Hall and several buildings overlooking Dublin Castle;
- Jacob's biscuit factory, Davy's pub by Portobello Bridge;
- South Dublin Union and James's Street area;
- Magazine Fort in Phoenix Park.

Proclamation of Republic read by Pearse outside GPO. Lancers charge down O'Connell Street. Looting starts. That afternoon the British counterattacks begin.

Tuesday, 25 April 1916:

City Hall retaken by military. Shelbourne Hotel occupied by soldiers and machine-gun fire forces rebels to retreat from St Stephen's Green to the College of Surgeons. British reinforcements, including artillery, arrive. Martial Law proclaimed.

Wednesday, 26 April 1916:

Liberty Hall shelled by *Helga*, backed by field guns. Artillery put into action against buildings on O'Connell Street. Kelly's Fort evacuated. Metropole Hotel occupied by rebels. Troops marching from Dun Laoghaire halted by rebels at Mount Street Bridge. After many hours of intense fighting and terrible casualties, the military gain control of the area. Clanwilliam House burns to the ground. Mendicity Institution retaken by the British.

Thursday, 27 April 1916:

Military shelling of O'Connell Street intensifies. Fires on O'Connell Street begin to rage out of control. Hopkins & Hopkins and Imperial Hotel evacuated because of the inferno.

Friday, 28 April 1916:

General Sir John Maxwell arrives in Dublin. Metropole Hotel evacuated. Rebels evacuate GPO. New HQ established in Moore Street.

Saturday, 29 April 1916:

Non-combatants murdered in North King Street. Rebel leaders in Moore Street decide to surrender. Four Courts garrison surrenders.

Sunday, 30 April 1916:
Rebels in remaining outposts surrender – College of Surgeons, Boland's, Jacob's and the South Dublin Union. Deportation of prisoners.

Wednesday, 3 May – Friday, 12 May:
Fifteen rebels, including the seven signatories of the Proclamation of the Republic, are executed by firing squad.

INTRODUCTION

PREVENTION OF EPIDEMIC

Persons discovering dead bodies should inform the Police or
the Chief Medical Officer of Health, Municipal Buildings,
Castle Street, immediately.[1]

When wars and conflicts are studied, the usual method is to
divide the participants into friend and enemy, us and them; and
in the case of Ireland, the rebels and the British. But sometimes
the more interesting division is into combatants and non-
combatants, armed and unarmed – those who were doing the
actual fighting and those who were just caught up in it.

When the rebellion of 1916 had ended, more than 400
people were dead and over 2,000 wounded. More than half
of these were civilians, and while it could be argued that the
casualties among the rebels were in control of their own destiny
and that those on the side of the authorities were at least doing
their duty, the stark fact is that the destiny of the civilian
casualties was out of their hands. They were in their homes or
travelling to work or shopping. Some, of course, were simply
fatally curious.

Many books have been written on the history of the Rising
– who did what, where it was done, why they did it, what
the outcome was. While these usually address the civilians'
predicament to some degree, in general they are written from

a factual point of view – how many were killed, who the looters were, etc. Apart from the effect the rebellion had on the unfortunate civilian casualties, few, if any, histories examine what effect it had on the general population.

In recent years the Bureau of Military History has made many hundreds of witness statements relating to the Rising freely available on the Internet. However, while these histories are important, and indeed fascinating, they are largely confined to participants and concern *military* history. So, are there statements from civilian eyewitnesses about the week of rebellion in 1916?

Thankfully the answer is yes, although not in as official a capacity as the Bureau of Military History's collection. Many people at the time had an acute awareness of the fact that history was being made before their eyes and that present and future generations would want to know about it. So they wrote diaries or sent letters, some of which still survive. Some witnesses wrote memoirs or an autobiography in later years and included a chapter on the Rising and how it affected them. In other cases, newspaper or magazine editors with an eye for the human story published contributions from civilians who were directly affected.

This anthology is an attempt to bring together a number of these civilian accounts of the rebellion in 1916, to give the reader the non-combatants' unedited point of view. Many of these accounts have never been published before and others, although having appeared in print, have languished for decades between the covers of long-defunct magazines or as minor chapters in otherwise obscure memoirs.[2]

In compiling the collection, I've been very aware that the vast majority of affected civilians would have had no opportunity, and even no ability, to keep a record of events, so I've tried to include as broad a range of contributions as possible – from the letter telling a mother that her daughter was shot dead, to the report by a Post Office engineer on the difficulties faced by GPO staff; from the six-year-old who was forbidden entry to Stephen's Green, to the last Lord Chancellor of Ireland, who managed to continue reading Plutarch, 'notwithstanding the sound of machine-guns and cannon'. Despite their different social standings, the writers quoted in this book were all civilians, for whom the rebels' charge on the GPO heralded a week unlike any other they'd ever experienced, filled with events beyond their control.

Some common themes are present in the accounts. For instance, a fear of going hungry, which resulted in constant, and dangerous, attempts to stock up with supplies. There was also a grim understanding of what the rest of Europe had been experiencing over the previous two years: 'We know a bit what War is like now.' For some, there was even an undeniable element of excitement – one witness writes: 'now that it's over, none of us would've missed it for the world.' After watching a woman shot in the street, another witness notes that he 'saw a man rush out and take a snapshot'. Elsewhere, there were 'crowds looking on as if at a sham battle'. For most, however, it was the kind of excitement they could have done without: 'Our world of security and unchanging values had been burnt to ashes,' remembers one man, while another writes of 'the sickening sight of corpses littering the streets'.

Many of the incidents mentioned in the accounts may already be familiar to those who have read histories of the

Rising; however, while eyewitness accounts can sometimes conflict with known facts, the fascinating thing about them is the personal point of view, the human detail, the emotion, which is absent from official or academic histories. So if you want some understanding of these events as they were experienced by the people of the time, then you'll find it in details such as the number of typing errors on Sheehy-Skeffington's manifesto, or in the description of the Proclamation by one who had just read it as 'a long and floridly worded document full of high hopes', or in gruesome descriptions of sights such as the girl found 'leaning on the window with the top half of her head hanging off'.

For Ireland the Easter Rising was probably the most momentous event of the twentieth century – on an individual level it was also probably the most momentous event in the lives of any of its citizens who experienced it. And although opinions changed over the years for many people, the fact is that, at the time, the Easter Rising was disastrous for the civilian non-combatants, as can be seen in these accounts. Of course, for many citizens it was fatal, and the hundreds of civilian dead included very old and very young, men and women, boys and girls. One witness remarked: 'It was very melancholy living in Glasnevin in those days immediately after the Rising as funeral corteges followed one another in quick succession.'

Eventually this devastating effect on the civilian population of Dublin could no longer go unnoticed by the combatants, and when the rebellion finally ended, P. H. Pearse's notice of surrender tellingly began: 'In order to prevent any further slaughter of Dublin citizens …'

'THE STREETS ARE NOT EXACTLY HEALTH RESORTS'

Robert Cecil Le Cren was an insurance official, aged about thirty-eight at the time of the Rising. He wrote this account of events from the Kilworth House Hotel, an establishment with frontages onto both Kildare and Molesworth Streets.[1]

Kilworth Hotel
26/4/16
(Wednesday)

Dear Girls

I may as well begin a letter tho' of course I don't know when it will be collected.

We have been in a state of siege since Monday but the arrival of three troop ships today should relieve the situation very soon. The Sinn Feiners (pronounced Shin Fainers) suddenly mobilised on Monday morning, occupied the railway termini, the GPO & entrenched themselves in Stephen's Green – at the top of Kildare St. They also invested the Castle & one or two of the barracks by occupying the surrounding houses & sniping from the windows & roofs. The telegraph & postal system is entirely suspended & we have no news of the outside world. I have had no sleep for 3 days & 2 nights as firing is going on all over the city & bullets are hopping about outside the house & machine guns are rattling from the roofs of buildings.

I ventured out this morning soon after dawn as it was believed the Green was cleared but the sickening sight of corpses littering the streets soon sent me home.

They have practically surrounded the Green now & occupied various houses. This afternoon we witnessed from a side street a pitched battle where the troops – English lads just landed, were endeavouring to drive them out. The soldiers were dropping like flies & the Red + were bringing out a constant stream of dead & wounded. It was dreadful to think of the poor fellows enlisting to fight Germans & being murdered by ruffians over here.

In some places the rebels have a whole terrace of houses – communicating by holes knocked through the walls & when the troops advance to bomb the buildings they are fired on from unsuspected houses at the side & rear.

Not a policeman has been seen since Monday & looting is rife – whole streets of shops ransacked without any restraint.

Thursday

Last night was quieter & we all went to bed. Heavy guns have been brought up at last & I believe the troops are shelling the GPO & a large factory.

Reynolds came over last Thursday & I dined with him & his wife on Sunday evening at the Shelbourne Hotel in Stephen's Green. He intended crossing on Monday night but they are presumably still in the hotel which is occupied by the troops & barricaded.

There has been a great fight around the Castle – about

200 casualties & the Sinn Feiners are now evicted from the neighbourhood.

There are all sorts of rumours about the rebellion in the provinces but an RIC official assured me that all was quiet except in Galway – although they let loose the Germans interned at Tullamore!

The city is under martial law & the latest proclamation is to the effect that anyone seen out of doors after dark will be shot at sight. The hospitals are all full & private houses are being commandeered for the wounded.

I hear the German submarine & the vessel flying the Norwegian flag which landed machine guns & ammunition on the Kerry coast were both sunk by a British destroyer.

A man here is going to try to get out of the city & I'm giving him this to post.

Bob.

Thursday evening

Our friend has come back having been unable to get away.

It is now impossible to cross the town. Our neighbourhood is quieter & the principal fighting appears to be in Sackville St in which the GPO is situated.

Half the street is in flames – an extraordinary spectacle.

From one of their strongholds the Sinn Feiners telephoned to an adjoining hospital to know if the latter could take in 200 of their wounded!

The St John's Ambulance men are going round requisitioning bedding for the emergency hospitals.

This moment the maxims at the top of the street are going off at a fearful rate.

It's reported that Asquith stated in the House that the PO was retaken – this is certainly not true yet, but now there are 20,000 troops in the town & armoured motor cars constructed out of Guinness motor lorries it shouldn't be long.

Friday morning
The 5th day of the battle of Dublin & Reign of Terror.

Firing never ceases. Last night about 10 p.m. we were ordered to extinguish every light in the house under pain of being fired on, so everyone had to grope their way to bed in the dark – no easy matter in this rabbit warren.

The looting of shops proceeds merrily but many people are starving & bread is being distributed by the military.

We are getting a limited dietary – no groceries – such as sugar – & no fruit being procurable.

Noon
It is reported that the GPO is really retaken now. More troops & heavy artillery have arrived from France. Howitzers will be placed in the mountains to shell Jacobs biscuit factory, a stronghold the military have not yet been able to approach as every house in the vicinity is a sort of Sidney Street episode.[2]

I have just given a card addressed to you to a man who hopes to post same at Kingstown from where it may be sent to England by gunboat.

Friday night
This afternoon was comparatively quiet & we sunned ourselves on the Molesworth St frontage but now firing is heavy & the conflagration is reaching terrible proportions – about four

square miles containing some of the largest shops & hotels.

At lunch & dinner today we had rations of two biscuits each in lieu of bread & Mrs S says she cannot feed us after Sunday.[3]

Visitors trapped here are in a desperate frame of mind as they [are] unable to communicate with their friends & relatives in the provinces.

Some people motored in from Belfast with the intention of spending Monday night only in Dublin & are now seeking a passport to get into the suburbs with a view to walking about forty miles to the nearest town north.

One inconvenience arising out of the rebellion is the absence of the laundry!

Saturday

If it were not for this 'diary of the war' I should have no idea of the day of the week. This is the ninth day of 'holidays' & sixth of 'war'.

Troops continue to pour in. They have passed without intermission along the other end of the street for hours this morning – artillery, field kitchens, etc., all complete.

An English newspaper of yesterday has been seen. Kut we hear has fallen[4] & Asquith has referred to 'slight disturbances in Dublin'.

Cold ham & biscuits for breakfast this morning, ditto for lunch, plus potatoes.

Sat. 5 p.m.

Great news – the main bodies of SFs have surrendered. I have been up to the Shelbourne & spoken thro' a window to Mr & Mrs Reynolds who are alive & well after six days immersed.

Odd snipers are still at work & the streets are not exactly health resorts. The main streets are still patrolled by soldiers & civilians are not allowed to pass.

It has been a most astonishing business & extraordinary rumours are afloat. Nineteen German transports are said to have been sunk & I believe it is a fact that German & Austrian officers are among the prisoners taken in Dublin.

A machine gun is still rattling two blocks away as I write & I expect desultory fighting with parties of 'no surrenders' and isolated snipers will continue for some days. However I hope tomorrow we shall be allowed a larger orbit of perambulation & that letters & papers will arrive once more.

There is no use in posting this letter tonight so I will keep it open till tomorrow.

Sunday evening

There is still desultory firing. The 'garrison' of the College of Surgeons near here surrendered this morning & I saw them being marched off to prison. There were 110 of them – a scratch-looking lot with only a dozen uniforms between them. At the head of the column marched Countess Markievitch [*sic*] (an Irishwoman) in male uniform – such a scarecrow. As she is an arch conspirator & socialist, an abetter of Larkin the strike manager, it is to be hoped she will be shot.

A few English papers were in today – selling at 1/- each & you may be sure they are eagerly sought after – the first news for a week.

This morning we were regaled with home-made scones but as they were rather more deadly than the dum-dum bullets used by the rebels, I contented myself with biscuits for my cold ham.

The bakeries are opening this evening however so we may get some bread once more.

It is very doubtful if business will be resumed tomorrow or even for some days. This has been an eventful week in my life.

It is quite strange to hear children playing again in the street outside.

Monday (1 May)

Except in one fairly remote part of the City there is only an occasional exchange of shots between soldiers & snipers, & the public were for the first time for five days allowed to go through the main thoroughfares. Sackville St – or rather the site of – was an appalling sight. Large hotels, churches, theatre, picture palaces, banks & printers' offices also & nearly 200 shops (173 I see in the official estimate) entirely destroyed.

Several side streets were also burnt out & the scene is just acres of ruins with a few shells of buildings standing here & there.

Apart from all this several houses are battered by artillery & hundreds of innocent people burnt to death or shot. Imagine the raging inferno & no assistance for the helpless people trapped.

If they escaped into the Attic it was only to face a hail of bullets or to be crushed by the falling masonry.

There were at least 500 casualties among the troops & there must have been as many Sinn Feiners & civilians killed & wounded.

I went round to Reynolds' hotel to get him to despatch telegrams from England but found he had left early this morning having got a passport & proceeded to Kingstown by road where he probably found a steamer for Holyhead.

It is said the Banks will open tomorrow – I hope so, as no one has any money & I shall open the office in case any of the clerks turn up.

Wednesday 3/5/16 (at office)

Nothing happened yesterday. We were allowed to walk freely within the City but communication with the suburbs is difficult & none of my clerks have turned up. As there is no postal service yet there is no work to be done & the shops are not reopened. By tomorrow, business will have been suspended just a fortnight.

Keep the diary for me. Love to all. Bob

'AS HE LAY ON HIS BACK
HE SPOUTED BLOOD LIKE A
FOUNTAIN'

Shrewsbury School in Shropshire, England, has an impressive list of famous past pupils; among them is the author Nevil Shute, or, to give his full name, Nevil Shute Norway, son of Arthur Hamilton Norway, head of the post office in Ireland in 1916. When the rebellion began, the then seventeen-year-old Nevil was on holidays in Dublin, and got involved as a volunteer stretcher-bearer, a position which put the youth in many dangerous situations and afforded him some gruesome experiences. The following article appeared shortly after the Rising in The Salopian *(Shrewsbury School magazine) – it's unattributed, but was clearly written by Nevil Shute.*[1]

Before setting out to comply with the request of the editors to send them an article on the rebellion in Ireland it is essential to say a few introductory words. Such an article is in the circumstances bound to be based largely on personal experiences and it is an extraordinarily difficult and endless task to decide which of the thousands of different and, in a great many cases contradictory, rumours are to contribute to the material of such an essay.

The class of the rebels varied between poets and cornerboys, but the vast majority of the men were men who were in government pay or other good positions. This may perhaps make it easier to understand why the rebellion was so formidable while it lasted. It was not numbers, which could not have exceeded 4,000 men, that produced the stubborn resistance, but the fact that all the principal buildings throughout the town were betrayed by their own inmates into the hands of the rebels. To some it may seem extraordinary that the insurrection was so formidable for a week and then came to a sudden collapse. The reason for this was that against the rebels in their strongholds rifles were no use, and even machine guns were very little use. It naturally took some days to get artillery over from Liverpool or up from Athlone, and this only arrived towards the end of the week. It was after a short taste of big guns that the rebel leaders realised that all was up and that they had been out-trumped.

During the first few days, life in Dublin was one of the most striking sights I have ever seen. Up till the middle of the first week the population were allowed about without passports and the oblivion which seemed to reign in one street when men were being picked off every five minutes in the next street was extraordinary. A great many people were sucked as it were by a whirl-pool into places of extreme danger by an indomitable spirit of curiosity and excitement. Except for the fact that they had to convey their own food home in baskets or other receptacles, house-keepers were behaving as though nothing had happened. Old ladies were exercising their dogs in the squares on which they lived, blind men were being led about for their daily walks, street Arabs were playing marbles on the pavements, steam-rollers were still to be seen at work. The only uncommon sight was that there were no wheeled vehicles about; the familiar sound of the electric trams was conspicuous by its absence. It is perhaps slightly incorrect to say no wheeled vehicles; there were motor ambulances, milk-carts and bread-carts but no others, barring a few bicycles. It almost transformed the city streets into suburban terraces to see one's neighbours all on their doorsteps in deck-chairs doing needlework, smoking and interchanging rumours. Some of these rumours were of course true, but it is beyond doubt that a very great many were false. For example it was believed in a country town, about 11 miles south of Dublin, that a whale had escaped from the Dublin Zoological Gardens, had swum down the River Liffey and was devouring the inhabitants of the city.

During the first half of Easter week one might see bread-carts and milk-carts, standing in the road with a crowd of hungry urchins and mothers all round them waving pennies and sixpences at the miserable drivers. I once saw no less than 8 bread-carts and three milk-carts at the same time in one street barely 150 yards long. After the barricades had been put up however the poor could no longer do this and excellent photographs were afforded of crowds of poor people behind barricades waving jugs and money at the soldiers who had commandeered the carts and were serving the sufferers across an excellent counter of sandbags and kitchen tables and sofas.

Such as these were the common sights in the quieter side of civil life, but it must not be forgotten that all this time there was the danger of being hit by a stray bullet or a ricochet, though only in some cases by a direct hit. It is with this subject that the remainder of this article must deal.

Two remarks I should like to make before starting this second half of my narrative. Firstly, I am writing everything exactly as I saw it or heard of it and I am giving the editor a free hand with anything that may be too morbid, so that with him the blame for such must lie. Secondly if such experiences seem tame or pointless it will be because they have been censored as giving too much information. They are mainly a disconnected collection which I am not attempting to make into a continuous whole.

On Monday afternoon I saw a great friend of my father's drive up to his hall-door in a motor-car. His two sons got out and went indoors and he was about to drive off again when a man came up to him and putting a revolver to his head said, 'I must ask you to step out; we want your car.'

'And who are you, might I ask?'

'I am an officer in the Irish Republican Army.'

My friend refused, and the man pulled the trigger. It was a miss-fire and my friend laid him flat on his back in the road and drove off. The revolver fell open and he had forgotten to load it.

I was going out to buy a sack of flour for a hospital one morning and as I was passing a bridge, I saw a postman being stopped and asked for his passport. He had none. He was suspected and searched. The military found the whole of his coat and waistcoat and other clothes simply padded with ammunition of all sorts. He was shot on the spot.[2]

A friend of mine at another bridge saw a similar scene. A milk-cart driven by two women was driving along towards one of the rebel strongholds. A sergeant-major signalled to it to stop, whereupon the driver stood up and whipped up the horses into a gallop. She whipped the sergeant-major also but he was too late to do anything. An officer then jumped forward and caught the horse by the reins and stopped the cart in spite of a hail of blows from the whip. The men then came to the rescue but not in time to save the officer being stunned. They took down the women who turned out to be men and found the cart full of ammunition. The two were shot there and then.

I witnessed another instance of men disguised as women in a different spot. There was a barricade under fire at the top of one of the streets joining Mount Street, a name that may be familiar. Three women wanted to pass this barricade and were told to do so at the double. They were not so good at disguising themselves as to be able to remember that they were women at a moment of danger. They scuttled past the lane at an unmistakably manly run and their men's clothes underneath were sadly betrayed by the raising of their skirts when they were in a hurry.

A friend of mine was riding his motor-bicycle along one day when it got clogged somewhere. He got off and started settling it and while doing so started to smoke; he also gave a cigarette to a passing Tommy, who was sympathetic. He was then accosted by a man in mufti who asked for a cigarette. He replied that he had not one. Upon this the other man put his hand into his breast pocket and my friend saw a knife appear. When he saw the handle he did not wait for the blade but hopped on his bicycle and rode off. He looked back to see the man holding the dagger open, which had so nearly been the end of him. This story is told more as an example of the way in which the rough element in the city took advantage of the rebellion, (as the police were confined to barracks), than in connection with the actual Sinn Feiners. (Incidentally this name is pronounced Shin Faners, as a good many do not seem to realise.)

So far these incidents have been such as are exclusive of

bloodshed other than bloodshed in execution. There are many more like them which might be told were it not for lack of space. Similarly the following are only a selection from the many instances that might be told of wounded and dead men.

I was standing in a window of our house dressing one morning, and I was looking towards a military barricade at the corner of the square. There were several soldiers passing along behind it, and the word was being passed from one to another to keep low as the barricade was under fire. One poor fellow was just beginning to speak to the man behind when he dropped. A doctor from a house at the corner ran out barefooted with nothing but his trousers and medical coat on and picked the fellow up in his arms, and carried him single-handed to the hospital that was next door. On examination he was found to have been hit between his left eye and the bone just to the left of that. The bullet had gone on in underneath the bone and had come out at his ear which was in ribbons. It was one of the closest shaves I have seen but he is doing well.

A friend of mine was walking along and saw an old man walk out of a lane with a barrow. He had gone very few yards when he was hit in the knee. He sank to the ground and my friend was just endeavouring to pick him up when another bullet went clean through his heart and took off the top of my friend's little finger on the other side.

Another civilian was walking along and came to a military barricade. He was halted but lost his head. He started to turn and run away and, was naturally fired on. He dropped. The stretcher bearers went out and got him in and we took him into the theatre of the hospital. There was only one surgeon present and he was unfortunately not a general practitioner but a nose, throat and ear specialist. He found the man had been hit in three places in the abdomen. It was a horrible sight. As he lay on his back he spouted blood like a fountain. It was an impossible case and the poor fellow died very shortly. Up till the very last he was in agony, calling for his sister and asking to be shot. With the exception of men who had been shot dead this was the most grisly case I saw.

Another poor fellow that we carried in was shot by a sniper. He was walking quietly along in a street hitherto quiet under the impression that there was no danger. A muzzle however pointed out from some area railings and shot him in the ankle. He had to have his foot amputated.

One poor servant girl that had to be seen to, had just opened a top storey window and had barely put her head out when the whole top of her head was taken almost off by what must have been a machine gun or more probably a Lewis gun as the military had more of them and were using them more in the neighbourhood. She was found exactly where she was standing, leaning on the window with the top half of her head hanging off and the window sash besmattered with her brains. Death must have been instantaneous.

Several men were shot dead, and of course had to be brought in whenever an opportunity occurred, but, in as much as the soldiers were sitting on our door-step to fire and to be fired at, it was foolhardy to look after any but the wounded men till after dark, when things grew calmer. And indeed it is only too easy to distinguish between the dead and the wounded. Having once seen death, one would almost prefer to feel it than ever to see it again.

'THE POOR DOG IS NEARLY OUT OF HER MIND'

We can see from the 1911 census that Bella Gloechler was an Englishwoman living in No. 8 Killarney Avenue, near Amiens Street (now Connolly) Railway Station. Her unusual surname came from a marriage in about 1906 to Karl B. Gloechler, a hotel waiter from Austria, six years her junior. By the time the rebellion began in 1916, however, Karl was no longer in No. 8; Bella was 'in the house all alone as my landlady went to Naas for Easter'. She now found herself in an area full of danger – 'machine-guns were firing up and down Killarney Street', just metres from her front door, 'people have been risking their lives all day to get food', and 'a tenement house up Buckingham Street, half a minute walk from here was shelled nearly all day'. Under these conditions, Bella began to write a diary which, all these years later, still conveys her worries and her fears, as well as her concern for her neighbours. Unpublished until now, the diary was kept in a small envelope, simply titled: 1916 Irish Rebellion.[1]

24 April

This afternoon an army of Sinn Feiners took possession of most of the big buildings including the GPO. They also entrenched themselves in Stephen's Green, digging trenches and blockading the outside with tram cars, carriages, motor cars and every kind of vehicle which came along. All traffic is stopped, business is at a standstill, a few of the military were called out, but they were soon shot down and barracks were surrounded. Passed by Westland Row Station which was closed, barricaded and held by the Sinn Feiners.

25 April[2]

The firing was continual all last night. All the riff raff have turned out and are looting all the shops as the Police were called in, several having been shot. Firing nearly all day, Killarney Street, Gloucester Street and Buckingham Street cut off from rest of city. No one allowed to pass. At 6.30 the Streets were cleared and machine guns were firing up and down Killarney Street, Gloucester Street and Seville Place. Everyone ordered to keep in. Firing continued all night and all today (26 April). We can't go out and get food. Machine guns continually firing, Liberty Hall was blown up yesterday by the gun boats in the river. It is impossible to settle down to do anything as the shots are terrifying. The poor dog is nearly out of her mind, am in the house all alone as my landlady went to Naas for Easter and couldn't get back. There is a big gun on top of Amiens Street Station (held by the Military) which fires straight up Talbot Street and another which has a range over Westland Row and others in different parts of the city. O'Brien's were selling things out of the back of their place as we can't get round in the front as a soldier orders us back and would shoot if we didn't obey. It is simply awful. Mr Quin who lives in No. 5 and drives a DBC cart had the cart riddled with bullets yesterday,[3] then he wasn't allowed to take the horse and cart back to the stables so they were left at the Fire Brigade Station. We know a bit what War is like now. It is simply awful. Here there have been battles at Clontarf, Phibsboro and Drumcondra. A tenement house up

Buckingham Street, half a minute's walk from here was shelled nearly all day. There is not much firing now (10.30) Sackville Street is on fire. The sky is all red from the fires.

28 April

The firing all night was terrible just round here but as I slept pretty well I didn't hear much of it. The firing has continued all the day. At 9 o'clock the streets were cleared to work the big guns. The soldiers told everyone to keep in. They have been firing up and down Buckingham Street and Killarney Street and Gloucester Street also Portland Row all the morning. They wanted to work a gun from the top of O'Brien's house. As a lot of Sinn Feiners lived round here I hear there is some talk of searching the houses. There were four trains in readiness at Amiens Street station last night to take as many people as possible if necessary. The gas has been turned off since Monday night. People have been risking their lives all day to get food. Thanks to the goodness of neighbours I am not starving yet. I might run short of fuel though.

29 April

The firing all last night was terrible. Got up very early and was out looking for milk, got a little also some provisions. Then went with a neighbour over to O'Rorke's near the Custom House to try to get bread. I was told I would have to fight to get in and that I would be killed. When I saw the crowd I knew it was no use trying to get into that so after waiting about thirty minutes I asked a soldier with fixed bayonet to get me six loaves. I was sorry for the poor man after as when he brought the bread to me he had a crowd of women clamouring round him.

No men were allowed to pass the sentry. There was a lull this evening about 5 o'clock and crowds hurried out to get things. The military opened some stores down at Seville Place and all the people were helping themselves to bags of flour, oatmeal, etc., and some were dragging coal after them along the road. A neighbour invited me to tea this evening. It seems as if we are going to have a quiet night. I heard the GPO was burnt to the ground today. It was held by the Sinn Feiners and they had thirty soldiers as prisoners.

30 April

Big guns were booming the whole night and I heard there was hell at the North and South Walls and Swords. A proclamation was issued today to say people are not allowed out of doors between 7.30 p.m. and 5.30 a.m. This will do instead of the 'Daylight Saving Bill'.[4] The last newspaper I saw until today was the *Daily Sketch* on Easter Monday. *Lloyds Weekly News* was sold today in Dublin. It gave an account of the insurrections. Managed to get to Mass and back without excitement. The Archbishop said although the bells would ring for Mass no one need go as it was dangerous. The weather is perfect, no one is allowed over any of the bridges without a permit, then only one to the address given; so we don't know how our friends are on the south side of the City.

1 May

We were allowed up into the City today (or what was the City). Sackville St, part of Henry St and part of Earl St are a mass of ruins. It goes to one's heart to see the desolation. Some of the fires were still smouldering. Only the walls of the GPO, the

Coliseum, and the Metropole were left. Hopkins, Reis, DBC and Clery's were all burnt to the ground. Not much damage in Grafton Street; the boot shops seem to have suffered most. Some of the Shelbourne Hotel windows were broken. I tried to get to the American Consulate and was escorted by a sentry with fixed bayonet from the end of Merrion Square.[5] The consul hadn't been in since Saturday week so I was escorted back in the same manner. Shots are still being fired. The Morgue I believe is filled with the bodies of women and children. No one is allowed along Nassau Street or Westland Row. There was a great rush for the *Irish Times* when it came out this evening about 5.30.

3 May

Nothing exciting happened yesterday. At 7.30 last evening there was heavy firing apparently in Mountjoy Square vicinity. I see by tonight's paper that Mr Kevin O'Duffy, an old friend of my father's, was shot while walking along the street and died in hospital.[6] Have heard several shots today. Three rebel leaders shot today, one had a shop in Amiens Street.[7]

4 May

Soldiers knocked at the door last night at 10.30 and told me to put out the lights at once. Managed to get to the Consul today. Mrs Mooney and her sister came back from the country so am not alone now. Went to Ranelagh. The soldiers searched every vehicle passing over Leeson St Bridge. A few trams were running today. Business is gradually being resumed. Today's papers give the names of more rebels who paid the penalty of the law, one being Joseph Plunket [*sic*] whose marriage yesterday was given in today's announcements.

7 May

A new order had come out. The public may now remain out until 8.30. Everything is quiet now, but since the firing ceased it has rained incessantly. The Police are making house to house search. The houses here were searched yesterday. One of two soldiers found in the ruins of the Coliseum has lost his reason.[8] Two soldiers were found in the ruins of the GPO but were all right.[9] During the looting people were seen to change everything they had on in the streets and put on all new clothing.

9 May

The gas is not yet on because of an explosion in Sackville Street yesterday. The fires are still smouldering.

10 May

Gas turned on at last.

Mr McKenzie who was accidently shot at his shop in Cavendish Row escaped the *Lusitania* disaster last year.[10] The day after his death was the anniversary of the sinking of the *Lusitania*.

The milkman turned up after 10 days; he was held a prisoner for two days near Church Street by the S Feiners. Hundreds of cases of looting continue to be tried in the Police Court.

BG

'WAIT A MINUTE – HAVE A LOOK AT OUR CORPSE FIRST!'

In 1916 Michael Taaffe was seventeen, living in what was then the outskirts of Dublin, near 'where the Donnybrook tramline came to a lonely end'. His quiet life had already been shattered by the deaths of two cousins in France, but he was nevertheless seriously considering joining the army, a decision that was hastened by the events he witnessed during the Rising. His memoirs include a chapter called simply 'Rebellion',[1] and although a non-combatant, Taaffe managed to fire a single shot from a rifle, in what can only be called unusual circumstances.

On Easter Monday the Rebellion of 1916 broke on Dublin like an unheralded thunderclap. The predictive lightning had been there for all to see, but few had heeded the warning. Least of all were the members of my family and their kind conscious of impending disaster at home.

They were preoccupied by more distant rumblings from across the water where a bitter and bloody holocaust was soon to begin in the shell-pocked wilderness of the Somme. Already two of my cousins from Cork had lost their lives in France; Cousin Frederick lay, severely wounded, in hospital in England; worst of all, the stolid, dependable William had been killed near Ypres. In the press of these tremendous events and in a common anxiety for the other members of the family and many of our friends, who were serving in various branches of the armed forces, indications of local trouble had gone comparatively unnoticed.

(When people in Dublin had had the time to sort out their feelings regarding the unexpected and catastrophic pheno-menon of the Rebellion, it seemed that they were compounded of annoyance at the inconvenience caused to everyone, grief and shock as the list of those known to have lost their lives grew longer, and, I think, an uneasy element of shame on behalf of the theatrical figures who were brave enough to risk every-thing – even the possibility of looking ridiculous – in embark-ing on an unco-ordinated venture which many of them must have known was bound to end in initial disaster. Who was to know, then, that the repercussions of this lunatic project, set on foot by the believers in the dictum that England's difficulty was Ireland's opportunity, were to be wider, stronger, and speedier than even the most optimistic insurgent of Easter Monday could have hoped?)

The first news of the insurrection, doomed *per se* to failure from its ill-timed beginning to its squalid and pitiful end in the rattle of the firing parties, reached us when my father was away in Cork. My sister's school in England did not allow holidays at Easter, so my mother and I were alone in the house.

'Avice says Stephen's Green and the General Post Office are full of rebels,' announced my mother, putting down the telephone receiver. Her cheekbones were flushed with ex-citement. 'You know how your aunt exaggerates, but all the same I'm going to Northumberland Road to see if Mother is all right.'

'Rebels?'

'Yes. Sinn Feiners, I suppose. Get my bicycle!'

To my suggestion that a telephone call to Grandmother would be safer, since there might be trouble afoot even in our remote and quiet suburb, she turned a deaf ear. 'Get my bicycle!' she commanded again, pinning on a large velvet hat, quite unsuitable for cycling.

I pushed the wooden-rimmed machine round to the front door and watched her arrange her skirts over the protective netting of the back wheel, mount, and pedal determinedly down the road. I realised for the first time that in her there was something of the spirit of Grandmother. I feared for her a little and then consoled myself with the thought that if the telephones were still working, things might not be so bad as Aunt Avice had made out. Since William's death, a sorely stricken Aunt Avice had lived in a cloud of pessimism and everyone knew that she tended to put the worst complexion on any event.

These were uneasy days for me. The loss of William who had died at the head of his platoon in some minor attack, shouting, 'Come on the Connaught Rangers!' had been a stunning blow. It was hard indeed to believe that the serious, long-faced declaimer of the Indian Fakirs' speech lay in a shallow grave in Belgium with a bullet-hole in his head.[2] The fact that Frederick had been wounded was an additional burden on my conscience. Reason told me that even if I, too, had been in the Army, the fate of my cousins would have been unaffected. It was true that they were both older than I was, but Frederick was my senior by less than a full year and I fancied I detected sometimes a look of reproach in Aunt Avice's face. It was true, also, that if I had not damaged my leg while playing Rugby (a kick had resulted in a stubborn infection of the shinbone, necessitating my removal from school for lengthy specialist treatment in Dublin), I should still have been a schoolboy, about to enter my last term. I clung to reason and tried to believe that these circumstances constituted a justification for my inglorious status as a civilian, but reason was an insecure prop. I was, in truth, acutely unhappy about my position and the feeling was growing in my mind that I must take some decisive action before very long.

I thought of these things as I watched my mother pedalling away down the road. Even she, I reflected, was taking some sort of action to deal with the present situation, whatever it might be. She must be quite forty, I thought, while I, soon to be eighteen, was lurking *embusqué* at home.[3]

Suddenly it became imperative to get out of the house ...

There was no tram at the Donnybrook terminus so I made my way on foot through the village and along Morehampton Road to Leeson Street. I stopped on the bridge and looked down the length of the street towards the trees of Stephen's Green. There were fewer people about than was usual, but otherwise the situation appeared to be normal. I was half-way down Leeson Street when a shot rang out from somewhere in front. It was the first time in my life that I had heard a shot fired in what I supposed to be anger and the flat, echoing sound was a daunting reminder that Aunt Avice's description of the situation in Stephen's Green and elsewhere might not be so wide of the mark. The shot was followed – or answered – by another. I turned into Pembroke Street and made in the direction of Merrion Square, noticing as I did so that Leeson Street was emptying rapidly.

I had left the house with no fixed idea of my destination,

feeling merely that I ought to get closer to the scene of operations and discover for myself what was going on, but now it was suddenly clear that I must go to Trinity. There, I felt, I should find myself among people who would be able to tell me what was happening. I crossed Lower Baggot Street at a trot, uneasily conscious of how close I was to the north-east corner of the Green, hurried down Merrion Street, and sprinted across to the Lincoln Gate. The sight of Massey, the porter, in his peaked velvet cap and coat with brass buttons, was reassuring. The fact that the heavy iron gate was locked was not.

'What's going on inside?' I asked through the bars, as he opened the gate and passed me in.

'Ah, they're all up at the Front Gate, arrangin' what I heard tell was a plan o' campaign,' said Massey. ''Tis quiet here,' he added placidly.

In truth it was tranquil in the backwater of Lincoln Place, with hardly a soul in sight. But – 'a plan of campaign'? I wondered uneasily what that might portend.

Crossing the College Park, I became aware of a solitary figure approaching. Tall and remote he strode, the rusty black pants flapping about his lean shanks. Under a sombrero-like hat, his white hair fluffed round his ears with an abandon belied by his unsmiling, bespectacled countenance.

'Good afternoon, sir,' I murmured, tipping my hat.

He inclined his head and passed on. *Penicillium Glaucum*, as the Professor of Botany was known to the irreverent, was a character whose massive preoccupation with his work brooked no interference by men or events. Neither at that time nor thereafter did he evince a sign that he was aware of the happenings convulsing Dublin. Like the persistent rhinoceros, he followed his accustomed path, contemptuous of change. When, after the Rebellion was over, a belated night guard was mounted on the armoury of the Officers' Training Corps, the Professor, deaf to challenge, strode across the parade ground each evening and let himself out through a side door to which he possessed a key, while some former pupil, now in khaki and bored with his vigil, juggled uneasily with his rifle and called upon him vainly to halt. It was a miracle that the venerable 'Blue Mould' wasn't shot.

At the Front Gate there was a certain quiet animation, slightly furtive in character. The inner wooden doors were shut and a single electric bulb shone dimly in the high, vaulted ceiling of the vestibule. As I entered the gloom of the archway a small figure in khaki bounded aggressively from the porters' lodge. He came to a halt in front of me, legs widespread, his gloved hands holding a short leather-covered cane. The ribbon of the Military Cross was bright on his tunic.

'Well, thank God for that!' he said, grinning. 'Another medical student's turned up! Jolly good! Come to win the war?'

From somewhere beyond the closed doors the noise of firing ripped through the silence. I winced. He continued to regard me steadily.

'Can't have too many men,' he barked, his round, little boy's face incongruous under the khaki hat. 'Got to defend the Library at all costs, y'see,' he added.

I had a nightmare vision of a last stand at the Library windows, ammunition spent, while a horde of rebels with fixed bayonets swept in line across the Fellows' Garden. Still, I thought, here I was of my own free will and even the meanest of men would have done anything sooner than lose face in front of Boyd-O'Kelly. Hadn't he been a First Year Medical up to a few months before I had entered Trinity? Hadn't we all been nauseated by continual reports of his intrepidity? Slightly wounded, he was now at home in Dublin on sick leave and the story was that he wore his MC ribbon when swimming at Tara Street Baths.

'What can I do to help?' I muttered uncertainly, feeling that the words severed my last link with the haven of civilian life.

'Well, you'd better come up to the Regent House and see Lawford,' said Boyd-O'Kelly. 'No! Wait a minute – have a look at our corpse first!'

He threw open a door beside the porters' lodge.

Eight months in the Medical School had made me familiar enough with death as exemplified by the mummy-like subjects that had once been human beings. When the initial repugnance to sinking a scalpel in the flesh of these anonymous and pitiful cadavers had been overcome, one thought little about them as people. As little, maybe, as the bona-fide student over at the Dublin Metropolitan School of Art thought about the carnal charms of the young woman who, her wedding ring her sole covering, posed nightly in the life-room.

The young man on the floor of that stone-walled niche was different.[4] He rested as quietly as any of the subjects in the dissecting-room, but he was new to death and looked as if he might get up off the flags at any moment and go about his business. His drab uniform melted into the colourless stone so that his hands with their fingers upcurled and his face, startlingly white in the gloom, seemed to have no true connection with the rest of him, like those figurines carved of wood with ivory extremities. His mouth was slightly open, showing regular, discoloured teeth; long lashes rested on the pallor of his cheekbones, and there was a small black hole in his temple. Beside him lay his hat with its draggled plume.

'What happened?' Boyd-O'Kelly seemed to expect me to say something.

'They came through an hour or so ago on bikes, heading towards the GPO,' he said. 'Didn't expect anyone to be here, I dare say. We got this chap and winged another, I think, but he kept on going. Daly and I brought him in. Come on up to the Regent House!'

Daly, the porter with the Kitchener moustache, clicked his tongue gently against his teeth and closed the door on the remains of the young man who had set out from somewhere unknown that morning to help in the conquest of Dublin. Climbing the stairs to the Regent House, I wished that wars could be fought without casualties.

In a chair in one corner of the magnificent room over the Front Gate drooped an ancient Fellow in a baggy tweed suit. He was fast asleep, a rifle between his knees. Despite the weapon, he looked less formidable than on the last occasion on which I had seen him, gowned and declamatory on his rostrum. At a table under the high window sat Tom Lawford, the brewer, in his captain's uniform, writing busily. Boyd-O'Kelly advanced and saluted. Lawford flicked an acknowledging finger in the direction of his bald head and they conversed inaudibly.

'Are you in the OTC?'[5] Boyd-O'Kelly's question floated across the chamber. The don woke up with a start, gazed fiercely at me, snorted, and went to sleep again.

'I'm afraid not,' I answered, feeling inadequate and trying not to make my voice too loud.

'Oh – well,' said Boyd-O'Kelly dispiritedly. He turned to Lawford, shrugged, saluted again, and came towards me. 'The Army's due to send someone to help us out before long,' he said. 'But anyway, you'll want to see what's going on above. You can get to the roof if you go out that way.' He pointed. 'But watch yourself! There are snipers all up Dame Street.'

I climbed upwards once more with the feeling that Boyd-O'Kelly's eyes were boring into my back. The trapdoor in the leads was open and I scrambled through, keeping my head low and wondering uneasily when the lynx-eyed rebels on the rooftops all around would fire. I crawled forward in the depression formed by the meeting of the roofs of the central pediment and the long wing to its side, and was confronted suddenly by the dirty face of Pinky Wilson, a student of divinity whom I knew slightly. Peering round at me over his shoulder he muttered hoarsely: 'Thank God you've come! Another five minutes an' I'd have given in!'

'What's wrong?'

'God!' said Pinky, slithering towards me. 'If you hadn't come I'd have had to do it up here. D'ye know I've been here for hours – for hours, dammit? Someone should have come to take over long ago! You know the orders?'

'I'm not here to take over from you! I'm only–'

'Can't help that,' said Pinky urgently. 'If I don't get to a lavatory this minute, I'll not be responsible for what happens, I tell you! You'll find the gun an' all up there in front ... orders are to treat everyone you see who isn't in khaki as a rebel.'

'D'you mean, to *shoot* at them?'

'Of course! That's what you're here for!'

'Have *you* been shooting at everyone?'

"Course I haven't, but those are the orders. I think it's that bloodthirsty little sod with the MC.'

'Oh!'

'Now, look! *Will* you take over?'

'But I can't, I tell you! I'm not even in the OTC. I'll – I'll stay until you come back, if you like, or send someone else. But don't be long, will you?'

'Oh, all right,' said Pinky. He was already half-way through the trap. 'Will I *ever* get there!' he muttered in his agony, and vanished.

I inched forward into the lonely wilderness of grimy stone. Close to the parapet were a .303 rifle, several clips of ammunition, a tin of Gold Flake, and a box of matches. Sixty feet below and in front the empty vista of Dame Street led away towards Dublin Castle. To the left and right, Grafton Street and Westmoreland Street were deserted. I scanned the rooftops hurriedly. No doubt every chimney-stack hid a rebel sniper, but I could see no one. I picked up the rifle and drew back the bolt gingerly. There was a round in the breech. I closed the bolt, put down the rifle, and lit one of Pinky's cigarettes with an unsteady hand. I had never felt so alone.

The minutes crawled by. It seemed a long time later, but was probably about a quarter of an hour, when I was suddenly aware of movement in Grafton Street. Instinctively, I grabbed the rifle.

Ten feet between each man, the soldiers came slowly towards College Green, hugging the walls on either side of the street. Their rifles were held at the port and here and there a bayonet flashed as it caught the light. The khaki figures moved forward yard by yard in silence, looking like toys to me on my eminence. In the middle of the street and slightly in front of his men walked an officer, a drawn sword erect in his hand. He led on slowly into the cobbled space directly beneath me, came to a halt, turned his back on Dame Street, and faced the College railings. Behind him the bronze hand of the Grattan statue was raised as if to ward off the shot I expected to hear at any moment.

Daly and another porter ran out to unlock the gate in the railings and the soldiers filed in, the scrape of their heavy boots now loud on the flags. When the last man had disappeared below me, the officer sheathed his sword and walked calmly towards the gate.

'Why can't he hurry!' I thought, in an agony of apprehension for him. As he came closer I could just make out the cap badge of the Leinster Regiment. He walked on deliberately and vanished from sight.

Cuddling the rifle in what I imagined to be the professional manner, I looked along the sights. To this day I don't know whether it was by accident or design that I squeezed the trigger. The rifle jumped against my cheek and across the street a white spot appeared high up on the stone facade of the Bank of Ireland.

As my ears stopped ringing, 'What the hell do you think you're shooting at?' hissed Pinky, emerging from the trapdoor.

My mother looked upset.

'How did you get on?' I asked. 'Is Gran all right?'

'Those soldiers in Ailesbury Road!' she said explosively, ignoring my question. 'There were a lot of them with bicycles.'

'Oh?'

'Ignorant yahoos! D'you know what?'

'English soldiers?'

'Of course they were!'

'But, Mother, you always say the Irish are yahoos, you know!'

'*Will* you listen to what I'm trying to say?'

'Sorry, Mother!'

'I asked them how long all this nonsense was going to go on.'

'What did they say?'

'They had the cheek to say that Dublin would be cleaned up soon, but it might take longer to round up the hill tribes.'

'The – *what?*'

'The "'ill troibes"! That's what the man said. Did you ever hear–'

'Well, after all – maybe he's served in India?'

'Nonsense!' My mother looked at me in exasperation. 'How dare they! How dare they talk like that about Irish people!'

'Well, after all, they're rebels, you know.'

'I don't care!' said my mother fiercely. 'They're Irish whatever else they are.'

I left her fulminating and went to put her bicycle away. My mind was seething with the day's happenings, but all that evening and later, when I lay on the edge of sleep, I thought mostly of the young Leinsters' officer, who didn't look much older than I was …

Throughout the tragic fortnight that followed, the sun blazed down on a city from which, very soon, wavering fingers of fire began to reach towards the cloudless sky. The initial shock of the outbreak was followed by a mounting list of minor tragedies, in themselves insignificant details on a large and formless canvas, but combining to stain the picture blood-red and to fan the more consuming flames of bitterness and hate.

Grandmother's first reaction to the Easter Monday activities of James Connolly's Citizen Army and the Volunteers who came out with Padriac [sic] Pearse was one of contempt and disparagement. 'The Fenians', as she insisted on calling them, would very quickly be put in their place and the whole business would be 'settled' in a day or so. The Dublin Metropolitan Police might not be very efficient, it was true, but surely they would be capable of dealing with a band of hooligans? The news of the prompt arrest of Sir Roger Casement who had landed from a German submarine at Tralee on Good Friday served to confirm her belief that matters were well in hand.

The death of Posnett awoke her sharply to the fact that the menace loose in the streets and on the rooftops was more than the lawlessness of a few roughs. Posnett, in common with a number of her friends and acquaintances too old for active service, had joined a non-combatant organisation. The uniform was olive-green, with a brassard carrying the letters *GR* in red. *George Rex* very soon became 'Gorgeous Wrecks', by which disrespectful nickname the members of this voluntary corps were known to all.[6] Their duties included meeting the leave boats and trains, finding overnight lodgings for individual soldiers in transit, assisting overworked Railway Transport Officers, and similar tasks. They helped a great many bewildered young servicemen and did no harm to anyone. Occasionally, to remind them that they wore the King's uniform, they were paraded and taken for a mild route march.

When returning from one of these outings, Posnett's unwitting unit was fired on as it passed the corner of Haddington Road, a stone's throw from Grandmother's hall-door. The surprise was complete and in a moment several of the defenceless old gentlemen had been shot down. The remainder scattered to the shelter of nearby houses, leaving Posnett and some others dead or dying in the dust of the roadway, pitiable victims of the law of probabilities and chances. The incident aroused great local indignation, but was speedily forgotten by most people in the excitement of more important events. Grandmother, however, did not forget. She was deeply shocked and in her was born a fierce determination to do everything in her power to fight those whom she regarded as the murderers of Posnett. She had not long to wait for her opportunity.

Reinforcements from England began to arrive on the Wednesday. They disembarked at Kingstown and marched along the tramlines into Dublin. The rebels, wise in their own terrain, had taken possession of a corner house at the south end of Northumberland Road, from which they had a splendid field of fire in three directions, including the route along which the troops came. The casualties among the soldiers, many of whom were untried recruits, were heavy. At the other end of Northumberland Road, rebel snipers in the tower of Haddington Road Church were active. Grandmother was now in the thick of it and presently she became more deeply involved when, to her great satisfaction, a platoon of the Notts and Derby Regiment was quartered in the house and garden.

At last the opportunity had come to live life as it should be lived – with a spice of danger. She ripped up her second-best bed linen and brushing aside the protestations of Uncles Louie and Bertie, set them to making bandages. Bridget, Alice, and Mrs Fitzharris (possibly against their political convictions) were turned on to converting the spare bedroom into a casualty ward and the kitchen into a species of military cookhouse where the young Sherwood Foresters could bring their rations and their mess tins. She organised the making and distribution, at fixed hours, of hot soup liberally laced with sherry. This was very popular. She was up and down the steep stairs continually and in and out of the garden a dozen times a day, to ensure that all was well with her beloved garrison. It was with some difficulty that she was dissuaded from climbing through the trapdoor that led to the roof in order to see how the snipers were 'getting on'. If anyone had been unwise enough to put a rifle in her hands, she would have let it off with enthusiasm.

The exchange of fire between the church tower and the roofs of Northumberland Road was intermittent and casualties were negligible, but the noise was nerve-wracking. Several stray shots entered the house. The drawing-room windows were smashed and the *Relief of Lucknow* was damaged by a bullet that pierced the hall door, shattered the glass of the picture, and lodged in the wall behind it. Grandmother, having a liaison of long standing with the tradesmen in Baggot Street, managed to stock up, after dark, with enough food to tide over the household for several days. She then commanded Alice and Mrs Fitzharris to stay away for their own safety and settled down to ride out the storm with her sons, Bridget, and the platoon.

It was over very soon. The snipers were dislodged from the church tower and the fighting moved away towards the centre of the city where it became confined, in its closing stages, to a few rebel strongholds that fell one by one. Grandmother bade her platoon a regretful farewell, set out her penknife and half a dozen of the 2B pencils she used for all her writing and settled down at her portable desk to catch up on her correspondence. Never had she had so much to write about.

'NOTWITHSTANDING THE SOUND OF MACHINE-GUNS AND CANNON, I WAS COMPLETELY ENGROSSED IN MY READING'

Sir John Ross was the last Lord Chancellor of Ireland, losing the office when it was abolished in 1922. He was also a judge of the High Court, and in 1924 he published a book of memoirs, including Chapter XXVIII, titled The Dublin Rebellion of 1916.[1]

In the afternoon of Easter Monday, 1916, Colonel A.H. Courtenay, CB, one of my colleagues on the Officers' Selection Committee,[2] rang me up at Oatlands to inform me that a Sinn Fein rebellion had broken out in Dublin, and that the insurgents were digging trenches in Saint Stephen's Green.[3] I at once telephoned inquiries to Dublin Castle, and the reply confirmed what I had learned. I asked if I should be required at the Castle, as I anticipated that a proclamation would be necessary. I was answered from the Under-Secretary's Department that the police had been called in, and so it was best for me to remain at my own house, as the insurgents were looking for hostages.

The weather, during the rebellion week, was like summer. I accordingly was able to sit in my garden reading Plutarch, and, notwithstanding the sound of machine-guns and cannon, I was completely engrossed in my reading. We received no newspapers or letters, but our ordinary supplies of food, somehow, continued.

On the Wednesday, my wife and I, while walking on the road, met a young rebel in uniform, carrying a short, serviceable rifle; this was the first we had seen of them. We entered the grounds of Mount Merrion, which then belonged to Lord Pembroke, whence we witnessed, across the valley, an extraordinary sight. The *Helga* gunboat, which had been brought up the River Liffey, was demolishing, with its guns, Liberty Hall, the headquarters of the Transport Union. After every shot, dust and smoke rose in the air.

British troops began to pour into Dublin from Kingstown, sometimes marching by the upper road past our gate-house, but more often by the lower, or sea road. The Sherwood Foresters, advancing by the latter way, as soon as they reached the suburbs of the city, were heavily fired on, and had serious losses of officers and men, before they succeeded in capturing the house from which the shots came.

The telegraphs and telephones were seized by the military, and no news could be obtained through them. On one occasion, I was rung up by the military in the Shelbourne Hotel, giving me a message from some lady detained there, which she hoped I should be able to convey to her relatives. While I was listening, I heard the weird noise of a machine-gun in the hotel pouring bullets on the insurgents in Saint Stephen's Green.

At night, I used to go up to our observatory and watch the great fires in the city. From another standpoint I could sometimes see the dark figure of Nelson on the top of his column in Sackville Street, standing out against the red glow of the flames.

News began to trickle in from various sources. A small company of the veterans, mainly Civil Servants over the military age, who had been out for a route march on the south side of the city on the Monday, were returning to Beggars Bush Barracks, unarmed, but in uniform.[4] Suddenly, rifle fire was opened on them from a house in Northumberland Road, and several were killed on the spot, among them Mr J.F. Browning, one of the examiners in the Land Registry. He was a most accomplished and able lawyer, and had done great service in assisting to raise the 'Pals' Irish regiment.

Every day we heard of the death of some of our friends. We were much grieved by a report that Mr John Colles, QC, brother-in-law of Lord Ashbourne, and Master in Lunacy, had been killed.[5] He and Mrs Colles had been invited to tea at Oatlands on the Thursday following. To our surprise and delight, they both appeared on the Thursday afternoon at the hour fixed. It then appeared that one of the lunatics under his charge had gone about circulating the report that the Master had been shot in the streets.

The Very Rev. F.J. Watters, president of the Catholic University School, a very popular priest, was struck down at his own door in Leeson Street by a stray shot, and killed. At another place, a man was shot in the streets by a sniper on the house-tops, who kept firing to prevent any person from coming to his assistance, when the Most Rev. Dr Donnelly, the Roman Catholic Bishop of Canea, a colleague of mine on several boards, bravely walked out and stood by the fallen man until people could be induced to remove him.

The St John Ambulance Brigade, under Sir John Lumsden, KBE, their chief commissioner, were on duty attending to the wounded from morning till night. One of them, Mr Stodart, while so engaged, was killed, probably by a stray shot. As the hospitals were all full of wounded, it was decided on the Wednesday night to convert our War Hospital Supply Depot in Merrion Square into a hospital. It was situated close to Mount Street Bridge, where the hardest fighting took place, and the house was full of surgical dressings, ready to hand. In a few hours, the depot became a hospital with fifty beds and an operating theatre ready for the first operation, an amputation, which was performed at six o'clock on the Thursday evening.

As the firing went on very briskly round the square, it was impossible for the VADs to leave the depot, and they had all to sleep on the floor for the next ten days.[6] Sometimes, when a man fell outside, a surgeon would rush out and bring him into the depot in his arms. Some of the wounds were dreadful to look upon, as though made by explosive bullets. When death occurred, the bodies were carried out to the stables.

On the Saturday morning, a maid-servant, while looking out of the window of a house close by in Mount Street, was shot through the head. Mrs Hignett and two VADs ventured to go to the house, but found the poor girl dead, part of her head having been blown away; they were able to secure the services of a priest, and buried her body temporarily in the garden.

The roofs of the houses round Merrion Square were occupied by snipers, who kept up a ceaseless fire night and day. The soldiers vigorously returned their fire. Casualties in the houses were constantly occurring, and several ladies were wounded.

Long after the fighting was over, householders made the unpleasant discovery that there was a sniper's dead body on the roof, and there has been many a grim surprise, since, for the cultivators of urban or suburban gardens.

The heroism of the ladies who worked in the depot when

it was turned into a hospital is past all praise. Hardly one of them had ever seen a shot fired in anger, or been present at an operation.

Lieutenant-General Sir John Maxwell arrived on the Thursday with plenary powers. On Friday, and Saturday morning, the firing was quite as intense as ever, on Saturday afternoon the leaders began to surrender, but the snipers seemed to be more infuriated and redoubled their fire.

On Saturday the Countess Markievicz surrendered the Royal College of Surgeons dramatically.[7] Marching out in her green uniform, she walked up to the officer in command, saluted, and kissed her revolver before handing it to him.

During Mr Wyndham's tenure of office, on several occasions I had met the countess at the chief secretary's lodge.[8] I believe she was distantly related to the Wyndhams. She was then a very beautiful and graceful woman, and extremely sympathetic in cases of suffering. Her husband was a Pole, and he seemed to me an artist of considerable power. At all events, I have seen one very fine painting representing the German legend of the demon wood-witch turning again into a tree, after luring a lover to his destruction.

When Lord O'Brien was having his portrait painted by her husband, the countess invited me to visit the studio during the sitting, to criticise the Work.[9] I considered the artist was not successful in getting a good likeness, and I thought the portrait too youthful and flattering, at which criticism his Lordship was far from pleased.

A piece of news that reached me in the early days of the rebellion, and grieved me extremely, was that the big policeman usually on duty at the gates of the upper Castle Yard had been shot dead.[10] It proved too true. He was a most kindly man, and a great favourite with children, to whom he was much attached.

One of our retired Judges had a strange adventure with the insurgents. Having taken possession of the roof of his house from the adjoining one, they next descended, and demanded food and drink. The judge, though an invalid, being a man of the highest courage and resolution, when they entered his room, addressed them on the heinousness of their conduct, expounded to them the law of high treason, and finally announced that neither he nor his servants would, on any account, supply them with what they demanded; at the same time, he informed them that as he was unable to resist their illegal requests, it was open to them to take, in spite of his protest, what they required. To their credit, they listened with respectful attention to his observations, and ascended once more to the roof, without taking anything.

It was striking to note that all the popular sympathy was, at the beginning, on the side of the military, and against the rebels. The soldiers were often cheered in the poorer streets, and supplied by the people with tea, food and tobacco. At a later period, however, after the execution of sixteen or seventeen insurgents, including all those who had signed the Sinn Fein proclamation, the tide of sympathy suddenly turned in favour of the rebels. Three of those executed were poets of great merit, whose works I had read with much pleasure, and I could not but feel regret for their untimely fate.

Everybody, whether Loyalist or Sinn Feiner, condemned Mr Birrell with one voice, and soon after, he resigned. I could not help being sorry for him; he was an extremely kind and well-meaning man, his only error was in coming into such a difficult and dangerous country as Ireland. From his admirable lectures on the Duties and Liabilities of Trustees, I think if he had persevered in the practice of the law, he would have succeeded; but his bent was otherwise and he enriched our literature with a number of charming books marked by a type of humour that was solely his own. I was very glad that, at the time of his resignation, the great-hearted Edward Carson, in the House of Commons, spoke kindly of him and his intentions. He departed, amid the smoke and flame of a minor rebellion, and as Hadrian said to his soul, we may sadly say to him: 'Nec, ut soles, dabis jocos?'[11]

When the fierce sniping had somewhat abated, it was interesting to go about the streets. Large numbers of prisoners were being deported to England; some of them looked depressed, others were proud and defiant. Among them, I was much amused to find two Derry apprentice boys and Orangemen, who had come up to Dublin on some loyal business. They were on the point of being shipped off to England in company with a crowd of insurgents, when they were recognised and set at liberty.

The Prime Minister, Mr Asquith, came to Dublin, and I met him at dinner at the Viceregal Lodge, where we had some conversation. He told me that it was the government's intention to set up a judicial tribunal for the hearing of appeals from the prisoners interned in England, and that Lord Justice Atkin and I were proposed for this duty.

I told him I would undertake it. It has always been my view that when any government calls for the services of a Judge in a case requiring the application of trained judicial impartiality, no Judge should decline to act.

On occasions when my services were requisitioned by different governments, I always consented to act. In this case, however, for some reason, Lord Justice Atkin and I were dropped, without explanation, and Mr Justice Sankey and Mr Justice Pim appointed in our stead.

During the first week of the rebellion, and for part of the following week, the ordinary Judges were unable to sit, as the Four Courts were occupied by the insurgents. When we did assemble, we came to the conclusion that it was necessary to have a special act of parliament passed to provide for the difficulties that had arisen.

I was surprised to find that although the door of my chamber had been broken open by the rebels, no other damage was done; my books, my robes (full dress and ordinary), my wigs, and papers, had been respected.

On a later occasion, when I was acting as chairman of the committee appointed to deal with appeals in the Irish internment-camps, I found I had before me the rebel commandant of my wing of the Four Courts. He said they had been careful to do no harm to my property, and I took the opportunity to thank him for the consideration and care shown to my equipment, by him and his men.

'WITHIN THREE HOURS OF THE OUTBREAK OF FIGHTING, AN AMPUTATION WAS GOING ON'

In 1966 the Electricity Supply Board (ESB) published a special commemorative issue of the ESB Journal, *containing 'accounts of participants in, and witnesses to, the events of 1916' – all by current and former staff. Here we reproduce* The St John's Ambulance Brigade, *by Staff Officer P.J. Cassidy, which gives 'the only living member's recollections of Easter Week'.*[1]

I had been in the Brigade about a year-and-a-half when the Rising broke out. From the humanitarian point of view which members of our Brigade had been trained to adopt, all casualties, whether civilians, or Volunteers, or British troops, received our aid.

When the position became clear, i.e., that there was heavy fighting in the city, as many members as possible were mobilised, and casualty stations set up, from where the seriously wounded were taken to the nearest hospitals.

Casualties were varied and many. I was serving in the Battle of Mount Street, with our casualty station at Baggot Street Hospital, under Sir John Lumsden and Surgeon Meldon. Over 200 casualties were treated there. One incident in all the excitement stands out in my memory. It concerned a casualty at Mount Street Bridge.

He got across Mount Street Bridge into Power's Court, where someone fitted him with a very long DMP overcoat and an old cap. I picked him up and took him to hospital.

As we were coming up the steps the people round the door began to shout: 'Another Shinner! Here's another one!'

Underneath the overcoat he was wearing the uniform of the Sherwood Foresters. He was very much an Irishman though, and said to me: 'Thank God I don't have to fire on my fellow countrymen any more.' He had a badly shattered wrist.

As we were the only non-sectarian, non-political First Aid group in the city at that time, we carried most of the burden of attending the wounded and dying. Several members of the Brigade were afterwards decorated for their gallantry under fire. One of our officers, Corps Superintendent Holden Stodart, was killed at Carisbrook House while going to the aid of a wounded soldier.

A noteworthy fact was the respect granted to us by both sides in our efforts to render assistance to those lying wounded in exposed places. There were many examples of human charity, where a temporary cease-fire enabled us to carry the dead and wounded from danger areas.

Many officers and men of the Brigade – including the Chief, Sir John Lumsden – were on duty non-stop for almost the whole week, catching a meal and a rest whenever they could. I was allowed to return to my home in Ringsend near the end of the rebellion. There, I really got work to do, attending to several people who had been hit by stray bullets – canal boat men, I remember, and many local people who knew of my St John's Ambulance Brigade training or noticed my uniform.

One young lady was killed on Ringsend Bridge, outside

Boland's Mill. A member of the Boland's Mill garrison, making his escape from the railway nearby, and going in the direction of the present Central Stores, was shot through the neck and jaw and in the arm. I got him to hospital.[2] He recovered, and for forty-six years he was looking for me, to thank me for saving his life. He eventually found me in 1962, while he was on holiday from Halifax in England, and we have kept in touch since then.

An interesting connection between the Board and the Rising is the fact that No. 40 Merrion Square, now part of Dublin No. 2 District Headquarters, and at that time the War Hospital Supply Depot, was turned into a temporary thirty-bed hospital by a unit of the Brigade under Lady District Superintendent Dr Ella Webb. Within three hours of the outbreak of fighting, an amputation was going on in the improvised operating theatre, and fifteen of the beds were in use.

While serving in non-combatant capacity in Easter Week, I had many anxious moments, as my brother and many of my schoolmates were in the Boland's Mill garrison.

'ALL THAT MADE LIFE WORTHWHILE WAS BEING TAKEN FROM US FOREVER'

Another account taken from the 1966 commemorative issue of the ESB Journal *is* The Refugees *by Eustace Malcolm, whose family in 1916 lived on Eden Quay in the middle of what became a war zone.*[1]

Six-foot letters fixed to the front of the building still proclaim the success of a business started by my grandfather and carried on for three generations.

The quays were quiet in those days. Few people strayed beyond O'Connell Bridge. Most of the business of the block was involved in the Shipping Companies and Forwarding Agents whose offices were close by.

We hadn't seen any excitement since the strikes of 1913, when we watched fascinated from a top window as crowds surged down the quays, eddied and surged away again leaving a body in a pool of blood opposite the turn off to Marlborough Street. Next day we children stood near the Liffey wall speechless before a pool of blood. Afterwards a cross was painted on the wall and was repainted regularly for many years.

Easter Monday, April 24th 1916 was fine and sunny. After Father had drawn some funny faces on our Easter eggs (hen, not chocolate) as they came out of the pot, there was talk of a trip to Booterstown for the afternoon. This set us humming with excitement and extra milk was taken from the milkman who always rattled his pint measure on the spout of his milk-can as he came along the quays.

About lunch-time we heard the sound of some rifle fire but although there was an air of curiosity about it nothing was said. A visiting Aunt offered to take the three older boys (including myself) to the pictures at the Masterpiece Picture House in Talbot Street and the Booterstown project fell through.

After lunch we turned off Eden Quay into Marlborough Street and along to the Earl Street–Talbot Street crossing. As we turned right into Talbot Street for the 'Masterpiece' several shots rang out from the general direction of O'Connell Street and there was a lot of shouting. My Aunt decided to investigate and literally rushed us up Earl Street towards Nelson Pillar.

Usually crowded on a Bank Holiday, the 'Pillar' was almost deserted. A horse lay on the ground near the 'Pillar' and without further ado my Aunt, trailing us by the hand and apparently oblivious to the sound of firing strode over to the animal. She poked it with her umbrella and turning to us said 'It's dead, Children! We'd better go home' and home we went.

My Mother, not realising the seriousness of the situation, was surprised to see us home so soon but my Aunt made it clear that things in O'Connell Street were very serious indeed.

On Tuesday the Milkman called as usual and told us he could not be sure of calling again as very limited supplies were getting into the city. Most of the supplies of essentials were being requisitioned by either side at the first strong point reached. He also told us that most of the shops in O'Connell Street had been broken into and looted. I anxiously enquired about Lewers & Co., a boy's outfitters near the corner of Earl

Street, where a suit of mine had been returned for alteration. According to the Milkman the premises of Messrs Lewers & Co. had provided most of the juvenile looters with outfits for a lifetime. Maybe my practically new suit contributed to the (temporary) comfort of someone less fortunate than myself. Although these were not my thoughts on the subject at the time.

Later in the day we heard a dull but persistent hammering on a level with our top floor. It seemed to get louder for a while and then ceased altogether. Long afterwards we were told that some members of the Citizens' Army were endeavouring to make a freeway along the entire block by breaking down the intervening walls at this level to give themselves greater firing command. Afterwards they decided to evacuate the position instead.

My Father would not allow any of us to stand upright near a window as firing was coming from the Tivoli Theatre (now converted to house the *Irish Press*) across the river and coming in our general direction. At this stage we had British soldiers in possession of the Tivoli Theatre opposite our house and the Citizens' Army in possession of Liberty Hall on our left which left us in a very unenviable position. To cross the rooms we had to go down on all fours and keep below the level of the window sills. We children thought this was a great game but an occasional bullet drilling neatly through a window pane and embedding itself in the walls took all the fun out of it for our parents.

That night mattresses from all beds were carried to the top floor and the beds were made up on the floor. Our parents talked long into the night and for the most part the beds were fairly comfortable.

On Wednesday morning no milkman arrived and with a baby under two years to care for, the enormity of the situation penetrated even to our irresponsible level. Then Father announced that there was no bread left and that the last of the home-baked had been finished the previous evening. Firing was now coming continuously from the Tivoli Theatre and sometimes carried the chatter of machine gun fire. It was replied to by bursts of rifle fire from Liberty Hall. Any attempt to leave the house to look for food would have been almost certain suicide.

My Father never believed in waiting for a miracle to happen. Using the back of a roll of wallpaper taken from stock he painted in large letters WE WANT BREAD. This was fixed in the top floor windows and an hour afterwards the miracle arrived in the person of a British Officer. He said 'We (the British) are quartered in the Tivoli Theatre opposite and understood this entire block was empty but for Liberty Hall.' After some conversation with my Father he said 'We will be shelling Liberty Hall or/and the General Post Office in the near future from the river and these premises are directly in line for any misses.' He then said, 'I'll send some of my men over to escort you and your family to the Customs House where at least you'll be safe until this is over.'

We hurriedly packed our valuables in a pram, seating the smaller children on our 'treasure,' tying up some bundles of night clothes and changes for the baby. We took a last look round what had been our home and that of our parents for so many years. All toys and treasured possessions had to be left as they were and we felt that all that made life worthwhile was being taken from us forever. The sharp thumping of a rifle butt on the hall door brought us sharply to the present and we found about a dozen British Tommies with rifles slung over their shoulders waiting on the pavement.

Telling us to walk steadily and without undue signs of haste they formed a group around our very frightened cavalcade and escorted us up the deserted and explosive Eden Quay and into the Customs House. It was the longest short trip I have ever made and it can be put on record that notwithstanding our exposed position and the easy target provided by the soldiers not a shot was fired in our direction from either side.

Safely inside the Customs House we were escorted up an interminable spiral staircase to the top floor. Here we found ourselves in company with evacuees from the Metropole Hotel, the Hammam Hotel and other premises in the Danger Zone. All women and children were kept in one large room and another running along the side of the building was reserved for the men. The windows of this room were situated behind the ornamental balustrade that runs round the top of the Customs House building. A sniper was stationed in this room where he had a clear view up the quays to O'Connell Bridge and to the right as far as the corner of Abbey Street. This placed Liberty Hall and the whole of 'our block' of Eden Quay under his control. He drew a bead on anyone coming to Liberty Hall steps and attempting to signal to whoever was inside. He paid no attention to others who just passed that way concentrating on their own affairs.

In 'our' room where the women and children were together a woman from the Hammam Hotel began to scream and shout about valuables she had left behind in the hotel. She became so violent that she had to be strapped to a stretcher for several hours.

Tea was army-style, great mugs of tea with biscuits and bread and butter and a hot meal in the middle of the day. Considering the conditions the fare was excellent but sleeping on the hard, hard floor was a bit of a trial.

Exploring our limited quarters with a freedom only accorded to children used up the rest of the day. We soon found that the spiral staircase reached to the basements from our top floor and we heard that prisoners were being brought in 'down below.' Devoid of any political leanings we felt vaguely that the 'prisoners' were responsible for our present condition. We launched a punitive attack by spitting on them down the well of the staircase. Needless to add our childish contribution disintegrated before it passed the next floor! Early Thursday the sound of cannon fire uncomfortable [*sic*] close brought us scrambling on window sills to peer through our protective balustrade. Apparently shells were being lobbed onto Liberty Hall from some point behind us and to our left and out of our limited range of vision. They seemed to be reinforced by shelling from Tara Street direction and a kettledrum accompaniment came from the machine gun at the Tivoli. Smoke began to fill Liberty Hall and suddenly tongues of flame gushed out through the already smashed panes of glass. Every moment we expected to see the building collapse but it stood firm although the inside was gutted by fire.

Afterwards we learned that the admiralty boat *Helga* had shelled the building by trajectory fire. The shells were directed up and over the railway bridge connecting Tara Street and Amiens Street railway stations. The bridge prevented direct aim and probably saved the front of the building. A smaller cannon was operating from somewhere in Tara Street but did not seem to have much effect. The Citizen Army had 'got wind' of the proposed bombardment and had wisely decided to preserve their numbers by evacuating the premises.

On Thursday evening I reaped the full reward of belonging to the local Boys Brigade, familiarly known as the 'BB'. One of its Members was a boy named Cecil Davis whose father was caretaker of the Customs House where the family had their living quarters. On one of our sorties we came face to face with Cecil and he brought us to his play room and offered us the use of his Meccano and other toys. When his Mother learned that the Malcolms were sleeping on the top floor (and I mean floor) some mattresses were produced and sent up to us. For the remainder of our stay we at least slept in comparative comfort and were doubtless envied by the rest.

All that night the uncurtained rooms glowed red from the City Centre fires and now the sound of firing was augmented by the crack of splitting timbers and the roar of crumbling walls. The rush of crimson light and the roar of roofs collapsing into burning buildings brought us creeping again and again on to the ledge inside the window. From our edge-on view of Eden Quay we saw sheets of flame gushing from the buildings and were convinced that our home was destroyed. That night and all the next day (Friday) the fires raged on destroying the entire east side of O'Connell Street and all but a small portion of the west side. The entire upper block of Eden Quay from the river front through to Abbey Street was reduced to a heap of rubble. It was this section of the fire that convinced us that our home was gone. In fact the fire never crossed to our block which contained the Abbey Theatre etc., and the only real damage was that sustained by Liberty Hall during the bombardment.

The sniper lost his job as Liberty Hall lost its interest for everyone after the shelling. He had been sniping on the French Front and there was an impressive number of notches on the stock of his rifle. I think they were only increased by one or two during his Customs House vigil. Some bodies watched on the steps of Liberty Hall with the abandonment of death.

Dense smoke hung over the ruins throughout Saturday. Heavy firing seemed reduced but the unnerving chatter of the nearby machine gun kept jabbing at our tired minds. There were rumours and counter-rumours; that the Citizen Army was victorious and the British had surrendered; that a truce had been signed; that the Irish had been defeated. Although we listened to and noted the talk we could not be expected to take it seriously with Meccano to play with and mattresses to sleep on.

Mr Davis the caretaker said we would be home soon but Saturday passed into Sunday with big mugs of tea and more biscuits. Sunday afternoon we were told by the Commanding Officer that it was safe to go home. Suddenly we remembered that we had heard nothing but an odd rifle shot during the whole day. We quickly returned our mattresses to Cecil Davis and his Mother and thanked them for their kindness and consideration. Collecting our pram from the ground floor we made a sad and bedraggled cortege as we left our sanctuary and entered a City as strange as the most distant country in the world.

Our house was there unharmed, but further along, the top part of a woman's body hung over the sill of an upper window. A poem learned at school called 'Barbara Frietchie' came to my mind. There had been no command from a marching column to save *her* life.[2]

Well loved places in the upper part of Eden Quay had vanished. The Seamens Institute where I had played violin solos for Seamens' Concerts and been rewarded with plenty of tea and cake afterwards; Smiths the Ironmongers where you could buy a good magnet for a penny; Hopkins the jewellers where unbelievably beautiful watches ticked in the windows and a chronometer in the centre window set the time for DUBLIN; and everywhere the smell of burning.

In our Home a few things had been stolen and every press and drawer had been burst open. The old office safe was hauled to the middle of the floor and hammered unmercifully but it had not yielded up its contents of about £200. We put our home to rights, got some provisions and a stone of flour. By Monday we were reasonably re-established.

But in the six days since we had left it our world of security and unchanging values had been burnt to ashes. For many a year we were to walk in fear.

'THE LITTLE WAR UP IN DUBLIN LEFT MAYO UNMOVED'

Katharine Tynan was a prolific and well-known writer in her time. She wrote many poems, as well as dozens of novels, plays and short stories. Among her many books are a number of autobiographical works, and The Years of the Shadow, *published in 1919, includes several chapters dealing with the 1916 Rising.[1] She begins by writing about a visit to Dublin just a month before the rebellion. At home in Mayo when the fighting started (with her magistrate husband), Tynan gives an insight into how the 'row up in Dublin' was viewed from a rural, uninvolved, point of view. She follows this with a description of her experiences in Dublin in the aftermath of the Rising, visiting from Mayo in June 1916.*

The Rebellion

The streets that March were full of serious-looking young men in twos and threes with absorbed faces, walking or talking in groups, whom we put down as Sinn Feiners. One day a Sinn Fein officer in full uniform clanked down Grafton Street to the amazed interest of the other officers in khaki. People were puzzled about Sinn Fein. It was certainly becoming very daring in its appearances and doings. The prevailing opinion was that there was nothing to be afraid about. The good citizens of Dublin for the greater part looked on it as play-acting. Some talked of shirkers, and even of cowards – in their ignorance.

Already these young men must have been under stern discipline. The passing crowd sometimes showed what it thought of them. Young ladies stepped aside ostentatiously as they went by. One would have said that the quick Irish blood would have been up, but they did not seem to notice. They were too absorbed in something. Perhaps knowing what they knew the insult passed them by.

Never was such a deceiving, disarming thing as the openness of Sinn Fein that spring. It manoeuvred in the streets, practised street fighting, and brought off a sham attack on Dublin Castle while the Dublin Metropolitan Police looked on and scratched their heads in bewilderment. How could anyone believe in the seriousness of a conspiracy that so flaunted itself?

An old college friend of my husband, an official in a Government Office in London, visited Dublin about that time. He wrote on February 23, 1916 – we just missed him in Dublin:

> There is a remarkable difference of opinion among the people I have met as to the importance of the Sinn Fein movement. Some people think it is merely theatrical heroism without risk. Others think it may mean serious business, even to the extent of bomb outrages. I saw a detachment of their Volunteers marching up Grafton Street on Sunday, which inclined me to the former view. First an advanced guard of cyclists and foot-men beautifully uniformed and armed to the teeth, carefully scouting down King Street and along the Green, in case of an ambuscade, leading you to expect that a regiment of a thousand or so was following. Then the main body headed by eight pipers in saffron kilts, but consisting of twenty men only, in all sorts of costumes, a few carrying arms, but most of them poor specimens, all taking themselves very seriously …

A month went by, six weeks; and one morning there were no letters – a disquieting and annoying circumstance in a household which lived on its letters. The postman had left a mysterious message to the effect that there were no letters; there might be none for a week; there was 'a row up in Dublin'.

'A cock-and-bull story!' I said sharply, out of my disappointment at getting no letters: 'the line is under water'; for, of course, there had been the usual deluge before the magnificent weather which hung the gold and blue as a background for the tragedy of Easter Week.

But that day as the dull hours passed the sense of calamity travelled by the earth and the air and the wind and the water. Out on the bog-road, where the slender trees looked down at their images in the water, we talked to the man at the level crossing. He, too, was an exile. He came from Nobber in Meath. No trains had passed through since Saturday: Sunday was a *dies non*. Perhaps it was a strike on the railway …

The next day and the next, the rumours came thick and fast. And with them Fear: Fear, not of Sinn Feiners, but of a possible German invasion. One imagined the spiked helmets coming in a line above the tops of the hedgerows. There would be the mountains for refuge, but not so near as at Shankill: the nearest mountains were seventeen miles away, and every one would be making for them, and there would be the question of food.[2] The bogs – if one knew them well enough, there was safety in the bogs and destruction for the enemy; not knowing them, there might be a quagmire and a slow, living grave for the one who sought to escape that way …

I think the first rumour of a Sinn Fein Rebellion reached us on the Tuesday afternoon, but the days passed, and the Sinn

Feiners had not at all emerged from the fog and the terror of the silent hours. I did not associate this wild melodrama with gentle, smiling Thomas MacDonagh, hat in hand and bowing politely, as I remembered him. Nor with Pearse, of whom I had heard but vaguely as a schoolmaster of ideals; it would have seemed a mad thing to think of that shadowy youth, Joseph Plunkett, whom I remembered as a baby, a commandant of the Irish Republican Army. Yet the week was not over before some one said to me: 'This will be a terrible thing for the Plunketts'.

I had wrung my hands before that over what I foresaw. I remembered mornings long ago in the Land League days, and the days of the Invincibles, when one prayed not to wake till late because there was a hanging at Kilmainham Jail, which was only a good stretch of country road and a few fields away from the home of my girlhood, so that with the wind in that quarter one might have heard the tolling of the dead bell.

'There will be all that over again,' I said, little knowing that the sons of old friends and people I had met in ordinary social life were of those who were going to die.

Mayo is given to minding her own business. Having given birth to the Land League and accomplished that Revolution, Mayo has ever since been quite well content to rest on her laurels. A 'strong' farmer came away from his tillage one of those days to ask us for news. 'And now we shall get no more money for Land Purchase,' he said sorrowfully. 'Was ever anything so uncalled for?'

The little war up in Dublin left Mayo as unmoved as the Great War – in our part of it. I stopped an old man coming from the fair one of the early days to ask if he had heard any news. One asked news of everybody, in those strange days when we seemed to be enclosed, shut away from the world, as though by a wall. He answered that he had never known a worse fair for pigs: there were no buyers. I asked him if any news had come in from Dublin … 'Oh, aye,' he said, 'bad work, bad work', and he went on his way.

The woman at another level-crossing, when the Rebellion was sinking down into its ashes, remarked that it was a terrible thing: it had stopped the fairs all over the country, the people couldn't get their pigs to Limerick; and another woman asked: 'Isn't it a desperate situation them villains have made for us? The man that comes collectin' eggs is stopped, an' I've five score on me hands.'

On Monday, the 1st of May, we motored to Tuam. We were not sure that we should not be held up on the way. But all went smoothly, and it was an enchanting day. In Tuam we found a different point of view concerning the Rebellion, although they did not talk freely, because of my husband's official position: but their silence was eloquent. They did not consider it as a matter of fairs and markets. They are quite a different people once you cross the imaginary boundary-line between Mayo and Galway.

At Tuam we succeeded in getting the *Daily Sketch* and another English illustrated paper. But already news had begun to come through. The local paper had a long tale of the events in Dublin, fairly accurate, as it proved.

One of these days the boy and girl met on the road a motor car containing three nuns, which was being driven very fast by a man, obviously a gentleman, who slowed down to ask them the way, and being told, went on at great speed. At first our imaginings went no further than that they were refugee nuns, from perhaps Athenry, where things were rather desperate.

Later on hearing tales of Liam Mellows and his hair-breadth escapes we began to wonder. Mellows will occupy a sort of Robin Hood place in the Irish popular mind by and by, if he does not occupy it already …

An English colonel at the Shelbourne told Barry O'Brien, who told it to us, this tale. His daughter was motoring in the West of Ireland, driving her own car, when the Rebellion broke out. She drove right into the midst of Mellows' men and was captured and her car commandeered. She was with them a day and a night, during which she was treated with the most perfect courtesy and consideration. At the end of that time Mellows himself arrived. He made profuse apologies for the inconvenience the action of his men had caused her. He asked if she had any complaint as to her treatment and she answered, none. He said, 'You are perfectly free to go now. If there was any chance of your listening to me I should make a request, which, of course, I have no power of enforcing.'

'What is it?'

'That for twenty-four hours after your leaving us you give no information that may lead to our arrest.'

'I promise that,' she said.

Barry O'Brien asked: 'Was she very much frightened?'

'You may believe that I was,' the father replied. 'But she, not at all. She said they behaved perfectly.'

After the Rebellion – Kathleen Tynan's experiences in Dublin in the aftermath of the Rising
I believe, after all, we learnt more about the Rebellion than those who were in Dublin at the time. Of course, one must always miss seeing the thing by one's own eyes: but beyond that

all our friends wrote to us of their experiences, and when we went up to Dublin in June they came and told us long stories, so that we got it from every point of view ...

We went up to Dublin on a beautiful June day, passing with joy from the bareness and monotony of the great bog which stretches nearly all the way from the West coast to the lush greenness and the distant mountains of County Dublin. People had said to us, 'You will cry when you see Sackville Street'; numbers of people had cried at their first sight of it after the burning.

I did not feel inclined to cry. I looked curiously and with a sense of aloofness at the ruined city, the hollows behind the shattered windows as though a skull grinned, the occasional high bit of wall standing up like a jagged tooth. What I felt was the something sinister that was released or came to life out of the ruins. People said that at first there was a positive stench. There were whispers of bodies under the ruins. Whether such or any remains of them came to light I never heard. But something escaped. Something of suspicion, of menace, of fear has been in the air of Dublin since Easter Week. No sooner am I come to the old town that I love as if it were human than I feel the chilly and subtle miasma that makes me afraid and distrustful.

Depression came down upon us with Dublin, and the Shelbourne [Hotel], which had always been so cheerful. The windows yet retained the irregular star-shaped marks of the bullets, a sinister reminder of what had happened. When we went upstairs to our bedroom facing the Green, there was a little comedy going on outside. A number of small children carrying streamers of the yellow, white and green tied to sticks for flag-poles, were piping *Who fears to speak of Easter Week?*

Now and again an enormous Dublin Metropolitan policeman gave them chase amid shrill peals of laughter from the children – after which they formed up and the same thing was acted over again. ...

Over in [St Stephen's] Green there were the shallow trenches which the rebels had thrown up while they held the Green – I was told afterwards that they were only for the sentries who commanded the approaches – covered up like graves.

In the days that followed we went over all the ground of the Rebellion. We had peculiar facilities. The two areas in which the fight had been hottest were Ball's Bridge and North King Street. In the latter narrow street there was desperate fighting. It took the troops thirty hours to gain a hundred and twenty yards of the street, hand-to-hand fighting all the time.

Close by North King Street are the church and monastery of the Capuchins, the special priests of the poor in Dublin. Attached is the Father Mathew Hall which provides a meeting and recreation-place for the people. ...

The Father Mathew Hall had been used as a Red Cross Hospital during the Rebellion Week. The dark stains were still on the boarded floor the day we were there, while in a room off the hall the competitions for the little 'Feis' – i.e., festival of music, singing, and poetry like the Welsh Eisteddfod – which is held every year at the Father Mathew Hall, were going on. The competitors were small children, some of them wearing the yellow, white, and green, oddly, in many cases, side by side with the regimental button of a soldier father. Pretending ignorance we asked one small boy what the knot of ribbon meant. 'Irish Republican colours, ma'am,' he answered. I had already been rebuked for talking about a Sinn Fein flag.

Accompanied by Father John we went on the track of the Rebellion. We climbed up the stairs of the Louth Dairy in North King Street, to see the bullet holes in the wall where what was called 'The Affair in North King Street' took place. We climbed to the high turret-like room of Monks's Bakery, riddled through with bullet-holes, where an intrepid sniper had kept picking off the soldiers who were trying to mount a machine-gun on the roof of the Broadstone Station which should sweep North King Street and Church Street. Many things we saw and heard which are better unpublished, for the present, at all events.

From this dreary pilgrimage we went on to tea at a Unionist house full of wounded officers. The days were full of such contrasts. ...

But everywhere there was the feeling of distrust, of suspicion. One day I was told that I myself had been arrested – a confusion with Dr Kathleen Lynn, I suppose – and I really felt as though I had.

Many people would not talk of the Rebellion, and they gave one the creepiness more than the ones who talked. The big man whom I met at a crossing – one of the finest and bravest men in Dublin, who shook his head with a sick look when I asked him if he could tell me anything, for I knew from the newspapers that he had touched against the Sinn Feiners: 'No, no,' he said, 'I can't talk about it. They were green boys. We were digging them up for weeks afterwards, out of gardens and dunghills, and all sorts of places.' He had got a grue.[3]

'HERE AND THERE YOU HAD TO STEP ASIDE TO AVOID A DEAD MAN'

In another chapter of her book, The Years of the Shadow, *Katherine Tynan writes: 'A priest who went up to Dublin on the Easter Monday, and was shut up there during the Rebellion week, was in great request when he got back again to Claremorris. He must have been tired of telling his story over and over, but he was very good natured about it.' What follows is his story.*

On Easter Monday Father Michael and myself went up to Dublin to see poor Father C__ who is lying very ill in the hospital in Leeson Street. We went by the 9.15 train which reaches the Broadstone at 2.30. As we intended to return the next night we had only hand-bags with us.

Nothing at all happened till we reached the Broadstone, but I heard a porter cursing the Sinn Feiners. As soon as we got out of the train some people came up to us and said, 'I wouldn't advise you, Father, to go down into the city at all. There's some terrible bad work going on there. Ye'd better wait for the next train back to the West.'

Well, we didn't know what they meant at all, but, of course, we were up to see poor C__ and we weren't going back without seeing him. There wasn't a cab or a car to be seen – that was the first queer sign – so we just set out to walk, thinking we would pick up a tram on the way. We hadn't gone far before we met a very respectable-looking young man, and he said to us much what the people at the station had said, bidding us to go back for there was bad work in the streets. 'What is it?' we asked, 'a riot?' 'Something of the kind,' said he. 'They were firing off a lot of rifles at the Post Office a while ago, but they've stopped now.'

We thanked him, but we said we'd got to see a sick friend, and we went on, wondering at the emptiness of the streets. There wasn't a tram running or any other vehicle. But when we got into Sackville Street we saw a great crowd on before us all round the Post Office, and extending as far as the Hammam Hotel where I always put up. There was nothing else in the street, but a few soldiers here and there, and in the middle of the street three or four dead horses lying. Now and again there came a foot passenger hurrying along, and every one of them said the same thing: 'For the Love of God turn back. There's terrible work going on in Dublin today.'

We went on towards the Hammam, but I wasn't long in finding out that the crowd in front of me was a very bad one; the slums of Dublin were out, and on for mischief. So we thought it the best thing to turn back and take rooms at the Gresham.[1] We had a meal there, and then we set off to visit our poor friend. No one at this time seemed to know what was up. Every one was asking the other, and no one at all guessed at the real seriousness of the matter, thinking it was only a street row, and that the worst of it was over.

We avoided the Post Office, going round by the side streets, which were very quiet, and once we left Sackville Street behind us the town was as quiet as possible till we got to Stephen's Green, where there was a barricade of tramcars and motor cars and such things from Grafton Street corner across to the gate of the Green with the arch over it; and there we saw the Sinn Feiners in uniform standing by the barricade and guarding the path where it was left open. They didn't hinder us passing and were very civil and respectful. So we went on and spent a couple of hours talking and laughing with poor C__, and cheering the poor fellow up.

It was about 5.30 when we left him. As we walked back we could see the Sinn Feiners in the Green digging themselves in; but we didn't even know yet what was happening till we turned into Grafton Street and saw the looting going on. It wasn't as bad there as it was in Sackville Street; but the way of it was you'd see a group of men and women coming along, and suddenly a man would take out a stone and smash a window, and then they'd all begin to smash and drag out handfuls of whatever it might be, jewellery or boots or toys or anything else. There was something horrible about it. There wasn't a creature to interfere with them, and they looked an uncommonly nasty lot, so we walked along in the middle of the street and no one minded us. Once a couple of men in the Sinn Fein uniform came along and they looked at the crowd with disgust in their faces, and I saw one of them snatch a handful of jewellery from a fellow and fling it in the roadway. It was as if, being out for a big thing, they asked themselves if it was for such people they were doing it.

We got back the quiet way again, and I said to Father Michael as we walked along, that as we'd seen poor C__ we'd better get home that night instead of waiting for the next day, but when we got back to the hotel we found the doors closed. They opened to let us in, but as soon as we'd got in we were told that the place was closed for the night, and there was no getting out again.

The night was quiet enough except for a rifle shot now and again, and the morning was so quiet that I was able to slip up to Eccles Street and say my Mass. That was the last time I was out till the following Monday.

Through the day troops kept arriving, but it was pretty quiet at our end of the street, though the looting had been going on all night, the police having withdrawn from the streets and no one to hinder the looters. But, of course, as we were not allowed to leave the hotel, we could see nothing of that. Some time that evening a knocking came at the door and there entered a sergeant and four soldiers. We all had to appear before him. 'I am very sorry,' he said, 'to be so unfriendly, but, till I know all about you, you are under suspicion.' There were about a hundred guests in the hotel, many of them English people over for the holiday. As soon as he had satisfied himself he gave the word to his men, and they dropped down in the hall, just as they were, and slept like logs.

They were the only people in the place that did sleep. The noise that broke out in the night was beyond all description: and it became worse the next morning when the gun-boat was bombarding Liberty Hall. That night the looting went on fast and furious.

I had a front room and I made good use of the window, although no one was supposed to look out, and the blinds were drawn. Tuesday night we were all forbidden to sleep at the front, so I took my mattress and laid it on the floor in Father Michael's room and got what sleep I could there. Our guard had got up on the roof and were hiding among the chimney-pots sniping now and again. There was one young lad, a terribly wild lad, maybe you know him, he is the son of K.C. (We did know him. He was at an English public school with our boys – KTH)[2] and he enlisted when the war broke out. The sergeant was heart-scalded with him. He couldn't be kept out of danger, only exposing himself everywhere, and the sergeant said if he took his eye off him maybe it is out in the street he'd be – and as time went on to be in the street was certain death, for the guns were firing from the Rotunda, and they were firing from O'Connell Bridge, and it was just a rain of death all the time.

I'll tell you some of the sights I saw from my window, for all that I was forbidden to look out. I saw three men suddenly come out from Britain Street[3] and stand on the edge of the pathway near the Parnell statue. They looked as if they were strangers and confused, and asking each other questions. There came a volley and the whole three were on their faces stone dead. I saw poor old John O'Duffy killed. He came hurrying along the pathway, wearing his top-hat, like a man in a dream. There wasn't a thing in the street but himself and the dead horses and the fire from the guns. 'My God!' shouted I, 'is the man mad?' I'd hardly said it when he went down. I heard he was looking for his favourite grandson and couldn't be kept in. Another thing I saw, and stuck at the window to see it, was the shelling of the houses opposite – the YMCA and the Richmond Institute for the Work of the Blind – where a most persistent sniper was on the roof picking off every soldier that came in sight. From the Rotunda end of the street there came an armoured motor-car; it made observations and went away. Then came a machine-gun, and I saw the men digging up a place for it in the roadway. Soon after that the shelling of the city began, but before that I left the window. Afterwards I saw the ruin the shells had made; but we were getting used, by this time, to the terrible noises that shook the place till every minute you'd expect it down about your ears.

Thursday night was the worst of all, for it seemed that the whole city was on fire. Outside the windows everything was red, with great columns of black smoke ascending to the sky. The houses at the corner of Earl Street were burning, and there was a strong south wind blowing all that day. When there was a sudden gust of wind the flames licked by your window and went off again. We gave ourselves up for lost. I never saw a stranger sight than I saw that night. All day the Catholic ladies had been coming to me and Father Michael asking to go to confession, and we explaining to them that, not belonging to the Dublin Diocese, we had no faculty to hear confessions, though we could give absolution if the necessity arose. The manager had got through a message to the Fire Brigade, but they had answered that their men had been shot at that day driving the engines and they would not expose them again. All the women were on their knees in the billiard-room saying the Rosary, and the queerest thing of all was to see the English and Scotch ladies, who were Protestants and Presbyterians, down on their knees with the Catholics joining in as far as they knew how. There was certain death in the street, but we were in the mind to do something desperate, when, by the Mercy of God, the wind changed at about eleven o'clock.

We were on very short commons by the end of the week – a slice of tinned meat, dry bread, and tea without milk was served out during the day. The air of the place was very bad, for you must know, with all these people shut up, not a door nor a window had been opened during the week, and, tight as everything was, the stench of the dead horses seemed to creep through – they were a horrible sight by this time, for the sun had been blazing hot for several days.

On Saturday I saw the surrender of the rebels at the Post Office. Oh no, before that I must tell you, I had seen eight men pass from the burning buildings about Earl Street across the street to the Post Office. You know the width of Sackville Street. And it was swept by gun-fire from end to end. Suddenly I saw them scurry out and run like rabbits. The guns blazed. One fell, but picked himself up again and followed the others. They all got safely as far as I could see.

The surrender – well, somehow I thought it a terribly sad thing. The Sinn Feiners were lined up by the Post Office. There was a firing party at each end, and soldiers scattered about among the rebels. They came forward, took off their bandoliers, and laid them down in a heap, laid down their arms, and went back again. There were old men there and there were boys in knickerbockers. Some of them couldn't have been fourteen. I knew what their madness would have cost us, had cost us, but I could have cried like a child.

The next morning I got up early and went downstairs. In the hall I met the sergeant. He was a fine, pleasant fellow, and we all liked him. Everything seemed very quiet after the noises of the last few days. 'Are you going out, sir?' he asked.

'I am going to the Cathedral to say my Mass,' I replied.

'If you'll wait I shall give you a guard of my men.'

'Oh no, thank you,' I said, 'I don't want a guard.' For the queer thing was, you seemed to have grown so used to death that you didn't care a bit about your own skin.

The streets were very quiet as I passed through them, only here and there you had to step aside to avoid a dead man. The ruin and destruction of the place was borne in on me suddenly. I had an inclination, like an animal, to howl and scream. It was as if my mind was going from me with the terror of the sight I saw.

However, I conquered myself and went on. Entering the Cathedral by the sacristy, the first thing I saw was a little girl fast asleep on the vesting-table. I didn't disturb her. When I went out to say my Mass I saw men and women all fast asleep lying about the altar. They were everywhere, under the seats, and in the gangways, all dead asleep. There was hardly any congregation. Indeed I don't know if there was any. I said my Mass before a congregation all dead asleep. They were starving and exhausted, the creatures! There were a couple asleep under the altar while I said my Mass.

Another thing. We travelled back with an English officer: there were one or two others, very pleasant and kindly. This one told how he had captured a Sinn Feiner, and was so much interested in his prisoner and the splendid fight he had put up, that he asked him if he would join the Army, that if he would, he would try to see him through. 'I fear I may have been going outside my province,' he said apologetically. 'I don't know that I could have done it, but I should have tried.'

'I can't see that it would be right to join the Army,' the Sinn Feiner answered, 'but we'll argue it out. If you can beat me in the argument I'll join.'

'There wasn't much time to argue it, but I said one or two things and he pondered them, and then he said, "No, I can't do it." So I had to send him off to the barracks. I could have hugged that man.'

On the other hand a man came to the Broadstone when we

were there. He looked very sullen and downcast as he asked for
the officer in charge.

'What do you want?' the officer asked sternly.

'To give information.'

'You're a Sinn Feiner?'

'Yes.'

'I'm an Englishman and I hate a traitor. Go over there with
your information.' He was a white blackbird. They were all saying that there were no informers among the Sinn Feiners.

I forgot to tell you that at the corner of Leeson Street and
the Green we met an old man and a little boy. 'You're a priest,
Father?' he said.

'I am,' said I.

'I want to get into the Castle,' said he, 'if you go with me
they'll let me in.'

'What do you want to do at the Castle? I am only a country
priest. They would not let me in.'

''Tis the poor boys,' he said, and burst into tears. 'They're in
the Post Office. They're the best boys ever stepped. If I could get
into the Castle and tell them about the boys … they wouldn't
maybe … be too hard on them.'

I'd have given anything to help him, but, sure, what could
I do? A poor country priest! God help him! I wonder what
became of the boys?

'THE CHIVALRY, THE MADNESS, THE INEVITABLE END'

The following account also appears in Katherine Tynan's book, The Years of the Shadow, *and was written at her request by one John Higgins, who she described as 'a young man in rather delicate health, living on a little western farm'. He had gone into Dublin to consult a doctor, and so had happened to be there for Easter Week.*

How do you begin writing about a rebellion? Beside it war is a comparatively easy matter, an affair of progressions. Human interest is led in a fortifying way along a sort of emotional path graduated with incident, each event going one better than its predecessor. From the *casus belli* to the diplomatic queries, to the scare headings, to the Parliamentary announcements, to the lonely soldier with a bullet in his heart across the frontier, and so from the confusing tangle of ambiguities and strident journalese to the last step – the straight issue of war. It does not so much break out as stand aloof to be broken into at the end of a sequence. But rebellion is a different thing; the essence of it is surprise. You ask for a match under the old regime and light your pipe under the Provisional Government: and, because the contagion of surprise spares no one, gentle or simple, it is impossible to reproduce happily the sudden and violent contrasts that burst above the level surface of our routine when a few hundred men in dark green swept into the General

Post Office on Easter Monday of 1916, saluted an unfamiliar flag in one long, racking volley, and proclaimed our country a Sovereign State.

It was all done under our eyes in the midday light, and, as it so happens (it is almost like ritual with us) that you cannot leave the city decently without first wasting a few minutes at Nelson's Pillar, O'Connell Street had half-choked itself with Bank Holiday folk, motors chasing northwards to the Fairyhouse Races, overladen trams flying eastwards and southwards to Howth, Sutton, and Tallaght, side-cars plying everywhere, and great crowds and processions of people peculiar in their enjoyment, loitering here and there, industriously doing nothing. For all these the volte-face might have been arranged to startle them out of their dull, thoughtless wits: but not one man or woman of us had, I think, an idea then that we were looking at anything more than an unconsidered prank. We could not see that every moment was a historic moment, every incident a link in an epic. For, believe me, you can take humanity by the throat, as it were, and leave it incredulous: and men and women are born into the world, grow up, marry, and die without ever getting a grip on the realities that meet them daily in the streets and newspapers as movements and propaganda. To our unreceptive intelligence the attempt to blow up the Pillar was – even as an artistic protest – something of a nuisance, spoiling the holiday.[1] Everything was, from that naive standpoint, wilful and wrong. Upon the spectators the noise and alarms produced a frantic disintegration, filling up the street, followed by a regrouping here and there to which individuals were drawn like atoms to their affinity. Windows were being riven with butt ends of rifles; somebody was reading a manifesto in the sincere, dignified style of Pearse; reinforcements kept pouring out of Abbey Street, where employers and customers alike had been bundled into the street and Volunteer guards stood on duty. From Cork Hill there kept coming a nervous rapping of rifles which, by and by, extended to other parts of the city near and remote. Across the open space near the Pillar one could catch the flash of bayonets inside the Post Office, and note the dive and bob of heads back and over as the intruders piled up material for palisades – all was movement and breathless excitement, but without confusion. It was like a stage setting for some stupendous notion of pageantry. With the long, barking volley the curtain went up, as it were, on a turning-point in history. Above our startled heads waved a new flag – the old flag – with an officer standing proudly by, bareheaded. At that moment the dream that had been dreamt through countless generations of our island story took form and substance, and the men who had taken for their portion the sorrows of Caithlin-ni-Houlihan [*sic*] looked into the infant face of their ideal incarnate. We see it now in the retrospect with its solemnity, its terror and wonder, but for the moment it was lost on us. Whatever malignant god controls the unmanly promptings that lurk – despite every pretence – in the recesses of our humanity, was even then active. Perhaps it is to such uncertainties that all strange enterprises are born. Men fled from the anger of the stars when Caesar died that Rome might live, and we, who looked upon the cradle of the Irish Republic, looked – at least in bewilderment.

Everywhere the same scene reproduced itself. The crowd flying from O'Connell Street, ran full tilt into a similar crowd hurrying from Liberty Hall. Around the Castle it was impossible to know where to go or which force was in possession of the building. A narrow street off the river brought us to a laneway opening on Dame Street. From an archway beside the Empire Theatre we tried to take our bearings while stray bullets ricocheting from the walls fell in the street outside.[2] We could not, of course, see the Castle, but the City Hall was plainly in possession of the Volunteers, a circumstance which led us to believe that the more important building was theirs also. That subject was one of warm discussion for forty-eight hours afterwards; the number of people who saw the successful storming of the Castle gates surpasses belief. Except for a few sentries inside the railings, Stephen's Green was quieter on Monday evening than I ever remember seeing it. Occasionally a Volunteer or two would pass along the walks by the lake, but as for that liberally circulated activity of trench-digging, I could see nothing of it.

By the way, those trenches are something of a mystery. For the life of me I could never find them. I did come across some broken earth, but it struck me as being less a trench than a London clerk's imitation of a potato furrow.

When a party of Lancers appeared at the Rotunda an old sea-captain, just arrived from the home of revolutions, South America, suggested crossing over to the Post Office side – the larboard side, he called it. Cavalry against a fortress had a touch of Quixote about it. Their officer, a good-looking, finicking sort of man, was fitting on his gloves as the party trotted along. Somewhere beyond the Hammam Hotel they were met by a volley that brought down some horses and sent the remainder clattering away in retreat. Of the casualties one was the dandyish officer, who passed, poor fellow, into the shades with the second glove unadjusted. Further up the street another man reeled in his saddle and fell. Above the corner, whence came the discharge, a little cloud of smoke curled casually upwards. For the present the fighting was done, but we, who were hoping against reason that something would emerge at last – some counsel, some compromise – to settle everything, saw in that one incident the irrevocable step, the gauntlet backed by the deed – the first challenge of the infant State.

All that evening crowds paraded the streets, watching Volunteer companies with fixed bayonets marching to their posts. The Government might have thrown up the sponge, so completely was it eclipsed; not a soldier, not a policeman in view. The more adventurous clustered round the Post Office, exchanging jokes and gossip with the defenders, scrunching plate glass under their feet, and making a respectable show of unconcern at the little colonies of rifles staring at them out of every window. Until nightfall, when the people began to melt from the streets, everything was quiet except for a forlorn rifle-shot in the distance, but the sense of expectancy was strong. There was a general impression that the military were being hurried hot-foot from the Curragh for a midnight attack, and on the strength of that feeling I doubt if there was a single unshuttered window in all Dublin that night. By midnight the looters were providing a strong counter-attraction, burning whatever could not be stolen. At Earl Street and Abbey Street groups of Volunteers in shirt sleeves filled up barricades, the men sweating and coughing in the smoke of a burning shop that swept in low, dense masses along the ground. Now and again the red shirt and brass helmet of a fireman would emerge from the murkiness to take counsel with his fellows, when some fresh outbreak threw red tongues of fire, lascivious and insinuating, into the night. With an east wind blowing, the Liffey at full tide was distinctly a personality; but for a genuine all-round smell commend me to burning leather. In the unusual darkness the city gave one an uneasy impression of death and abandonment, but where the Post Office showed stolid in a halo of errant smoke, with never a movement or sign of occupation, there was always a sense of waiting on the alert and watching the night. Upon that building the minds and tongues of the whole city ran during the anxious hours. The *fons et origo* of the passionate dream, its fate stood for the fate of the whole adventure.[3] We sat and smoked for hours in the starriness with rifles chattering from Church Street and the Courts, trying to picture as we might the adopted home of so much surging faith and devotion. Night and the stars and our brothers in arms, what was and what might be, the chivalry, the madness, the inevitable end. There were moments, I think, when the whole mystery of our country's ideal stood faintly luminous but illegible by our side, when we seemed to look upon the sanctified heart that in every century beats for an instant, a world's romance of sacrifice and sadness – and dies.

As far as the north side is concerned everything had been set in order for an effective resistance during the night. A motley but quite forbidding barricade barred the way at Cabra Bridge. When out of curiosity I requested to be allowed to pass along, I was firmly but quite politely held up by a sentry, a youth in mufti, with no equipment save a single-barrel shotgun – a formidable weapon at close quarters, but otherwise useless – and a bag of the material that my grandmother used in her wholesome feather beds, crammed with cartridges. His impartiality was undoubted, for a very smart buggy, which almost deserved to get through for sheer display of élan, had to yield to the persuasions of the grim sentry and his shotgun. There was quite a display of suburban parlour furniture in that barricade, serviceable sofas and chairs, and in the middle our grocer's pony cart looking very plebeian and out of place. Seemingly there is a special providence that overlooks the affairs of small grocers – a very over-taxed providence I imagine – but it is noteworthy, in the context, that although the more luxurious elements were mere faggot wood by Tuesday evening, the familiar cart delivered a dozen of stout to some thirsty students next door on Thursday morning. At the Park Road Bridge, after an effort to spring a mine had proved futile, a barricade of barrels, boxes, and wire was erected. The sentry there, who might have been specially imported from Mexico for the occasion, with his swarthy face, picturesque muffler and hat, *comme il faut*, knew his business. There was no exit – orders! He was very sorry, but it was the Provisional Government now! Inconvenient – yes! But would I please step back – as if, with a bayonet at my chin, I had any intention of stepping forward. To every such defence groups of young men and women came strolling, their confidence – the sunshine was like a spray – inversely proportional to the omens. There was much laughing and small talk, many rumours of invasion and Volunteer dissensions, amateurist impressions of street fighting; in a word, all the irrelevant chatter that springs disconcertingly from our headless democracy brought in quick, familiar contact with unforeseen crises.

All that morning O'Connell Street kept carnival as if in derision of the *coup d'état* and the imminent consequences. At Moore Street corner the public-houses were being fast sold out. One met drunken men and women frequently. Drapery shops, jewellers, sweet and tobacco shops, spirit grocers in the vicinity of the Provisional Government's headquarters, had all been or were being looted. The swaying ant-hill of humanity, that came in its hundreds to look on the graver aspect, had its attention undermined by the wanton ruffianism of the gutters of Dublin minding number one. Men hawked watches shamelessly at so many a shilling; urchins in tall hats played at being knockabout comedians, golfing swells, or soldiers, running to and fro among the crowd, pausing only to get astraddle of the two dead horses. Unclean women in shawls bore off freights of costly furs and finery; one old hag literally dripped alarm clocks. Outside a fancy-store something similar to a football scrum open to the sexes was taking place. Heaven alone knows the motley loot that came hurtling and splintering through the windows to the crowd waiting ravenously below – picture-frames, ornamental knick-knacks, books, toilet outfits, royalty on postcards, Teddy Bears, hand-cameras. It rained fountain pens.

So it was that for the moment the seriousness of the emergency was smothered in ridicule. But, occasionally, the curious throng would fly apart as little convoys of motor-cars came whooping warningly through the street to glide under the sagging strands of barbed wire held purposely aloft on bayoneted rifles. A clear space before the Post Office seemed reserved for the professional confidences of the leaders, all of whom looked refreshingly neat and well-equipped. Despatch-riders came and withdrew, commissariat carts, sometimes bearing unimpeachably loyal names, rumbled up, mysterious vans, strongly guarded, followed, the whole varied activity going to a note of unrelieved seriousness and strictest military observance. Yet, if you believe me, whether it was due to the flashing sunshine or the raucous foolery of the mob, there was something unreal about the ensemble, something almost indecent. If I fail to make this picture convincing, it is because it was not convincing at the time. For a few seconds of the preceding night one seemed to have vision and understanding; but, in the morning, as if God was withholding the interpreting talent that sees into the very heart of life, the whole scene swam before and around us like some colossal melange of high purpose and buffoonery, austerity and profanity, mysticism and vagabondage, blend for blend, all thrown headlong by the Devil's own stage manager into the proudest street in Europe. I know a dozen men writing today with the faculty of making a revolution in fiction far more realistic than the one I myself experienced seemed to me.

Of the actual fighting I can only write briefly. I saw very little of it. Somewhere about two in the afternoon shrapnel began to play on the drawing-room barricades, followed by a shower of bullets from some unascertainable quarter. The defenders, taking to the houses, gave battle from the windows and roofs. Puff, puff, puff! Soon there was an opaque grey cloud over Cabra Bridge. Outflanking the position from Glasnevin, the military effected a surprise entry by the gardens and backyards – first fall for the Dublin Fusiliers. With that rebuff the position on the Park Road became untenable, and such of the defenders as were not captured withdrew citywards, leaving the northern entry open. Through that gate huge covered motors, like Boer wagons on trek, tore down the North Circular and Berkeley roads at nightfall, filled with soldiers, their bayonets glinting in the gloom. Short as was the fight, it had tragedy to spare. The fatuous spectators, lingering too long and heedless of the rain, ran amok when the fusillade opened. Not all of them escaped. Knots of hysterical people helped, with linked arms, some limp victim to hospital, face and clothes running blood. A priest, materialising from nowhere, hastened with the viaticum from a dying girl to a man with his brains splashed over his trousers. Two boys with head-wounds and dark clotted hair lay dead. An old man was shot – *blind*.

On Wednesday morning we had two surprising items of news – that Sir Roger Casement had been sent to the Tower – homely climax to his strange adventure by land and sea, to be run down by a peasant's daughter in Kerry – and that Sheehy Skeffington had been shot in Portobello Barracks. Poor Skeffington, the alert, good-humoured-looking little man, with his air of perpetually savouring a joke and hurrying to a mass meeting with some brilliant amendment up his sleeve – we were very sorry for him.

That evening I witnessed a delightful conflict between a Volunteer sniper and some soldiers. The former was either too humane for his work or too uncertain; the latter appeared too unnerved and amateurish. The exchanges took place across a green railed-in lawn, the combatants taking cover and behaving in the accepted fashion. War on these terms might become the most fascinating game possible, leaving the most pacific conscience without an objection. An almighty racket, plenty of movement, thrills galore, no casualties, and honour – I hope – satisfied. No one saw the sniper except the writer, and on fours the sniper could not have sniped the megatherium.[4]

About midnight a thin shaft of light showed white through the closed shutters of my room. Kneeling at the window I watched the quivering glare of a searchlight passing the roofs and chimneys in review. There was a venomous volley in unison – yet not quite so – and when I knelt down, wondering which bullet had got home first, thinking of the murderous hide-and-seek of those strange lonely vigils on the housetops of our afflicted city, thinking, too, that out there those abrupt dramas were being played, Irishman against Irishman on the holy soil of our country – I could only pray simply – God save Ireland. But God sees the confusions and implications of our worship.

The world knows how the following two days passed, position after position falling to the military, guns smashing desolation and horror by night and day into the burning heart of Dublin, troops closing in nearer, nearer. And on Saturday, with infinite relief and some incredulity, came the tidings of surrender, of another dream laid, of the end of good, impractical men's hearts' desire, the end of that Irish Republic that struck, in full confidence of victory, fifteen hundred against the greatest empire the world has known, in fair fight, struck and failed, but kindled for the generous imaginations of mankind a touch of romance that darkened a whole continent of armies. It is over now with its stresses and piteousnesses, its hopes, its prides, and devotions – over forever, except its enduring memory. Against every array of contumely I will still maintain that in its spirit and unselfishness this was something almost religious – in despite of which sedentary madmen in the coming days will write superficial devilment (as many of them are doing now) for the children of Ireland yet unborn and Ireland's woe. Time is a healer and novelty a philtre to close the eyelids of retrospect; but can one ever enter the new building, to buy stamps across a brand-new counter from a brand-new clerk, thoroughly disinfected of all dangerous sentiments, without thinking of the old building at the close of the red week, when the fabric of dream-stuff was shot and riven and the last gallant rally was made to the bleeding heart of an enterprise – the spirit heart of the Irish Republic!

'THE PEOPLE WERE THOROUGHLY COWED'

Sir John Evelyn Wrench was a tireless worker in the cause of developing the Commonwealth, and trying to bring together the English-speaking countries of the world, as a means of furthering world peace. One-time editor of The Spectator *magazine, Wrench wrote a number of books, including* Struggle 1914–1920, *in which he recalls his reaction on hearing about the Easter Rising, and quotes from an account written by his father, Frederick Stringer Wrench.*[1] *Although some of Wrench senior's notes are hard to believe ('had to drive through a force of 100 armed Sinn Feiners'), the accounts given by both Wrenchs are a good example of the sort of rumours and half-truths which circulated during and after the rebellion.*

While in Devonshire for the Easter holidays I received the first confused accounts of the Dublin Rebellion. There had been fighting at Ballsbridge, Stephen's Green and Westland Row Railway Station – places familiar to me since my childhood. I could hardly believe my eyes. A letter from London written on Easter Monday contained this sentence:

> F who is just back from his club tells me there are persistent rumours of the Germans having landed in Ireland and of a revolution there. What a world we live in! He also said there were rumours of the Germans having landed in England and all

the women and children in the towns on the East Coast have been ordered inland.

The papers reported the capture of Sir Roger Casement, who had landed off the coast of Kerry with an Irish companion in a small boat put ashore by a German submarine. What was the virus that had turned a man once high up in the British consular service, who had accepted a title and a pension from the British government, into a rebel? The Irish patriots had their eyes on America, and when I read the manifesto of 'The Provisional Government of the Irish Republic', in which the story was told how Ireland, 'supported by her exiled children in America and by gallant allies in Europe', had struck 'in the full confidence of victory', I was bewildered.

Apparently the sceptics were right. The underground machinations of the Irish Republican Brotherhood had been more widespread than I supposed. The Irish extremists, whom I had met in America, were apparently the real leaders of 'progressive' Ireland, and not John Redmond and his following.

This account of the Rebellion was written by my father at the time: On Easter Monday 24th April, 1916, I went into Dublin as usual by the 9 o'clock train from Ballybrack and called at the Kildare Street Club on my way up to the RDS show grounds at Ballsbridge, where I had promised to meet Mr Robert Bruce, our agricultural superintendent, to see that everything was ready for the opening of our Spring Show the next day.

Most of the cattle and other exhibits had fortunately arrived at the show grounds the previous Saturday. At the club I met a friend who had just come up from Cork. He told me that his district was very unsettled and that they had been expecting some sort of outbreak for the last few days. However I didn't see how that could affect our show, especially as I knew the southern cattle would be in, and I proceeded to Ballsbridge promising to come back and lunch with some friends at 1 o'clock.

Bruce and I did our business and agreed that the Show was a very promising one. I was leaving about 12.30 and was standing at the Show Entrance when two little telegraph boys dashed up on their bicycles shouting 'they're out' and that they had seen a man shot in Stephen's Green. Shortly afterwards we had telephone messages from the Dublin Society's offices in Kildare Street giving us all the information to be had. There was no use in trying to go back to Dublin as the streets were said to be full of armed rebels and spasmodic shooting was going on.

The first thing we did was to get a big hose, that was supplied with a powerful force of water, into position in case we were attacked. We then decided that there was no use in funking and that the Show should be held unless we were actually stopped. We soon heard that we need not expect any of our friends from the south, that troops were coming rapidly from the Curragh and that English regiments had also been telegraphed for. Fortunately our President, Lord Rathdonnell, was staying at Kingstown and we expected our judges and many friends from England to arrive by the boat that afternoon, and I undertook, if it was possible, to meet them on my way home to Ballybrack and to tell them what had happened in case they liked to go back by the next boat.

This brought us up to about 4 o'clock when I left the show to try and accomplish my mission. I had just secured an outside car when some poor people I knew in Wicklow came up to me, saying that they had come up to Dublin for the holiday and didn't know how to get back. So I said I would take them in my car to Kingstown whence they would be able to get a train to Wicklow. The husband, wife and a baby got up on one side of the car and a little girl got up with me on the other side, and I always thought it was a fortunate arrangement from my point of view. If I had been alone and not one of a holiday party, I might have been stopped, as about a mile from the show we actually had to drive through a force of 100 armed Sinn Feiners. On getting to Kingstown I found that my English friends had no ambition to witness an Irish rebellion, and most of them went straight back by the next boat.

Next day, Tuesday, 25th April, I was in Kingstown before 8 o'clock when a most unwonted sight met my eyes. Cavalry soldiers were bivouacking outside the St George's Yacht Club and inside every available inch was occupied by officers, many of whom had slept there, only too thankful to have a roof over their heads. I found out who were the commanding officers and told them that we were going to hold the Show but as there would be few visitors we could put up a considerable number of the military at Ballsbridge and could hand over to them the provisions that we had laid in for our expected guests. I then drove on into the Show with a carman I knew well and found that Lord Rathdonnell, our President, and Mr Doyne were the only other officials who were able to reach the Show.

When we had everything settled as to the arrangements for the Show, emergency judges, and the accommodation for the soldiers, the day looked as if it was going to be a day of fighting. I went back to Killiney for luncheon to see that my family was all right. After luncheon I walked up Killiney Hill with my glasses and watched Dublin and notably the Post Office in Sackville Street, which was occupied by the Rebels, being shelled with wonderful accuracy by the gun boats in Kingstown.

Then I went into the Show again and brought Matthews our shorthorn auctioneer, head of Messrs Thornton & Co. back with me to stay the night and discuss the extraordinary situation.

It was a very hot day and the English troops marched up from Kingstown and generally made a halt when they reached Ballsbridge before they got into the line of fire. One British regiment consisted of young recruits, such a nice lot of boys. We brought them lemonade, for which they were most grateful. Only six or eight hundred yards on they had to pass houses that were occupied by rebel snipers, and nearly two hundred of them were killed and many wounded. It always seemed to me such a wanton waste of life, though we tried to explain to them as well as we could the geography of the streets in that part of Dublin and what they might expect.

The next three days there was so much to do that I went into the Show and remained there all day. The military were getting the situation well in hand though there were spasmodic outbursts and we still had to have soldiers guarding our house. Wonderfully little damage was done at the Dublin Society's premises. We could see the bullet marks through some of the high iron roofs.

There was a very brisk sale of the prize-winning animals and I got 900 guineas for the Champion yearling Shorthorn Bull which was the highest price I had realised up to that time.

English newspapers and letters, of which we had been deprived for the first four or five days, began to circulate again, and by the end of the week things were becoming normal. On the 1st of May I was once more able to go as usual to the Land Commission Office in Dublin and learn the news, and on Tuesday for the first time I lunched at the Kildare Street Club. Dublin was a ruined city for the time being and Sackville Street a scene of desolation. With considerable rejoicing we heard of Birrell's resignation on the 4th of May, his feeble efforts as a ruler had brought about much of the Irish trouble. A new spirit of distrust of the people seemed to permeate every branch of the civil service.[2] Mr Asquith paid a visit to Ireland which did far more harm than good, and all the old spirit of friendship and goodwill, which was one of the great charms of Irish life, vanished overnight.

Several Roman Catholic farmers and dealers, good friends of mine, came to see me and talk things over. They complained bitterly of this changed feeling, and more than one went down to his grave saddened by the changed aspect of Ireland.

There were just two occasions when conscription could have been introduced with very little difficulty and when the people were more or less expecting it; the first was in the spring of 1915 when I wrote to six prominent members of the Cabinet and to Lord Kitchener. All the Cabinet ministers sent me replies and most of them appeared to approve of my suggestion. Lord Kitchener alone gave me only an acknowledgment and I heard afterwards privately that he disapproved of trying to conscript the Irish. The other occasion was shortly after the rebellion when the people were thoroughly cowed.

FW

'HER DEAR BOY IS AT NORTH WALL WITH HIS MACHINE-GUN'

The following letter by Margaret Mitchell to her sister Flora, written during the Rising, gives a good idea of the fear and downright panic felt by ordinary citizens, confined to their homes with supplies dwindling and rumours flying, while gunfire sounded nearby.[1] Herself and her neighbours are variously 'agitated' or 'very anxious', and one is described as 'having got the fever on her, which made it absolutely impossible to sit quiet'. Nevertheless, Mrs Mitchell shows herself to be resilient and resourceful under the pressure: 'We have made up beds & are ready for emergencies, & I shall pack up a few things for myself & family in case we have to flit in a hurry.' She also has an understanding of the significance of what she's witnessing and describing – she starts her letter with: 'I feel as if I must begin to tell you current events which will probably be history in a very short time', and later she writes: 'So good-night, dear people, I am sure you are praying for us all, & the city.' Here, it's easy to think she was aware that she was writing for a much wider audience than her sister.

Woodcote, Herbert Park
Dublin
                                              April 24th 1916

My dear Flora –

I feel as if I must begin to tell you current events which will probably be history in a very short time.

About 12.30 this morning, we heard a great deal of firing, &
I said laughingly 'I wonder if the Sinn Feiners are out.'

About 2.15, a neighbour of ours came in to warn us not to
go out, as the Sinn Feiners had taken Dublin, & there were 20
casualties already, & more occurring. I rang up Mrs Armstrong,
& Emmie answered that her mother had gone out, but that a
neighbour had been in to tell them of it, & that her husband had
been in town, & ordered by Sinn Feiners which street he was
to go up & which not – at the point of the bayonet – Sis and I
put on our things & went down to Ballsbridge.[2] There we found
crowds of people standing about in knots & no trams running.
Mrs Armstrong was not there, so we walked on to her house, &
found her very agitated, as she had been down to see the animals
coming to the Show yard for the Spring Show, which opens
tomorrow but was told by a Railway official that there would be
no more trains tonight, as the Sinn Feiners had taken possession
of Westland Row, & made the Railway men tear up the lines
outside the station, at the point of the bayonet – Kingsbridge
station was wrecked this morning & Harcourt Street Station.[3]
Mrs Armstrong is in a panic as she is afraid the Germans are
upon us & is afraid for the girls. I have offered them asylum here
if they wish, but they are going to their next door neighbours.

Arthur has just been down as far as Leeson Street Bridge, to
see the Whites but no further news.[4] He rang up the Club, &
the news from there (Sackville Street) is the Irish Hussars were
called out, got into Sackville Street, where the Sinn Feiners
opened fire upon them, killing several, & wounding several &
killing the horses under them. So the rest were sent back to
Barracks – the horses were still lying dead in the street, & the
casualties taken to hospitals.

They have taken the GPO & no messages can be sent. Of course it means something very serious, & we must only pray things may quiet down soon. We have made up beds & are ready for emergencies, & I shall pack up a few things for myself & family in case we have to flit in a hurry.

The Sinn Feiners have taken a bank on the corner of Stephen's Green, barricaded the streets with cars, carts, carriages etc., & are shooting at all & every such. They are digging trenches in Stephen's Green, why, I don't quite know. Some one says there are 16,000 Germans in Bantry Bay waiting to land! The plan is pre-conceived, as the Sinn Feiners have risen in Cork, Limerick & Belfast simultaneously!

We expect to have the telephone stopped at any minute. The housemaid went out for her holiday to Lucan at 12 noon. I wonder if she ever got there, or if she is one of the casualties. She will not be able to get back anyway. Now no more – I will add to this later tonight or tomorrow.

Tuesday 6 p.m.
The housemaid rang up about 7.45 p.m. to say she was unable to get through Dublin & was staying at home so that was a great relief. No one came to spend the night, but Arthur & I did not do much sleeping. There was intermittent firing all night & we could not sleep. This morning the milkman and baker both came, so we were able to get milk & bread. We were up early, I had breakfast at 8 o'clock. Arthur went round to old George to see what he was going to do as the Distillery was taken by the Sinn Feiners yesterday,[5] & they had taken all the floats & carts for barricades – George himself had been telephoned to yesterday, he was at Betty Glen, & had to walk every step of

the way to Bow Street, by a very circuitous route, & allowed in, but the place was occupied by ten or twelve Sinn Feiners & the caretaker was in a panic, however. It appears she stayed there the night, waiting hand & foot on the men, who ordered drinks & food, which she had to supply. It was useless to try & go in this morning. Mr Taylor tried & Mr Davie, but they were both turned back, & not allowed to cross the river at any Bridge. It has been a long day, & tales which we have heard are terrible. Shooting continued all the day, & at 11 o'clock Marshall [sic] Law was proclaimed, & all citizens were told to keep in their houses & they were given three hours to do it in. At 3 o'clock the military opened fire with big guns, & it was a terrible sound, the rifle firing, & the booming of the cannon. We could hear it all distinctly from here, but it seemed so strange that it was all within a mile, or a mile & a half of us where we were, walking calmly about with death going on so near us.

Mrs Hodge came in at 4.30, having got the fever on her, which made it absolutely impossible to sit quiet, so she put on her things & went out at 12 o'clock, & went into the town. She saw terrible sights, but felt drawn towards it. Dead horses, dead Sinn Feiners, & she saw one of the big guns firing from Trinity College right down Dame Street, & she went to the Shelbourne Hotel, & there saw the military who were in the hotel firing on the Sinn Feiners who were in Stephen's Green. They were in the trenches, & every time the military saw a movement in the trenches they fired, a volley would come back. She says she saw several dead lying in the Green. Yesterday the good old GRs went for a route march in the morning, came back at 3 o'clock not knowing anything about all this.[6] We saw them marching through Ballsbridge, down to Lansdowne

Road where they dismissed, and began wending their way to their different homes by ones & twos. Two were shot dead & several wounded, two so badly that they died shortly after. One was 'Chicken' Browning.[7] Charlie Power's great friend is lying dangerously wounded in Baggot St Hospital. It is really terrible – we heard this afternoon that troops have arrived from the Curragh and from England in a warship. Anyway the GPO has been retaken by the military. The Welsh Fusiliers were put on that job, & 70 soldiers are killed.

Kingstown & the telephone are mercifully in the hands of the military, but nothing but military matters can be posted or cabled. I hope you will not be getting anxious. Of course we are completely isolated as far as post & press are concerned. Arthur has gone to lie down, he is tired out, he was really quite seedy yesterday, & never slept a wink last night, poor fellow. We are terribly anxious, & if there is any likelihood of its continuing, he would like to get the girls out of the country if possible, as this *may* be connected with the Germans; & they would be safer with you.

We are all in God's Hands & can only pray Him to guide all things for our good & eternal Peace, but they are terrible times we are living in.

Mrs Le Peton was here this afternoon, & her dear boy is at North Wall with his machine-gun, & she is very anxious, & all alone, her husband is in England, so she may come up & spend the night here.[8] Torrents of rain fell for an hour after the cannon fired, but it is a fine evening. Percy & Billy Jones came in this morning. They had ridden in to the office as usual. Percy did not go in, when he found it was in the hands of the Sinn Feiners, but Billy rode right in, & found the gates locked

& a barricade of all the tables & chairs out of the offices, every window smashed, & ledgers & papers & deed boxes piled up in them for cover & men with rifles guarding them; one man accosted him, & he answered civilly, so the man allowed him to ride off again. The shops are being looted, or rather, were yesterday, & Sybil Robinson, who went right down to the Pillar saw the women and children taking the hats & boots & things out of the windows which had been broken. It certainly is a dreadful state of things, & cannot be put right for years, if ever. The loss of life is dreadful, & property is damaged, fires have been started, shops burnt to the ground, & we hear that Jacob's factory has been burnt down, but this may not be true. The telephone is ringing, but there is no answer when we take it up, it has been in the hands of the military for the last twenty-four hours, & we have not been able to use it. I wonder whether you have heard anything of it all, & what – Yes! it's Andrew ringing up, asking for news. He has just come from the North. I am glad he is home again, he evidently knows nothing.

Wednesday night 9 p.m.
We are still alive, but it has been a terrible day. Firing went on intermittently all night, & early this morning, Arthur got on his bicycle to ride down to Leeson Street Bridge to see what the chances were of getting into the Distillery. He managed to get as far as Stephen's Green which was open, he rode on & tried to get into the Green itself by the gate on the corner opposite the Shelbourne Hotel, & had only just got in, when two shots whizzed over his head, so he came out again, but not before he had seen two dead Sinn Feiners in the trenches & the ground strewn with rifles, caps, bayonets, etc. After breakfast

he went to see what old George was going to do, & eventually they started out together to see if they could get through to the Distillery; they parted company about St Patrick's Cathedral as Arthur did not consider it safe to go on, & George wished to. Three minutes after they parted, Arthur found himself in difficulties, & took hours to get home, as he was turned back from street after street, & had to go round by Harold's Cross Bridge, Portobello, etc., & so home. Comparing notes with George this afternoon, precisely the same thing had happened to him, three minutes after parting, and he had to take the same circuitous route. The girls & I sallied forth about 11.30, & went to see how the Armstrongs were getting on. They were all out, but we waited about 20 minutes & then walked up Baggot Street & met all very cheery, hoping the worst was over; laden with provisions. We fixed up about their coming to us this afternoon, as we had arranged about a fortnight ago, & we parted. Most of the shops are closed, & we had difficulty about getting anything. No butter or margarine to be had *at all.*

We walked home, & Arthur came in shortly after. About 1 p.m., the most dreadful firing took place *quite* close, & we found it was from a house immediately opposite the Armstrongs, on the corner of Pembroke Road & Northumberland Road, which the Sinn Feiners had absolutely commandeered from Mr Layne-Joynt [*sic*], & there they had a machine gun & waited for the military.[9] The soldiers arrived at Kingstown from England, & were marched every step of the way from there with their full kit, rifles and ammunition. They were marched right into the trap, & were mown down by the Sinn Feiners. It was terrible. The battle raged for almost an hour, & then silence. The next thing was along the Donnybrook Road came the next lot of troops, marching from Kingstown, the Notts & Derbys, evidently they had been warned about the lower road; they were fearfully hot & dusty & tired. The day being a real summer's day, intensely hot sun. Firing began again very heavily about 4 p.m. Of course the Armstrongs never arrived, & I am afraid they have had a very dreadful time, but we dare not go down till tomorrow. Then about 5.40, it began again, most dreadful to hear, & Sis & I made up our minds we would go to the bottom of Herbert Park, & try & find out where it was. Well it was awful, there were hundreds of troops coming from Kingstown, & they were halted just at the bottom while the ones in the front were engaging the enemy. Sis could see what she thinks were dead & wounded lying in the road, & the motor ambulance came up, but we did not stay long, because the proclamation[10] had told us to stay in our own homes, & not hamper the military, but it was hard to realise that there was a deadly fight going on so near, & crowds looking on as if at a sham battle. Whole families, Father, Mother, swarms of kids, pram with the baby & dog on a string, which was a common sight. Tonight there is a fierce fire raging. We can see the smoke & a flame or two, after heavy bombarding it is Boland's Bakeries next the Cats' Home, which the Sinn Feiners are in possession of, and the military have blown the whole place up. This morning, after heavy cannonading from a gunboat on the Liffey below the Customs House, Liberty Hall was blown up, & we hear there were 100 men in it. It makes one feel positively sick, & of course we have no husband or resources, as no provisions of any sort are able to get into the town, and it will be months before things are normal again. The looting of the shops has been dreadful, we hear all police are confined to Barracks, so there is no one to guard property & women & children are stealing wholesale. Lawrence's toy shop, & the shop next it utterly destroyed by fire, & I expect it will be Jacobs factory next. Not one of the five men who started for the Distillery this morning, & all went different ways ever got there. They had to return home. Andrew managed to ring me again at 7 p.m. tonight, but he cannot get in, & cannot realise what is going on, except that they could get no provisions, & had to motor to Balbriggan to get necessities. Oh dear, it is all very awful, & the worst of it is, one does not know friends from enemies, & dare not speak to anyone. As I am writing, firing has begun again, one can only surmise, but the different weapons have different sounds. The Sinn Fein rifles are feeble in sound compared with the military's rifles, which are generally fired in a volley, whereas the enemy's rifles are single shots. Then there is the pit-pit of the machine guns, & then the real heavy guns. Now Arthur is home from old George's, & wants us all to go to bed. So good-night, dear people, I am sure you are praying for us all, & the city.

27 APRIL 1916

3.30 p.m.

Fairly quiet night but such a morning, heavy cannonading & sniping. All sorts of rumours, but very little authentic, & most difficult to locate the firing. About 10 a.m. Arthur & I went up to Ranelagh on our bicycles, with a view to getting provisions. The shops were like a siege, all closed, & only a few women let in at a time & only small quantities of things being sold to each customer. I could only get a quarter stone of flour, & half stone of oatmeal, but I took all I could get, & two sides of beef. Arthur & I staggered home laden. Other people in the Park were clamouring for food & some had been left bread-less. Then about 11.30 we discovered about fifty soldiers resting in the Park, so after cogitating with myself I came to the conclusion they were worthy objects, so sallied forth with the half box of cigarettes, & two dozen boxes of matches I had for the Soldiers Buffet, eighteen pieces of chocolate, & acid drops, & Sis & I distributed them. They were so grateful, & we could have done with twice the amount. Other people were doing the same, so I hope every man got something. Then we watched between 2 & 3,000 troops pass with their full kit. Ambulance, provisions, a field canteen, Royal Engineers with all their equipment, Naval guns & blue jackets, such a host. The regiments were 'Notts & Derby' besides gunners.

The girls think McCrerick (can't spell it) but one of George's boys passed, though Sis thinks he was in a Somerset or Devon regiment. We hear five warships came into Kingstown this morning, & there is a proclamation today from the Commander-in-Chief ordering all civilians to be in their houses between 4 p.m. and 5 a.m. in the morning. A lady in the Park very kindly told me she had a way of sending letters to the Mail tonight, so I have sent you a card, which I hope you will get in due course.

We were misinformed about the Post Office being re-taken by the Military. It is still in the hands of the Sinn Feiners. Poor Mr Browning died last night, he was shot on Monday, returning from Lansdowne Road after dismissing from a route march of GRs on Easter Monday. His makes the first death out of that small lot, & there are still several wounded severely. If I get this through to you before the mails are running again, will you let Charlie Power know as he was such a great friend of his.

6 p.m.

Terrible news since writing the above, apparently a whole terrace has had to be demolished, Herbert Place, if you know where the Collards used to live. The Sinn Feiners were on the tops of the houses, & from the sound I should think the military have demolished it all. We could hear the houses falling after each gun-fire. The Red Cross nurses came to Miss Wade's school this afternoon in motors,[11] so the girls went out to know if there was any help wanted, but came back to say they were only collecting everything they could for the wounded. So the girls asked people about, & you should see the collection, enough for one whole ward anyway – mattresses, blankets, sheets, pillow cases, pillows, even *beds* people brought out & they loaded up the cars, sent them off, & returned for more, bowls, basins, towels, etc. It was grand work. Joan Armstrong & the girl staying with them came round this afternoon to tell of the awful time they had yesterday, but it is too long a story to begin on. Joan showed us a flattened bullet which they picked up outside Mrs Armstrong's bedroom door! & their windows were smashed & Mrs Armstrong was grazed by a bullet. They saw a man they knew, a civilian shot dead on his doorstep, as he was putting his latchkey in the door, to go in, & that was a shock for them. The worst is that so many civilians must be suffering & killed. It is like exterminating rats, & they are in twos & threes in different houses. There goes the machine gun again. God help us all. The city is in flames in many places like Sodom & Gomorrah; & it makes one feel quite *sick*. So far we are all well, & our nerves are steady, but one does not know from hour to hour what may happen. I must say here, that a great many things I have written down, I find are not the facts, only rumours. What we thought was Boland Bakeries last night was St Stephen's schools on the Northumberland Road.

'THE SOLDIERS HAVE COME AND WE REJOICE'

Isabel Fleming lived at 32 Northumberland Road where, in April 1916, she found herself right in the centre of the heaviest fighting the rebellion would see – what became known as the Battle of Mount Street Bridge. One of the main rebel positions was a corner house just across the road from her, 25 Northumberland Road. Her recollection of those days provides a fascinating account of a civilian caught up in events far beyond her control, and an idea of how she felt can be had from the title she gave her typewritten manuscript: 'Dublin During the Reign of Terror. At the Cross Roads'.[1]

The early hours of Easter Monday, April 24th, 1916, differed little from many of its predecessors, the usual crowd of holiday-makers gathered at the corner of Northumberland Road awaiting cars for the country, until about noon when I noticed there was some hitch in the tram service, and an incoming tram-car brought a body of police. During the afternoon I heard a couple of shots, which somewhat surprised me.

About 4.30 as I stand at an upper window I see a small detachment of the GR Veterans marching towards the City, the afternoon had been warm, they look hot and tired, a sharp report rings out, a man in the foremost rank falls forward on his face, to all appearances, dead – a ghastly stream of blood is flowing from his head. His comrades fly for cover – the shelter of a tree – the side of a flight of steps. Bullet follows bullet with lightening [*sic*] rapidity, the road is unusually deserted and silent, until one of the veterans dashes across it, and falls wounded at the feet of a woman who sets up a wail of terror.

I cannot bear to look and yet I feel impelled to do so, of the six or eight men by the tree only one is now standing – they must have lain down that they may not prove such good targets, but no – they have fallen on their backs, one over another – they are all wounded! Oh! the horror of it all, what does it mean?

A wounded man is being borne in the direction of our house – we rush to open the door and offer assistance, but they turn in next door. I cannot watch longer, I must go back to my mother who is sitting by the fire, she is old and frail, she must not know of what is passing, so I try to appear as usual.[2] After a time I return again to the window, I see a bare-headed, white-coated doctor drive up in a motor.

He disappears into one of the houses to tend the wounded, some of whom are then carried off to the hospital, the crowd which has gathered gradually melts away. Later on we find a bullet has come through the window, beside the door we had opened – was it intended for us as a punishment for offering shelter to the wounded?

Tuesday

Our road is quiet, yet I hear a sound of constant firing, from what quarter I do not know, neither milkman nor baker will tell us anything, I elect to stay indoors and await events. No police are to be seen, no postmen, the tram-cars are not running, nor yet the trains from Westland Row nor are there any newspapers.

At dinner-time bullets are whizzing by the windows.

Wednesday

The morning hours pass quietly, but at noon the sudden report of a rifle close at hand breaks the silence – I run to the window – khaki-clad figures are creeping along at both sides of the road, getting what shelter they can from the low stone wall supporting iron railings – I hastily close all shutters, fearing a repetition of the scene of Monday, but the soldiers have come and we rejoice. Alas! poor soldiers – neither we nor they knew of the death-trap into which they were about to fall!

We take up a position on a landing at the top of the kitchen stairs as being the safest spot, for more than an hour we listen to the sound of battle, there seem to be many men engaged, we think some are in our garden, or on our steps, they are attacking the corner houses nos. 25 opposite, 26 and 28 on this side of Northumberland Road. We fear they are wavering, I hear a voice shouting 'you won't give way now, boys.' Almost immediately there is a hurried knock at our side door, we run to open it. 'May wounded men be brought in here?' We gladly welcome them and hasten to give the little help in our power, bring water, towels, cushions to put under their poor heads. The two brought in are, alas! very badly wounded – the Adjutant of the Sherwood Foresters is unconscious, the young Lieutenant is in great pain, the doctor and some Red Cross men are with them, but so hurriedly have they been sent to Ireland that no medical supplies nor comforts are forthcoming, and it was sometime before any anaesthetics could be procured.[3]

We lose count of time, and meals are forgotten – except to provide tea and bread for the soldiers, who have had no proper meal since they left their quarters.

All day long the battle rages. The noise is terrible; revolver, rifle, and machine gun are doing their deadly work – more wounded lie outside – but can only be brought in under cover of darkness.

The Adjutant still lies unconscious on our dining-room floor, a Red Cross man keeps watch beside him. The doctor advises me to take my mother to another room, we try the drawing-room, but a bullet has crashed through the window, the mirror over the mantelpiece is shattered, the floor strewn with glass – it is too unsafe – I bring my mother back. The poor Adjutant is dead, they carry him to the hall.

Suddenly there is a tremendous crash, a bomb has been thrown, in order to drive the rebels from a house a few yards distant. Their aim was true, a cheer goes up – the glass round our hall-door is smashed by the concussion – upstairs in my mother's room a bullet has crashed through the window, but does no further damage.

About 8.30 p.m. the firing ceases, they tell us that the houses in our immediate vicinity are all now in the possession of the military, the wounded are removed, and we are left to take what rest we can.

All night we hear the sound of marching feet, no word is spoken, only a steady tramp and every now and then rings out the report of a sniper's rifle. The doctor tells me that a whole division consisting of more than 15,000 men have come to help us, thank God.

Thursday
Much sound of firing from early morning until about 6 p.m. More houses in the neighbourhood are taken by the military. A naval gun is brought from Kingstown on a cart which does

great execution and is taken back amid cheers. Soldiers are posted on the roofs of the houses between us and Mount Street Bridge … a dozen houses away. They fire continually towards the Railway Bridge (beside Beggar's Bush Barracks) which is still a stronghold of the rebels.

Our food supplies are getting short; the milkman cannot reach us nor yet the baker's van – neither can we venture out to seek for food.

Friday
Still more soldiers come! They halt before reaching the crossroads, a volley is fired, and in detachments of twenty-five or so, they take the crossing at a run. Poor weary fellows! I saw them sit down in the ranks while waiting for their turn, yet never a man fell out of all those I watched running for their lives.

Next come the ammunition wagons – the finest sight of all – they paused, a soldier sits on top, his rifle pointed towards the rebels' quarters. The drivers each whips up his pair of shaggy-hoofed horses and in one breathless moment they take the crossing at a gallop.

The terrible noise of firing goes on around us all day and far into the night. A strange contrast – the troops as they march citywards meet with a varied reception: from the houses which had been seized by the Sinn Feiners, a murderous fire from rifle and revolver is poured upon them: from others, not in the direct line of fire, sally forth ladies and their maids, bearing trays with cups of tea and plates of bread and jam to feed the hungry men. It made quite a festive scene under the bright sunshine which marked the days of the tragic week.

I heard it said that some of the soldiers when they were landed in Kingstown asked if they were in France, while a lad asked in this house if they had been brought over to fight Carson's crowd, so little did they know.[4]

Saturday

No bread. I rise early and go out to seek a bread-cart on some neighbouring road not subject to such continuous fire as ours. A young officer is kind and gets me through without a pass. I succeed and return in triumph with two loaves! Now we want milk, and having spent the day waiting to get a pass at the head quarters a few doors away, I sally forth armed with it and my jugs, but on hearing from a soldier that a Sinn Feiner has just been shot on the very road for which I was making, my courage fails me – I return with them empty.

Sunday

At noon there is an alarm. Suddenly there is a rush. An officer orders our windows to be closed – soldiers run into our garden and take up positions there. My mother being still in bed, I get her up hastily and bring her to the dining-room, where I finish her toilet. We spend the strangest Sunday of our lives, sitting in a shuttered room listening to the sounds of fighting all around – it must be that armed bands of rebels are being cleared out of all their strongholds near us. By evening comparative quiet is restored, but the sentries, who are posted very close to each other, still keep a sharp look-out, and soldiers lie on the ground on their faces, with rifles pointing towards the Railway Bridge.

Every night there has been tremendous firing, one knows

not where – the road is dark as pitch – no house is allowed to show a light, and no one moves except the military.

Monday

The tension is relaxed, we have our first visitor from the outside world (every one still requires a pass), our friends bring us food. We are, thank God, no longer in the firing-line.

'NOTHING TO SEE EXCEPT
A DEAD HORSE LYING
AT THE STREET CORNER'

In 1916 Andrew Bonaparte-Wyse was a high-ranking civil servant working in the Education Office, and living in Blackrock, Dublin. He described his experiences during the Rising in two letters to his brother, Captain Napoleon (Nap) G. Bonaparte-Wyse, on Ministry of Education headed paper.[1]

Herbert Lodge
May 3rd 1916

My dear Nap,

I am sure you will have been greatly excited over the Rebellion we have been having here for the past ten days, and will like to hear what I have seen of it. The London papers that I have seen, especially the *Times* and the *Daily Mail*, have very good accounts this week which I believe to be accurate & on the whole very fair representation of what has happened. But my own personal experience may also be interesting. So far as we here are concerned we are all right and except for a temporary difficulty about food (we have no butter yet) we suffered little inconvenience.

When the affair broke out on Monday, Maria & I were staying at the Royal Marine Hotel Kingstown where we went on Friday morning for the Easter Holiday.[2] Lulu was also with us,[3] but Nellie & May remained at Herbert Lodge with the servants, but came over on Saturday and Sunday afternoons & joined us at tea.[4] The weather was lovely for Easter & all went well. On Monday morning we hung about the pier & harbour enjoying the sun and no sign of any disturbance was apparent. In fact I thought it curious there was not much of a crowd in Kingstown for the Bank Holiday & said so at the time. In the afternoon at 3 o'clock I went to the top of Marine Road to meet the tram which was to bring Nellie & May from Blackrock to join us for the afternoon. The tram was a little late in arriving but Nellie & May turned up all right shortly after 3, and it was from them I heard the first mention of the Rising. They said that the tram they were in was held up for some minutes between Monkstown and Blackrock & that they heard the conductor saying there was firing of guns in town, and a sort of riot & that the trams would have to stop running, & that the Sinn Feiners were doing it. I returned to the Marine Hotel & found the guests there talking & laughing over the news (which was only vaguely known to them) & the thing was regarded as some sort of a joke & that the Sinn Feiners who drilled in the Dublin streets on several Sundays previously had gone a little farther this time & fallen foul of the police. A little later a report got about that the SF were in possession of the GPO, the Castle (this was untrue), the Hotels in Sackville Street, Stephen's Green, &c, & that the thing was serious. People were a little puzzled, but no fear or anxiety was expressed.

After tea, Nellie & May had to go back to Herbert Lodge, & at 6 I went with them to look for a tram, but was informed that all tram traffic was suspended from 4 o'clock, the rebels being in possession of the tram Power House. As trains had also stopped running, I thought it best to walk back with Nellie & May to Blackrock along the railway line. On our way we saw nothing unusual, but on my questioning an old railway man on the line near Monkstown he told me in a jeering way that Larkin's men were up in revolution, that Westland Row station was barricaded by thugs & all the wires cut – he added that the object was to let the people come into their sights, & altogether he was an unpleasant & slightly truculent old man. I have heard since that many of the railway men helped to destroy railway property. However we got home all right, & on leaving the children at home I rode back to the Hotel on a bicycle without any difficulty. On arriving at Kingstown I saw the mail steamer leaving for England at 7.15 instead of 8.20 as usual (another steamer did leave at 8.20) & I said to myself they are off now to get troops. Nothing further happened on Monday evening, but we went to bed in the hotel rather uneasy in mind.

It had been my intention to take the train into the Education Office on Tuesday morning as usual, & to return to Blackrock from the Hotel later in the day on getting back from the Office. But this course was clearly out of the question now. At 6 a.m. I got out of bed & ran to my hotel window where I saw the mail just arriving from England, & also noticed a 4-funnelled cruiser & a torpedo boat, which had arrived in the night. There was also a queer looking craft, which I am told was a 'monitor'. I returned to bed. At 9 o'c we went down to breakfast. Reports were now alarming. The boots said that the whole city was in the hands of the Sinn Feiners,[5] that John McNeill,[6] their president up to Sunday at least, was in hiding at Kingstown & that soldiers were looking for him there. While at breakfast we noticed a squad of soldiers halt with fixed bayonets before the Hotel where they remained for twenty minutes while their officer came into it – I understand [illegible]. There were no newspapers to be got, no post, no trams, no trains running, no telegraphs or telephones, but an air of suspense & uncertainty, over everyone. After breakfast we walked out in front of the hotel on the esplanade, but were ordered off by soldiers from whom I learnt that all the approaches to the Harbour were to be cleared of civilians & I saw then two warships come near in as if their guns were trained on the railway station & Marine Road. The hotel grounds were cleared of people too, the big outer gates were locked & sentries posted with fixed bayonets on guard.

These warlike preparations alarmed Maria exceedingly especially as it was freely reported that the rebels from Dublin were marching to seize Kingstown (this was one of hundreds of false rumours spreading about in the absence of newspapers) – I was not much alarmed as I knew rebels wd. have no chance in view of the warships in the harbour.

So the day dragged on & in the afternoon we decided to go home. By paying double fares we persuaded a cabman to drive us to Blackrock & we took a circuitous route round by the hinterland of Kingstown & Monkstown but arrived safely. No disturbance or signs of war in Blackrock and no reliable news to be got of any kind.

Next morning I was up early – still no post or papers & I determined to go into Dublin & see what I could discover for myself. I bicycled without interruption – no trams of course – to Anglesea Rd Donnybrook where my friend and successor in the office of private secretary lives and found him just over breakfast & full of the news. At 10.30 or so we sallied forth on

foot over Ballsbridge & by Merrion Square into College Green.[7]
Very few people in the streets, all shops shut – at Lansdowne
Rd corner we saw a private house belonging to a Mr Lane
Joynt (the crack revolver shot) with blinds down which was full
of rebels.[8] Lane Joynt had been ordered to leave on Monday
afternoon by a band of fifteen rebels who came to the door
fully armed & gave him 10 minutes to clear out. He describes
them as quite young fellows, except one or two leaders, and so
trembling with nervousness that one of them let off his rifle
by accident & frightened Lane Joynt's daughter very much. In
Northumberland St at the Canal bridge we saw a school on
one side and a Parochial Hall on the other occupied by rebels
– the windows were piled high with mattresses & benches &
over them one saw the barrels of rifles & the boyish looking
heads of the Sinn Feiners. They made no sound so we passed.
It was here they did their worst crime just after, they ambushed
a half company of the Veterans' Corps doing a Bank Holiday
march, killing six well known Dublin citizens, members of the
Corps, and wounding several others. In Merrion Square we
met a chap pasting up a proclamation of the Ld Lieutenant,
Dublin under martial law – which gave us great satisfaction
– & also managed to buy an *Irish Times*, which had nothing
but the aforesaid proclamation & news which had appeared
before Easter. At Grafton St corner there was an awestricken
crowd gazing down towards College Green, & we turned down
that way. We now heard the first firing of guns, & I found that
every window in Trinity College front was full of soldiers with
rifles. These fellows were it seems collected off the streets on
Monday as they were enjoying the holiday & were furnished
with arms of the OTC of Trinity.[9] At first there were only *four*

OTC men in the College, but the stray force which included many colonials ultimately amounted to fifty men. These fellows successfully defended TCD for five days & also prevented the rebels taking the Bank opposite or doing much in Dame Street. I went no further beyond the College, as there was too much shooting. The rebels were firing from the Pillar & the Rotunda I believe at soldiers who were skirmishing towards O'Connell Bridge from the south side. We then went up Grafton St, where we saw two or three shops broken into, but very few people about, and these seemed to be half dazed with fright – certainly they were not in any active sympathy with the rebels. At the top of Grafton St more firing, & a man said that soldiers were shooting from the roof of the Shelbourne Hotel & the Stephen's Green Club at the rebels in the Square & in the College of Surgeons. There wasn't much to be seen, except a sort of a barricade of overturned wagons & a motor car just opposite the Coll. of Surgeons.

We turned back down Grafton St when a man in the street said that if he were allowed to fight the rebels with his fellows of the Redmondite Volunteers they would knock them out of the Green in ten minutes. We next went up Merrion Square to the corner of Merrion Row & Stephen's Green – more firing going on with rifle & machine gun, but nothing to see except a dead horse lying at the street corner in a pool of blood.[10] Very few people here, but a few civil servants that I knew. Not a policeman or a soldier had I actually seen so far & there was no looting in this part of the town. We next went down to Westland Row to the Butt Bridge. The station at W. Row was barred up & nobody about, but I believe the rebels were inside. At the Butt Bridge there was a guard of soldiers & no one could pass. A small crowd was watching on the quays opposite the North Wall. Across the river we saw Liberty Hall, Larkin's stronghold, which had been shelled that morning from a gunboat in the Liffey. One end was a heap of rubbish, & there was a very neat round hole in the corner wall.

After this we turned back intending to go back to Balls Bridge by the Beggars' Bush Barracks, but I must reserve our further adventures for another letter, as this one is growing under my pen.

Will you send it on to Ealing. I just got your letter dated 2nd inst. this (Thursday) morning. It was a wonderful week, & the more I think of it the more amazed I am at the ineptitude of Birrell & our rulers. There was never a rising more wanton or unwarranted or with less justification. And the foolish Liberal newspapers are still calling upon the Govt. not to be hard on them – the fools!

> I must write more in a day or two.
> Goodbye till then
> Yours ever
> Andrew.

It was almost four weeks later before Bonaparte-Wyse was able to write his next letter to his brother.

Herbert Lodge
Blackrock
28/5/16

My dear Nap

The continuation of my adventures that I was to write you has been so long delayed through pressure of work etc. that it seems almost too late now to refer to the events of Easter Week again. However I must just mention briefly what happened from the time when I stopped my story. I was returning to Blackrock on Easter Wednesday morning. But before I got home that day I witnessed the Battle of Ball's Bridge where the Notts & Derby (Sherwood Foresters) regiment suffered so badly. I arrived back at Ballsbridge about 1 o'clock, just at the moment when about 600 S. Foresters had reached that point on their march from Kingstown, very hot, tired and dusty. These were the first troops to arrive from England & apparently they had no local staff officers to guide them, for they walked into a veritable death trap in Pembroke Rd. They were very well received by the people of all classes who flocked out to their doors along the road & gave them bread, & fruit, & cups of tea & milk, etc. & at Ball's Bridge I heard them cheered by a crowd of artisans' wives who live near there. Very different is the present attitude of these people who, now the danger is over, are abusing the English soldiers! Where Lansdowne Rd meets Pembroke Rd there is a house at the corner facing up towards Ball's Bridge & inhabited by Mr Lane Joynt whom I think I mentioned before. This house & one or two others near it were full of rebels. The soldiers stopped in Pembroke Road for some minutes & seemed to be conferring together. Several civilians spoke with the officers & told them of the house being occupied, but seemingly the officers were too proud or too suspicious to take notice, & after a bit decided to march on in close formation towards L. Joynt's house. I followed them along the pavement on the left hand side keeping in the cover of the garden walls on that side – in a moment shooting began

& many soldiers were hit. The front ranks opened out & took cover behind telegraph poles, knelt, & fired on the house. After a few minutes they were again fired on from a house flanking them in Pembroke Rd itself & then the whole regiment fell back to Ball's Bridge in a fearful stampede.

I thought things were getting too warm, and I took to my heels, but I kept well under cover in the small gardens before the houses, & got across to Clyde Rd. I did not stay to see any more then. I must say this first attack was badly fought. A good commander should have spread his men out into the gardens on the side of the road & have searched the houses on each side before making his attack. In this way few lives would have been lost. It was in this way that Lane Joynt's was taken later in the day, but little progress was made until the artillery came up, when houses containing rebels were fired into & generally the bursting of one shell inside brought down the roof & brought out the rebels who were shot or captured on emerging from the building.

For the rest of the week I didn't go in to town further than Ball's Bridge. At other times we went down near the sea wall at Blackrock & watched the huge columns of smoke & flame which were rising over the city from the burnings in Sackville St, Henry St, Abbey St, & the Quays. The canopy of smoke over the city was terrific, & as we had no idea at the time what streets were burning it looked as if the whole city was in flames. Indeed the devastation was enormous, as of course you know from pictures in the papers, practically every shop in which I dealt, e.g., tailor, bootmaker, hair cutter, shirtmaker, etc., was destroyed. The Education Office was occupied by the military early in the week but happily they had little occasion to fire from it, so that no damage was done there, beyond a few broken windows.

The city is quiet now, but there is a very menacing tone among the lower classes, who openly praise the Sinn Feiners for their courage & bravery, etc., & there is a lot of abuse of the soldiers. At the same time, the latter seem to be popular, at least with the female population. I could relate many facts about the position of the Castle & the under secretary, etc., but this has been published in the report of the Rebellion Enquiry.[11]

I am *amazed* at the attitude of English Unionists at present. Nobody with the least knowledge of this country believes in the loyalty of the Nationalists, & the idea of handing over the administration to a H[ome] Rule Committee as a reward for rebellion is simply appalling in its folly. The *sympathies* of the ordinary Irishman are with Sinn Fein – they want independence, & their only criticism of the rebellion is that it was *foolish* (not criminal or otherwise wrong) but just foolish because it had no chance of success. Had it a possibility of succeeding they would all approve it. To give this country, its police, its postal communications, its railways, into charge of Redmond & Dillon (Redmond has no authority here now) would simply mean that there would be another rising which would be acquiesced in by the Irish Government. From a military point of view this idea is unthinkable. I strongly suspect Asquith knows this & is putting the job on Ll[oyd] George in the hope of getting rid through failure of his rival in the premiership. But why, oh why, do English Unionists connive at this? Are they insane? The *Morning Post* alone seems to keep its head – I am disgusted at the *Times*. I send you an article from yesterday's *Irish Times* with which I thoroughly agree.

I must close now. Please pass this letter on to Ealing. We are all well here. The Williams are in Greystones for the past fortnight. We shall likely go there before the end of June.

Yours ever
Andrew

'HEAR TRAMPING ON OUR ROOF AND SO DISCOVER THAT SOLDIERS ARE POSTED THERE'

Lady Eileen Chance lived at 90 Merrion Square, near the National Gallery of Ireland, a house she was confined to when the rebellion began. Despite being busy with 'a crowd – fifteen in the house to feed', she found the time to keep a diary of events – one which is interesting not just for its content, but also for the fact that she regularly notes the time of day.[1] The houses surrounding Merrion Square all face each other, and it's clear that there was something of a community among them. In 1900 Eileen was married to Sir Arthur Chance of the Royal College of Surgeons, who was nineteen years her senior, and who she refers to as 'Father'.[2] She was his second wife, and became stepmother to four children.[3] Throughout the diary, she is constantly concerned for her eldest stepson Norman, nine years her junior. The residents of the house try to continue life as normal, but unsurprisingly, aren't successful – 'Play Bridge but very hard to keep our minds on the game with all the shots round us.'

Easter Monday, 24th April

Feeling seedy with influenza cold, remain in bed. Norman goes to the island for golf – Bill, George and Leslie for a day in the mountains, Father to the Mater Hospital. Duke is to play in competition with Alex Hodgson.

12.30

Father brings in story of Sinn Feiners having taken GPO. Says he saw men with revolvers and was advised by police to go home as soldiers were coming with guns. He returns by Butt Bridge and Westland Row where people say the Station too is held by Sinn Feiners. Fancy it is not serious.

2 p.m.

Telephone from George V Hospital to say Duke is to get there as fast as he can, but *not* in uniform.[4] Try to get him, catch him at Castle Golf Club, he is coming in.

2.30

They say Sinn Feiners are entrenching in Stephens Green and have taken College of Surgeons. Beginning to feel uneasy. All quiet outside, very little sign of life. News that the Harcourt Street Station is taken. Very anxious about small boys, they are to come via Dartry Tram. Will they do it or come some other way? Things must be really serious, no trams running, shots being fired at Green and College Green. Telephone Dartry to look out for small boys. They promise to do so.

4.30

Duke arrives disguised as C. Wisdom Hely.[5] There are some funny things about a rebellion and Duke at present is one. Wish we had news of the small boys and that Norman was home.

5.30

Telephone from Dartry – kids safe there, will be kept the night. All sorts of stories about people coming home from Fairyhouse

Races, that their cars are being taken and made into barricades in Stephens Green and elsewhere. Some shooting still going on in the Green.

7 p.m.

Norman home, and telephone from Duke so all is well. Streams of people who went out for the day returning to town on foot. They look very tired. Pity the children. No trauma at all. Early to bed.

Tuesday 25th

All go out to 8 o'c. Mass. No doubt of the Station being taken by Sinn Feiners. Call at 18 Westland Row[6] – Patrick had to walk home from Portmarnock. Make up our minds to get the kids from Dartry. Arrange for them to be left at Mrs A.H. Sullivan's and send Moore on foot for them. Telephone from Khyber Pass to get a message to Judge Fitzgerald.[7] Telephone now in hands of military, only doctors and hospitals can be called. Norman walks to Clyde Road with message to Judge Fitzgerald.

11.30

Bill, George and Leslie arrive. There is a barricade at Leeson Street Bridge they say – wish N was back. Constant firing at Stephens Green. Father and Edward go to look around, say there is a dead horse at the Green, a barricade of motors across the street, and a machine gun blazing away from the Shelbourne Hotel. We hear that yesterday the firing at Portobello Bridge was awful. Sinn Feiners in Davy's public house fired on the people and the soldiers. The R[oyal] I[rish] Rifles fired on them from the grounds of the barracks. It is feared that the Irish Regiments cannot be trusted. Certainly there are no soldiers about, and the police are confined to barracks too. Every moment fresh reports come in. Things seem very serious. Wish I had the kids out of town. No newspapers, no posts since Monday, no trains. Now they say that the Sinn Feiners are in the S[outh] D[ublin] Union, Bolands, Jacobs and a number of corner houses, even in Mount Street and Grafton Street. Nothing to do but sit in the window. Everybody else doing the same. See women going by with hats and all sorts of things. Whoever had a jumble sale must have done very badly with all this upset.[8]

2.30
Llama calls. He and Norman gone to look round. Every now and then great bursts of firing.

4 o'c
Norman comes in with weird stories. Says that TCD is sand bagged, a machine gun there rattled at the Hibernian Bank (held by SF) as they passed. He says he felt uncomfortable. Llama goes along addressing everyone as 'Citizen'. There is a proclamation pasted up warning everyone to keep out of the danger zone. Father bought a copy from a bill poster for sixpence. Funny there are no soldiers, it must be true about the Irish regiments. Glorious weather. Hard luck to be shut up. No news from Duke.

8 o'c
No telephoning now at all, except military calls. Norman goes to Stokes for Bridge – silly goat. Things are quiet so I suppose he is safe.

Wednesday 26th

Norman safe at home anyway. All quiet. Things must be nearly over. Still no posts, papers or trams. Firing all last night, very hard to sleep, must be in Stephen's Green. Sounded very near. We got a bit of beef on our way home from Mass. No hope of getting to O'Sullivan's. Sheridan's charwoman who comes from York Street reports having *seen* dead soldiers and dead Sinn Feiners in the Green. It is true that the SFs have the College of Surgeons, but it is the soldiers in the Shelbourne firing on the trenches in the Green that we hear. They say the OTC (Officers Training Corps, TCD) have saved things for us, that they command the Banks in College Green, and also Kildare Street which let the soldiers in the back way to the Shelbourne. The SFs can't hold out much longer. Troops must turn up soon.

12 o'c

All very quiet. I let Alice[9] and Esther take the kids to Stephens Green to peep round and see the barricade, the dead horse, etc. They may never see such a sight again.

Norman says he felt very uncomfortable coming from Bridge at 1 a.m. He says he ran like a rabbit with his posteriors tucked in passing the Leinster Lawn. He met Doris Lynch who tells a thrilling tale. At 4 a.m. last night a Sinn Feiner armed walked into her room, said they wanted the house and if the family did not clear out they would be shot.[10] The Lynches tumbled out and are now staying with friends in Merrion Square. Norman also says that Captain de Burgh Daly was standing in the window of the University Club when Countess Markievicz stepped from behind the statue in the Green and fired at him. Norman saw the hole in the window. She is said to be in charge of the College of Surgeons. Great firing now. I wish we had not let the kids out.

1 o'c

Kids back – the last trip I will let them take till this is over. Great looting going on – Lawrence's or Elvery's or some such place. Little children playing with cricket bats and Silver Kings in Denzille Lane. Still no soldiers – where are they?

3 o'c

Awful firing somewhere near – Mount Street or Grattan Street I think. Norman gone on roof with glass, can't see anything. Father gone to corner. Lambert, Sir G. Roche, Collins and others all still looking towards Mount Street.[11] What a row – it seems so near. Awful head from the constant firing. Poor people passing with all sorts of things, boots, etc. They say big guns are coming from the Curragh, part by rail and part by road. The Railway is torn up; Railway at Merrion torn up and a bridge on the Great Northern at Donabate torn up too. Telephone from Duke – all well. Walls of hospital lined with soldiers. An attempt on General Headquarters (beside George V) last night, but SF beaten off. SF hold the Four Courts and all the canal bridges so there is no chance of Duke's coming home. Martial law has been declared. There is a notice posted at the corner of Lr Merrion Street, but as Father hears you are sniped if you go to read it none of us have been. Still firing at Mount Street bridge, machine guns and volley firing, they do make a row. A new noise now – big booms now and then, not big guns I think, but much bigger and louder than anything we have had yet.

5 o'c

Less firing down Mount Street way, though lots everywhere else. There is a big fire somewhere near Mount Street.[12] Perhaps it is Boland's and they have been shelling it.

7.30

Play Bridge but very hard to keep our minds on the game with all the shots round us. Sometimes long pauses, then a burst of firing; some isolated sharp shots close to us. There are said to be snipers all over the place. We have taken an early dinner and high tea. It is very hard to manage for such a crowd – fifteen in the house to feed, wish we could get to Cabra but we seem hemmed in on every side. SF at Mount Street, Westland Row, GPO, Stephens Green and Leeson Street. No use trying to get away. Early bed after a very trying day. All our tempers getting short.

Thursday 27th

Wakened very early this morning – about 5 o'c – by really big guns somewhere. The usual 'crack-crack' all night, but this is something very big.[13] Fire down Mount Street burned all night and is now smoking. Beg Father to abandon ____.[14] Firing seems to come down from Westland Row. He thinks we should go. Round Westland Row corner with a very sinking feeling. Nothing unusual except that we walk to Mass on tea and sugar. People carrying off chests of tea; then taking bottles of sweets and smashing them on the pavement. Don't like the feeling of looters so close to us. After ____ urge the Sheridans to come to us as Westland Row is to be bombarded, also we fear a fire in Barrett's the oil people beside them.[15] They insist on sticking to their own ship. It is hard to know which is the safest place. Knock at Newmarket Dairy door, are let in with suspicion.[16] Think we had better get in supplies before all the shops are looted. Find Newmarket people removing their stock to the back of the shop – expect to be looted at any moment. We buy butter and cheese. Going home we meet Cooney going to see if his shop has been looted yet. Father returns with him and gets more beef. Come home to find that no bread or milk have arrived. The carts are being stopped and emptied in the streets. Norman and I go to Johnston, Mooney's, find it closed and a crowd outside. The man calls to us that there is not a loaf in the place. See a crowd round a baker's cart near Kildare Street. Run up to it; find it surrounded by poor women and people like ourselves from Fitzwilliam and Merrion Squares out for bread. Are lucky in getting a fair supply of fancy bread, as the women will only take plain loaves. Come home to find that Alice and Father have gone on a like quest. They return with the same result, so thank God we have bread.

10 o'c

Father makes up his mind to provision. Spots a man from Findlater's going along; gets him to open a side door, and Norman, Ethel, Moore and myself carry home by the back way flour, condensed milk, a side of bacon and a bladder of lard. I have rice, dried beans and dried peas in the house, so unless things are very bad we can't starve. We have a chest of tea in the house. We hate the condensed milk and long to see a milkman. Set the kids tasks to try and keep them quiet, but find it impossible to keep them from the windows or to keep from them ourselves. Hear that the heavy firing this morning was a gunboat which slipped up the river and blew down Liberty Hall. This is a good job anyway. Great fuss in the Square. No. 40 opposite has been made into a Hospital. VADs and Doctors in white coats are going round commandeering mattresses from all the houses. Glad they have not come to us.[17] Very funny to see all the people who don't get up early coming out on their doorsteps to look for the milk and bread carts. Story, O'Donnell, etc., all going out now to hunt for food. Needless to say they won't get any. Story just gone by with cabbage under his arm, and the Master of the Rolls with two loaves.[18]

12 o'c

Soldiers have begun to arrive and are going into the city. At this corner they pause and at the word of command run over the crossing to Clare Street.[19] Lots of them coming now; they look very tired. More and more soldiers. A big batch of them have settled down here. They are filling sandbags with clay from the Square. They are taking all the seats out of the Square and making a sandbagged barricade across Lr Merrion Street. We can't think what they are at. Soldiers filling sandbags have been fired on. They are running from the Square and have sandbagged a place just inside the gate opposite to us, and are firing over towards the South side of the Square. Our friends at the barricade are firing down Merrion Street. I have seen smoke coming out of the top windows of Sir A. Macan's, now a Convent,[20] and there are men on Martin Dempsey's roof right opposite.[21] With a glass we can see that the men on Dempsey's roof are soldiers.

Great firing from there. We have just now discovered that the convent has Sinn Feiners in it, and that the Martin

Dempsey's have been turned out for the soldiers. No. 1 has soldiers; the corner house of Mount Street and Grattan Street Sinn Feiners; and Lahmann's here beside us, and facing up this side of the Square is a stronghold of Sinn Feiners, so we seem to be in a very hot corner.[22]

1 o'c

Visit from Llama and Charlie Armstrong. They have persuaded N to go round to L's rooms. Silly of Norman, as an order was published this morning proclaiming martial law and warning us to stay indoors. Hard luck that the weather is so glorious. We have been sitting in the garden a bit, but some shots sound so close that one gets jumpy. There is a very troublesome sniper on the roofs of Dawson Street who has potted no end of people. They are blazing away at Stephens Green, and now they say that the SF have been driven out of the open and are all in the College of Surgeons. No word from the Mater. No telephone at all. It is rather dreadful not to know what is happening round the city. The SF seem to have had their plans very well laid. They have secured corner houses everywhere. The story of the Irish Regiments being distrusted is untrue. Their not coming out is due to the skill of the SF who have machine guns at Mount Street Bridge commanding Beggar's Bush Barracks; Portobello Bridge commanding the barracks there; the SD Union commanding Richmond Barracks; and the Four Courts commanding the barracks near the Park. They say the country is rising too. The feeling just here is that we are like rats in a trap. I am not feeling as happy as I was. Even the soldiers here are in a fairly tight place.

5 o'c

A new turn of events here. A bombing party have crossed the Square through the bushes. A firing party are lying along the path opposite with rifles towards the South side. The sentries are not allowing anyone to come down Merrion Street at all. I wish Norman was in. I have just spoken to the sentry saying that I will point out N when he comes. Have got cheek in return – 'If he is properly brought up he will go back when I order him.' Have got the soft side of another sentry with bread and tea. He promised to try and let Norman through. Awful young pup of an officer in command here. Bullying everyone, and clearly very jumpy. Asked by a lieutenant to give the soldiers bread at any cost. We have just sent out a tray full of bread and jam sandwiches, and big jugs of tea. No butter left. Lieutenant tells Ethel who has been out feeding the men that they are very hard up for food. EM and maids not allowed to cross the street. Men clearly very hungry.

5 o'c [sic]

Great excitement now. Gun carriages drawn by mules are going into town. They come slowly to the corner and then go galloping over the crossing. The troops just here have been landed at Kingstown; have been in training only three weeks, and think we are all Sinn Feiners. They cannot understand how it is that we all speak English. Some of the officers I hear won't let the troops take food or drink for fear it would be poisoned.

7 o'c

No Norman. He has not been let back. Our butter is finished and thanks to the soldiers who would not let Norman back our bread is very low. More condensed milk, it is horrid muck. No lights allowed in the front of the house after 7.30 – so we grope our way to bed in the dark. All evening long – 'Put that light out or I fire' – from the sentries. They have shot out the street lights all around the square. Awful firing in Sackville Street and now I am called from bed to the back of the house to see that half the city seems on fire. What is to become of us all? I wish the Sheridans had left Westland Row. It seems a very dangerous spot. Very little sleep. Anxious about Norman. Put everyone sleeping in back of house.

Friday 28th April
Wakened early by terrible firing in the street outside. Father and I leave our room in front of house hurriedly and go to back rooms. Sit and quake on nursery bed whilst volley after volley is fired right at our door. Feel really shook up this time. Miserable about Norman.

6 o'c
Slight pause in the firing. Dash into my room, grab my clothes and retire to the back to dress with my heart in my boots. Lock the doors of all front rooms to prevent a stray kiddy going to the windows. Come downstairs to find that the maids had set out at 6.30 to try and get bread. Breakfast on fried scraps of bread and tea. Hate the condensed milk. No sign of the maids. Am beginning to feel very gone in the knees. Put all the kids in the back drawing room in charge of George. Send Alice and Doreen to wash up with the old cook. Ethel and I go to make the beds. Heavy firing in front of the house has ceased. But all the time the sentries are shouting 'Go back or I fire' to people

trying to come down this way. No one it seems may round the corner of Merrion Row, and several times we see the sentries fire over people's heads who venture too far down. We are not allowed to open windows or doors so no chance of speaking to sentry. Feel sick with fright over the maids and Norman. Hope they will not venture home.

11.30

Hear tramping on our roof and so discover that soldiers are posted there.

11.45

Hear a volley of shots and a shout from Father 'Bring that man here. I am a doctor.' Rush to the window to see two motors stopped in the middle of the road. A man lying behind the second car kicking in the dust. The three other men still in the car with hands up. Recognise Sir Horace Plunkett in the first car.[23] Stretcher bearers come and help Father to bring the shot man in here. The two men from the car follow. Father calls to me to get beds ready. He thinks Mr Ponsonby is dying. Get beds ready with Ethel's help. I go to the drawing room to tell the kids to pray hard that Norman and the maids will get back safe. Lock them in and start downstairs. As I turn the corner of the stairs they are just turning Mr Ponsonby over (he is lying on the hall floor) and I see a bad wound for the first time. His whole back seems to have been torn away, I don't want to look and I can't look away. It was a horrible sight. Hope I may never see such a terrible scene again. I feel very shaky.

Mr Lane had his arm all torn, and Sir Horace had bullets through his coat in several places. It is decided on account of the children here to move the wounded to Dr Bewley's house next door. He has spare rooms. It appears that these three men who are Government officials were summoned to the Castle on urgent business concerning the riots, and were told to come by this route. All the morning no one had been allowed to pass the top corner of Merrion Row, and sentries on the South side prevented anyone passing that way. They (on the South side) had some sense, and on seeing Sir Horace Plunkett's pass let him through, so that the cars came very quickly round the turn half way down, and were close to these sentries before they challenged. All held up their hands and Mr P stood up in the car. This I suppose terrified the sentries who fired a volley. Ten shots went through the front car; how no one was killed outright I don't know. Mr Ponsonby is very bad. Father looking after him and Mr Lane.

12 o'c

Joy! Norman and the maids have returned safely. Shooting a Privy Councillor seems to have cooled these soldiers in front, and seeing the maids' aprons they I suppose made up their minds that they had no machine guns. The poor girls walked to Ballsbridge for bread, and have been sitting up at the corner of Merrion Street all the morning. Norman they found by the merest chance. He stayed the night at Llama's rooms, and just looked out of the window as the maids passed with their sack of bread. While they were sitting there a batch of Sinn Feiners passed on bicycles, flitting back and forward silently like moths, and disappeared into Hume Street. Our three wanderers have not had anything to eat and are half dead.

4 o'c

Mr P is still very bad.

6 o'c

Dr Bewley has just come to say that the insurgents have surrendered unconditionally.[24] Still lots of shooting. The fires in
Sackville Street are still blazing away.

7.30

Bed in the dark. Very thankful to be still alive.

Saturday 30th April

No hope of going out. Still heavy firing on all sides, especially
Westland Row. The news of surrender cannot be true. Father
has been sent for to the Castle Hospital. He has gone with
Alice, both in white coats and red cross armlets. They will bring
us back the real news. Mr Sullivan the butcher who lives on
Northumberland Road has been and told us the whole story
of the Battle of Mount Street Bridge, to which he was an eye
witness. The Sherwood Foresters were landed at Kingstown
and were marched by map to Dublin. Several people warned
them when they came near Northumberland Road that some
of the houses were held by Sinn Feiners. The Colonel, taking
for granted that all Irish were Sinn Feiners and traitors, would
not take any notice, nor allow his men to touch food or water.
The SF held the School House at Mount Street Bridge and
the corner houses at Haddington Road. The tired and thirsty
soldiers were marched past Haddington Road, and almost
onto Mount Street Bridge when the Sinn Feiners opened
fire with machine guns and rifles.[25] Killed 70 soldiers right

off. The rest dazed and terrified and thinking every house hostile, took shelter where they could, but the slaughter was awful.

2 o'c

Father, Alice, Dr Blayney and Dr Hayes have just come in by the back. Blayney and Hayes were in the Mater Hospital when the trouble began, and have been prisoners there ever since. Lucky, for the Mater have 50 dead, nearly all civilians. The Castle Hospital in a fearful way. Packed with wounded and very shorthanded as so many doctors and nurses were away from Easter and could not get back. Alice is getting great value. Some Sinn Feiners have surrendered, but those in Jacob's, Westland Row, and Lamans (here beside us) still hold out. No one except doctors and nurses are let move round. The fire in Sackville Street is still burning.

Sunday 1st May

A quiet day. Most of our time spent at the window watching ambulances fly by. Alice and Father are buzzing in and out all day; very busy at the Castle.

6 o'c

Duke came in this evening – first time since Easter Monday. He has had the time of his life. Two other men got to the hospital in time; both more or less physicians. All the surgery was handed over to Duke; the other two treating him awfully well. He has been operating day and night; has done nearly every major operation and is rubbing his chest and walking round himself. He has quite enjoyed the rebellion. Besides they had enough to eat. Still some firing and the wicked crack of the sniper. I hear they are picking off men all over the place.

Monday [1 May]
All quiet except for the snipers. We are going to take the kids to Cabra and leave them there. I will be thankful to get them out of town.

2.30
When a batch of kids were dumped at school today the nuns asked that we would send all out so I am going with a second party this afternoon. Longing to get out after all these days in the house.

4 o'c
Just back from Cabra. Sackville Street is an awful sight. Not a building standing from Pillar to O'Connell Bridge. All Earl Street, Abbey Street, and Henry Street in ruins. It almost makes me weep. A man has just been shot in Westland Row by a sniper. They are finding it very hard to get hold of the snipers. However the worst is over now; nothing remains but to pay the awful bill.

When we were passing the Mater Hospital today a great coal lorry was there taking away the bodies. Hundreds of killed reported and bodies being found every moment. Seventy were buried in the Castle hospital garden. They are burying in the hospital gardens, Stephens Green, anywhere, fearing an outbreak of sickness. A procession of prisoners has just passed, a couple of hundred headed by a naval gun. Such a sad, tragic sight; lots and lots of women and young girls amongst them.

There is hardly a whole pane of glass left in the south side of the square. Judge Boyd's daughter (sitting in her room) had her hip broken;[26] and Dr Richard Hayes' son his arm smashed in his house over there.[27] We have been lucky; only some bullet marks on the brickwork, no windows smashed.

'THEY'RE BARMY,' THE SOLDIER SAID. 'THAT'S WOT *THEY* ARE.'

In 1916 Michael O'Beirne was just six years old, living 'at the top of a respectable house in Clare Street near Merrion Square'. It was many years later that he wrote his autobiography, but his memories of rebellion through a child's eyes stayed fresh.[1]

The Green was in sight at last, but we'd have to cross the road, walk up to the corner and cross again.

'Always look both ways before you cross,' Maggie said, but there was no sign of motor-cars. There was a peculiar stillness as we neared the corner. Here a few people were standing, staring across in amazement at the shut gates of the Green.

On this perfect circle, my hoop, all my hopes of a glad sunny morning were centred. On the smooth walks of the Green how swiftly I'd speed, driving my hoop on its oval, slim shadow! But something was wrong. The space between the corner of Merrion Row and the Green looked different, oddly vast. It was a deserted space. We realised that the gates of Stephen's Green were locked, and a wall of sandbags had been piled against them.

A few men, like figures on a distant stage, stood staring from behind the bars.

'Go home!' one of them shouted. He was waving at us, and shouted again: 'Go home or I fire!'

This fellow came out in front of the gates with a revolver in his hand. For a moment I could only gape, not even feeling annoyed. The man had a startling appearance. He was wearing a leopard skin like the big drummer in a band. He waved his gun at us again, threateningly: 'Clear away home!'

The four or five people near us were just as amazed as ourselves. Like us they had wanted to go into the Green – and here we were, stopped! It was natural to feel angry, but the big people seemed more excited than angry. They had clustered together and were all talking at once in low tones.

'What's up?' Maggie said, going over. 'What's the matter?'

Nobody seemed to know. One man said, staring across at the shut gates: 'There's going to be trouble.'

Maggie grabbed my hand and said, 'Come on, Mazie, we'd better be going home.' It was exciting and strange; we turned away reluctantly. As we moved on we met groups of people all eager and astonished, all talk and questions. Someone pointed along the street. There was a tram there, overturned. Rumours were flying that the Irish Volunteers had marched into Sackville Street, there would be a war.

When we got home Maggie opened up the bottom sash of her window and leaned out, gazing left and right. 'The city is like a desert,' she said, 'not a soul on the streets,' but I knew them furry fellows were in Stephen's Green. I got my toy revolver and ran to the window. Maggie pulled me back. 'I want to shoot them furry fellows!' I shouted, but she pushed me from the window. 'Do you want us all to get killed?'

We were all there at home as the holiday Monday wore on, dull and boring. That evening my father said he'd ramble over for a game of housey-housey, but he came back soon. 'I seen a tram on its side,' he told us (we had seen it already). 'There's a horse was shot dead near the college, and they have King Street barricaded.'

Maggie said all this trouble was caused by the Irish Volunteers. Nobody knew exactly who they were or what they were up to. 'A lot of hotheads,' Granny said, 'that's what they are, hotheads and firebrands.'

Nobody in our family took an interest in politics, except maybe my aunt. If Maggie was pro anything I would say she was pro-British, reading out about the doings of the Royal Family. But she also knew about the Volunteers; in fact she had a photo of one of their leaders dressed in military uniform. She admired him because he was handsome and was named O'Reilly – her own name was Maggie O'Reilly. Only he named himself in Irish 'The O'Rahilly', which meant he was chieftain of all the O'Reilly clan.

At either side of our windows there were tall, narrow shutters which opened out as hinged panels. These were shut and barred. As darkness fell you could nearly feel the silence over the city. I went to bed with no notion of sleeping. Later, in total darkness, I lay listening to a mysterious noise down in the street, and it went on and on – the measured stroke, stroke, stroke of marching feet. Was it the Volunteers – or what?

Now in the darkness rang out the crackle of shooting, far and near. I knew about the war in the papers Maggie read, the fighting on the Western Front, rifle and mortar fire and bayonet charges. This marching and the banging of guns was all part of the war, it seemed, come nearer.

The next morning we peeped from our high-up windows at a line of soldiers on the opposite side. They were at our side too

– all the way along Clare Street and Merrion Square, into the distance. The soldiers were suddenly there, ranged along both sides of our street holding their squat, sloped rifles at the ready.

It was like a dream that went on, all the time more bewildering. Of course nobody could go to work. The fact that my father was there, at home, didn't seem to matter because he was only ordinary compared with a drama like this. He would sometimes take a quick peep through the curtains.

Maggie wondered if she could slip out to get milk and bread. I came beside her in the hall, saw the door swing open and the soldier outside with his leather-strapped rifle. He had a funny way of talking, not like us.

The soldier said in a grand voice that Maggie could go out if she wanted to, at her own risk. He was keeping a sharp look-out. 'Hit's the snipers on the roofs,' he said. "It and run, that's their mottaew.' Maggie was raging, because 'hit and run' sounded so cowardly.

'You can't deny that they're brave men,' she said indignantly. 'Whatever else!'

'They're barmy,' the soldier said. 'That's wot *they* are.'

Waving her milk-jug, remembering her namesake hero, Maggie retorted: 'I don't care what you say. The O'Rahilly is a splendid man, and a real gentleman.'

Later, when Granny was told about this it upset her. 'You and your O'Rahilly! You'll have them raiding the place next. And if they found that photo–'

'Well they won't!' Maggie put the photo down inside her blouse.

'All the same,' she went on, 'you'd really pity some of them poor Tommies. Sure they're only boys. There was one in the dairy drinking a glass of milk, and sis he, "Crikey," sis he, "it's werse than Flawnders!"'

Some of the people opposite – the quality – stood at their doors and chatted with the soldiers.[2] They even brought out tea and sandwiches to them, which Maggie said was Irish hospitality.

The sky greyed over and all afternoon the rain pattered, dimpling the shiny pavements. We knew by now that there were Irish Volunteers barricaded in the Post Office in Sackville Street. We heard – which seemed a hard and brutal thing – that they had shot down looters thieving from shops. Also that crowds had gathered to watch the big shop, Lawrence's, go up in flames. There had come a lull in the shooting, but it only made the interval more tense as we waited for what must happen next.

Maggie said it was a good thing, anyway, that Miss O'Leary was not in evidence. She had gone home to the country for Easter, and with luck would be unable to get back.

Late that night, when I had gone to bed, we heard the thunder of big guns. By Wednesday morning the war had really started. The city seemed to shake. The terrible noise went on, sometimes wavering, then suddenly strong and intense: the yap-yap-yap of machine-guns, the crack of rifle-fire, the shuddering crump of artillery.

For a house-bound child of six it would be hard to imagine a more thrilling or marvellous experience. The way at night they would shout: 'Put out that light!' Soldiers on horseback clattering along – the cavalry – had been shot down in Sackville Street. When I peered out a Tommy opposite stared up at me from under his cap's peak, before his gaze went roving on along the rooftops.

On Thursday night the Far Room was in darkness. We knew

that a great battle was being fought across the city. Pressing close against the window we could see the left side of Lincoln Place and Fanning's pub. High up, the ornamental roof of this building stood out in silhouette against a bright red sky.

We were beginning to feel sad, to feel a kind of sympathy for the Irish Volunteers. They were foolish men – hotheads all right, but they were fighting a losing battle now. You couldn't but feel sorry for them, even feel a sneaking pride.

Saddest of any news for Maggie was that The O'Rahilly was dead. He had been shot in Moore Lane, off Moore Street; she stood at the window and muttered a prayer for his soul. 'The whole of Dublin will be levelled,' she said. 'God have mercy on them – Jesus, Mary and Joseph protect them!'

The Volunteers in the GPO were holding out, though by this time the building and most of Sackville Street was blazing. Still the big guns pounded and the rifles cracked. Then all of a sudden it was finished. Quiet had spread over the city by Saturday evening, a great stillness. They had at last laid down their arms, a soldier said.

I remember being taken for a walk the next day by my father. We saw the tram on its side again, shop-windows broken by looters, bullet-marks in walls. We came to Westmoreland Street, and saw beyond it the piles of blackened rubble and the sky, an open space that showed the backs of houses in streets far away.

The walls that stood in Sackville Street looked ragged, as if my story book giant had lumbered along punching holes in them with his fist. Where the roads and pavements had been level people were climbing and stumbling, and standing to stare. From the acrid-smelling ruins a plume of smoke was here and there still rising.

'THE WORK HAD TO BE DONE WHERE FIRING WAS IN PROGRESS'

The GPO in Dublin's O'Connell Street served as the rebels' head-quarters throughout the Rising, and has unsurprisingly been the focus of many books and accounts ever since. However, some fasci-nating information is contained in the sometimes dry, but always businesslike and very detailed reports made by Post Office staff to their superiors in the aftermath of the rebellion. One such report is reproduced here, written by Superintending Engineer Edward Gomersall, for The Post Office Electrical Engineers' Journal.[1]

Gomersall's account is given almost in full, including its technical aspects, as it provides an interesting background to the building taken by the rebels on Easter Monday – 'an entirely modern building with up-to-date appliances', including two electric lifts and a bag-cleaning machine. The GPO had been undergoing enlargement and modernisation since 1904, and was entirely finished less than two months before the rebellion – a week later, twelve years of refurbishment had gone up in smoke. His account is also interesting because, for our modern purposes, he was an ideal observer of history – completely professional and businesslike, detached from the rebellion with no apparent bias towards either side.

And although his account begins in the most technical manner, Gomersall seems to adopt a lighter attitude as he continues – describing the rebels' comprehensive methods of disrupting communication and the dangers faced by engineering officers doggedly going about their business, bullets notwithstanding.

Many readers of the *Journal* will be interested to learn how the telegraph and telephone service was carried on during the recent troubles, and at the request of the Board of Editors I have prepared the following notes. The principal Post Office buildings in Dublin were the General Post Office in Sackville Street, the Telephone Exchange, 700 yards away on the south side of the river, and the Parcels Office near Amiens Street Station, 1,000 yards east of the Post Office. The General Post Office building accommodated the Public Office, Telegraph Instrument Room, Trunk Telephone Exchange, Sorting Offices, and the clerical offices of the Secretary, Controller (Postal), Controller (Telegraphs), and, in addition, a part of the Accountant's Staff. The local exchange at Crown Alley is a magneto-call auto-clear exchange with over 4,000 subscribers. The Superintending Engineer's Office is located at Aldborough House in the same buildings as the Controller of Stores Office and the Stores Depots.

The equipment of the telegraph instrument room included 4 fast-speed duplex repeaters, 4 forked repeaters, 11 duplex Wheat-stone, 11 DC Sx sets, 13 quadruplex, 26 DCS, 25 CB sounder, 1 concentrator 60-line, 1 concentrator 40-line, 5 Gells, and, of course, the miscellaneous apparatus, typewriters, etc., required in a present-day telegraph instrument room. The Trunk Telephone Exchange consisted of 6 trunk positions, a local and concentrator switch, 20 phonogram sets, and the usual miscellaneous equipment.

There was a standard carrying 20 wires on the roof of the Post Office, but the bulk of the wires were brought to the building underground in the following paper core cables:

50/20, 100/20, 30/40, 38/40, 96/40, 8/100 + 26/40 + 52/40 and two cables 8/100 + 52/20.

Secondary cells were used for telegraph working, and primary batteries for telephone trunk purposes. The batteries, charging machine, three pneumatic pumps and motors, and a compressor and pump for Creed working were in the basement. The whole of the buildings were heated by hot water, the heating chamber with three boilers and accelerator being in the basement. Much had been done in recent years to make the Dublin Post Office an entirely modern building with up-to-date appliances. A conveyor had been completed in the sorting office, there were two electric lifts in the building, and a bag-cleaning machine had recently been brought into operation.

The General Post Office had been in process of enlargement since 1904. The work had been divided into three sections. The first and second sections had been completed in 1912, and the third section may be said to have been completed on March 6th this year, when the new public office was opened, a spacious, ornate, and well-furnished office.

The rebels took possession of the Post Office soon after noon on Easter Monday and quickly expelled the staff, including an engineering officer who was on duty. Within a couple of hours a circuit to London was joined up at an intermediate point; thus telegraphic communication with the outer world was promptly restored, and as a matter of fact has been continuously maintained. The local telephone exchange received no attention from the rebels until after the arrival of the military guard which had been asked for by different officers immediately they heard the Post Office had been seized. Matters developed very rapidly, and some of the details which have appeared in the papers will be fresh in mind.

The engineering staff passed through a very trying and dangerous ordeal. Telegraphic and trunk telephonic communication was essential for military purposes. New telephone circuits had to be provided for military purposes, and the local telephone system had to be maintained. Many members of the staff could not leave the vicinity of their homes. Many of those who could were unable to reach their normal places of duty; but before Monday midnight supervising officers and men were concentrated at three points in the outskirts, including certain officers who had been despatched from Belfast immediately the fact of the rebellion was known there, and men were in attendance at the Dublin Exchange. These arrangements continued until Tuesday, May 2nd, after which it gradually became possible to operate without the same extreme risk.

On Monday night, at 11 p.m., when trunk telephonic communication was urgently needed, several men were sent by motor cycle and side car, supplied by the Chief Engineer, Irish Command, to points several miles outside Dublin. After midnight one important circuit was cut into on very high poles and diverted by means of subscribers' circuits into an exchange which happily was still in communication with the main exchange. The next morning the main line was damaged by the rebels. Linemen who went after the fault were threatened by the rebels and fired upon. The military headquarters were informed of the locality in which the rebels were, and in the evening it was possible to make good the wires. On the next morning, Wednesday, the rebels cut down the line again some miles further away from Dublin. Other trunks were extended to the local exchange under similar conditions of danger and difficulty.

In the meantime, additional telegraph circuits were being

joined up. During the fighting three temporary telegraph offices were installed at different points, and, in addition, cross-channel wires were joined up at two other places. Telegraphic communication with Great Britain, and with all the most important places in Ireland, was thus restored, and it was maintained throughout the operations although the wires were strictly reserved for military and official purposes. Simultaneously with the rising in Dublin the lines had been cut down at a large number of places – evidently a characteristic feature of the operations of the rebels – and the restoration of communication from these temporary offices had necessarily to be preceded by making good the external plant.

A general idea of the damage which was done will be gained from the following statement:

Nearly all the main lines in the vicinity of Dublin were cut, generally in two or three places. The method adopted was to chop down two or three, sometimes more poles, and to cut the wires. At many places telegraph and telephone instruments were removed from the offices and smashed to pieces in the road; block and electric train staff instruments and telegraph and telephone apparatus in signal boxes were battered and destroyed. I can name over sixty places where telegraph and telephone lines were cut, excluding plant inside the Dublin City and suburbs. It may be convenient if I here mention other damage done during the operations in Dublin. When the work of diverting the telegraph wires to a new office was begun it was discovered that the rebels had cut most of the underground telegraph and trunk telephone cables. I hold a cheap tenon saw, found in a manhole where the cables had been cut. It was evidently quite new, and though not of Post Office pattern, it served the purpose. Eleven cables were maliciously cut, fourteen aerial cables and four DP cables were damaged by gunfire, two distribution poles were burned down; and, in addition, numerous overhead routes were brought down during the military operations and by the succeeding fires, and wires, stays, etc., were damaged in very large numbers by bullets. Of many interesting cases I might mention one in which a bullet passed through a 75ft stout pole, 3ft above the ground, through the protection pipe, and lodged in the cable. The fault in this cable was not traced without difficulty! Sixty subscribers' instruments were maliciously damaged, and 250 subscribers' telephones and sixteen private branch exchanges were burnt out or disappeared in ruined buildings.

The provision of additional circuits for military purposes was a matter of much difficulty, and unusual methods had to be employed. It was necessary to commandeer a large number of subscribers' circuits and extend them elsewhere, and in some cases line plant had to be taken down and apparatus removed from subscribers' premises, that being the only method possible of meeting the requirements.

The provision and maintenance of the circuits during the rebellion was both difficult and dangerous – difficult inasmuch as it was necessary to find lines which were intact to replace others shot down, and dangerous because zones of fire had to be crossed and the work had to be done where firing was in progress. Much of the firing was from house-tops. A connected narrative of events would require more space than is available, and perhaps I could best give an idea of the conditions by a few short notes:

(1) A lineman, cycling along a line after a fault, was

instructed by rebels to turn back and was fired upon, the bullet striking the front number plate of the machine.

(2) A lineman carrying telegraph apparatus, required urgently, was refused permission to pass by a military officer. He insisted that he must pass, although firing was going on and a wounded man was brought from the thoroughfare along which he had to pass. He was allowed to proceed at his own risk and got through safely, although a man was shot dead a few yards from him.

(3) Two officers who went to repair an important telephone rendered assistance to a dying man under fire, repaired the telephone, brought doctor, priest and ambulance, and returned safely.

(4) Continuous attendance was given at the main exchange throughout the rebellion, and day and night attendance for periods at other exchanges. Some officers were continuously in attendance nine days. Cross connecting work, etc., in the test room at night had to be done with lights out. Many unusual duties had to be performed in the exchange, which was practically under siege, including operating duty at a trying time. These officers now have expert knowledge how to put a building into a state of defence, how to prepare for a fire which seems to be approaching, and they ought to be able to give the weight of a sandbag with accuracy!

(5) Engineering officers were compelled to remain in a temporary telegraph office for several days at a stretch except for occasional short and risky journeys to fetch apparatus, etc.

(6) A light engine, with improvised protection, was used in searching for faults on important wires in areas where firing was proceeding.

(7) Initiative was shown by certain officers, who obtained military guards, gathered a few men, and on special trains travelled towards Dublin picking up and repairing broken wires.

These are a few instances illustrating the character of the risk which was run. Every day the engineering officers experienced the uncomfortable nearness of bullets, and, either when they were at work or were making their way to places where work had to be done, frequently saw the bullets find a mark.

On Tuesday, May 2nd, it became possible to ascertain the extent of the damage, to approach the Post Office, and gradually to organise the work of restoration. The magnitude of the task was soon apparent. It was clear that a new telegraph office would have to be installed, and that this work would have to proceed simultaneously with the repair of cables and wires, the diversion of the wires to a new office, the diversion of trunk telephone circuits to the local exchange, and the restoration of the block signal and telegraph wires on the railways and of the damaged local telephone exchange circuits.

The cables at the Post Office passed through an external chamber at the north-east corner of the building, from which they were carried along an area to an internal chamber under the portico. Only the shell of the building remained, and in places the débris was still burning and the surrounding ground was extremely hot. The Fire Brigade was called to cool the débris in the ruins adjacent to the external chamber, and at 5 p.m. it was possible to enter the manhole. The cables and cable connection boxes there were found intact, and, the internal chamber being inaccessible, the work of proving the wires, in preparation for the diversions, was immediately started. On Wednesday, May

3rd, it was finally decided that a new telegraph office should be installed on the upper floor of the parcel office at Amiens Street, pending the reconstruction of the GPO. On the afternoon of that day requisitions were sent by telegraph to the Engineer-in-Chief for the necessary apparatus. The construction of the tables by Board of Works carpenters was begun in the parcel office the following morning after the removal of the parcel baskets. The first consignment of apparatus arrived on Friday evening, May 5th, and the new instrument room was brought into use on Tuesday, May 9th. Meanwhile, the smaller temporary telegraph offices had been kept working, but on Thursday, May 11th, all the wires had been diverted to the new instrument room.

With much difficulty 160 of the 208 72-ampere hour cells were recovered from the basement of the GPO – they had been very hot and were full of debris from the ceiling, but they appeared to be usable. They were carted to Amiens Street and there cleaned and set up. Heavy gauge cable was recovered also, and temporary arrangements were made for charging the cells. Meanwhile, the construction of the tables, the fitting of the apparatus, the diversion of the cables (including the laying of two pipes across five pairs of rails and two railway platforms and drawing in new cables), the provision of phonogram lines, and the wiring of the instrument room proceeded night and day. Two thousand primary cells were set up on the galleries …, as the secondary cells had not sufficient capacity and might not prove satisfactory.

The character of the trouble necessarily meant that only as the work proceeded would the full extent of the difficulties come to light, and cable after cable proved to have been cut by the rebels. The test-frame arrived on Sunday – it had gone astray and was found at the bottom of the hold of a ship! The weather was cold and very wet. In spite of all difficulties, however, the new installation was completed as stated above.

Two new sets of 126 ampere hour secondary cells were set up ten days later, and the primary batteries have been made spare. The lead-covered cables were carried on the under side of the galleries and fed down to the distribution cases on the tables. The spacing of the instruments and the method of wiring is from start to finish on standard lines for permanent work. ...

[In the GPO] The offices of the Secretary and other controlling officers in the building were destroyed with all the records, as were the sorting offices and all other rooms in the building. ... Some cable, one or two motors, a large number of radiators, some electric light distribution boxes, and some electric light fittings, conduit, etc., have been or are being recovered, but otherwise the whole of the valuable plant which was installed in the GPO has either disappeared or is recoverable only as scrap.

The office of the Dublin West Sectional Engineer in Sackville Street was totally destroyed. Aldborough House was held by a military guard. Some rooms were damaged and there were casualties in the building, but the offices fortunately escaped severe damage.

A new sorting office has been opened at Rotunda Skating Rink, a building in Marlborough Street is to be used as a supplementary parcels office, and the Sackville Hall is to be fitted for the Secretary's staff and for a temporary public office. A lighting scheme has been put in hand and partially brought into use at the new sorting office, and other requirements are being met as they arise.

The Ireland district had had two severe trials since the beginning of 1915. In February that year very serious damage was done by a gale. In November 1915, another gale, which was followed by others in December, caused widespread devastation. The repairs were completed in the week before Easter. But the dangerous and difficult work which the staff has had to face since Easter Monday 1916, is, I think, without precedent in the United Kingdom, and it is due to the staff that, with the most intimate personal knowledge of the circumstances and of the men, I should express my admiration for their courage and devotion to duty during the rebellion, and for their untiring efforts and splendid work in connection with the restoration of the telegraph and telephone service in Ireland.

'THIS LARKINITE
& SINN FEIN RISING'

A letter from solicitor Sir John Robert O'Connell to British politician Cecil Harmsworth, written soon after the surrender.[1]

Telegrams
O'Connell, Ballybrack.
Telephone 20 Killiney.

Ard Einin,
Killiney.
Co. Dublin
7th May 1916[2]

My dear Harmsworth

Just a line to thank you very sincerely indeed for all your kindness & to say that I quite realise that it would have been impossible to have done more even before this truly deplorable rising put all other matters into the background. We seem to have travelled a long way since I wrote you first only a few weeks ago. A great deal of the Dublin which you and I knew in our T.C.D. days has been wiped out. The G.P.O. which after more than 100 years was only completed three months ago is now in ruins, the Hibernian Academy is wiped out and the Curator Kavanagh a painter of some merit went down in the ruins.[3] The *Freeman's Journal* offices are gone as are also the supplementary printing works of the *Irish Times*. The loss of life has been very heavy not only amongst the military & the insurgents but amongst the innocent civilian population who imprisoned in their houses were forced to come out to buy food and were then sniped by soldiers or rebels.

The Alma Mater saved the situation on Easter Monday by preventing the rebels from getting the Bank of Ireland and in various other ways the O.T.C. of T.C.D. did wonders; and an entrance exam and a parliamentary election were conducted within the walls of old Trinity while the roar of the machine guns almost rendered the voices inaudible.

I do hope that the English public will have no delusions about this rising and that it will realise that it was as much directed against Home Rule and against Redmond as against England. And further that there is not a responsible man in Ireland – of any class or creed – who does not deplore this Larkinite & Sinn Fein rising more bitterly than any Englishman can do.

Again many thanks
Yours sincerely

John Rt O'Connell

'WI' THE SINN FEINERS IN DUBLIN'

'Bab M'Keen' was a pen name used by newspaper editor John Wier, when writing a weekly column in the Ballymena Observer. *M'Keen's column was used by Wier to report and comment on everyday life, and he wrote in an Ulster-Scots dialect common to the area. Visiting Dublin for the Easter holiday, M'Keen was staying in the Granville Hotel (now the Savoy Cinema) on O'Connell Street, and found himself trapped there when the rebellion began. He wrote about his experiences in two of his columns, on 5 and 12 May.*[1]

BALLYMENA OBSERVER, 5 *May*

It was a subject o' frequent conversation atween me an' hir (you ken wha I mean) whaur we wud go for a wheen days at Easter.[2] We had baith been workin' hard, an' feeled we wud be naethin' the waur o' a twa or three days idle set, an' various propositions were made an' discussed, an' finally we thocht 'at Dublin wudna be a bad place tae pass the time in. I had been there last Easter Monday mysel', an' was present at yin o' these great Irish Volunteer turn oots, but she said there micht be rows this time, an' I juist said, 'I wish there wud; it wud be a new experience tae see yin,' but a' the same I didna want that experience. It fell oot, hooaniver, itherwise nor I cud been daein' wi', but that's anither story.

I had a min' afore we started tae pye a visit tae an auld acquaintance in Dublin 'at kent me when I wasna the heicht o' yer knee an' am gled tae say she's aye in guid form, an' cud put some o' the younger yins tae shame in guid lucks yet. We got intae Dublin on Friday nicht, an' onther the circumstances it wud be a' loss o' time an' space tae tell hoo we got in frae then tae Monday mornin'. I micht say, though, 'at pairt o' the time was spent wi' fren's, an' jusit tae show 'at we wud be guid, we went tae prayers at the Chapel Royal at the Castle, an' heerd an auld M'Keenstoon[3] man preach an' heerd the loveliest music sung it cud be possible tae listen tae, an' we baith feeled we did oor duty on Easter Sunday onywye. An sae ends the introduction.

Am no' at liberty tae mention whaur we stapped for reasons 'at'll be ontherstood later, but I can say it was aboot the middle o' Sackville Street, atween the Post Office an' the Parnell Monument, for aboot eicht days yin o' the hetest places iver my fit was in. There wur aboot thirty-five visitors in this hotel, besides aboot a dizen o' a workin' staff, luckin' efter metters sae 'at you see we wurna by oor lanes a' the gither. Weel, efther breakfast on Easter Monday the auld woman an' me gaed oot for a bit o' a walk an' a luck roon. An' she boucht some post cards tae sen' hame, an' got them fixed in the post office aboot half-past eleven, an' awa we went on the tap o' a tram tae the Phoenix Park, 'at was fou o' holiday makers enjoyin' themsel's, men an' weemen an' weans, as innocent o' onythin' likely tae happen as the birds on the bushes abune them. It was a scene o' peace tae be changed in an oor or twa tae yin o' war but then naebody thoucht o' it. It's aboot this am gann tae write, an' if the editor prents it I'll be saved a heap o' talk, for since I got hame my throat's sair tellin' folk what we come through.

The First Shots

Weel, we got back frae the Park aboot yin o'clock, in time for a bit o' denner, an' juist as we got aff the tram ker I saw a crood o' folk doon the street a bit, an curiosity led me tae see what it was a' aboot. There was a side street leadin' intae oor's an' at the en' o' this an empty tramcar. On the tap a young lad breakin' up the sates an' throwin' them awa amang the crood. 'What's the meanin' o' this?' I axed a man stannin' near. 'It's the Feiners,' he said, 'an' they hae possession o' the Post Office.' An' wi' that there wur twa shots fired, an' hir an' me tuck tae oor baters, an' the folk rinnin' a' roon us. By some wye or ither in roon by back streets tae we come oot yince mair on Sackville Street, an' like hares got intae the hotel daur. Juist noo a troop o' lancer sodgers oot on parade walked past the hotel, an' I thoucht tae mysel' they wur in for trouble. They had nae airms o' ony kin'. Juist lang rods wi' a wee spike on the en' o' them, an' aboot thirty or forty had got past whun there was a brattle like thunner, an' immediately an officer rushes in an' tell't us tae close the daur an' tak' tae the back, an' a lot o' folk pushed through frae the street. Thinks I tae mysel' this is Hail Columbia,[4] an' we made oor wye back in dooble quick, the ithers wi' us, an' ony o' them no' belangin' tae the hotel wur let oot the back, an' the rest o' us made oor wye intae the hoose again.

When we got the length o' the smoke-room, an' it wasna mair nor ten or fifteen minutes, we foun' twa sodjers lyin' on the floor an' yin on the sofa: a doctor in attendance, an' ither folk in the room. The men were badly wounded, twa or three horses killed onther them, an' the hale place in an uproar. A priest was sent for, the men bein' Catholics, an' yin o' them, shot in the lungs, de'ed aboot twa oors efther. His last words in a lady's ear, as he departed bein' 'The Lord hae mercy on my soul.' It was terrible, an' touchin'. An' anither man shot through the groin, his horse killed, said 'tae be shot like this by my own countrymen.'

The dinner oor has lang passed, though duly announced, but naebody dined that day. The meal was there an' ready, but there was naw appetite.

The front daur was noo closed finally an' niver apened again tae Friday evenin' except in cases o' needcessity. Ithers o' the visitors as they made their appearance, tellin' their experiences an' nerrow escapes. Yin young man was goin' doon the street, a woman in front o' him, an' a Colonial sodjer on leave walking leisurely in front o' hir. Immediately a shot was fired, an' the woman fell dead, the bullet bein' intended, nae doot, for the sodjer, wha went back, an' wi' the help o' oor frien', carried the woman's remains tae the fitpad. An' it wasna lang tae oor frien' was in safe quarters in the hotel.

House Wrecking

On Tuesday hoose-wreckin' commenced, an' hunners o' wretches frae a' the slums roon aboot wur in them, upstairs an' doonstairs; the goods systematically thrown oot on the street, an' carried awa' in armfuls. Groceries, draperies, shoe shaps, sweety shaps, an' whaur ony o' these were used as dwellin'-hooses the furniture an' beddin' was thrown oot an' carried awa' wholesale. Noblett's sweety shap, an' Tyler's boot shap got special attention, an' crowds went back an' forrit carryin' awa' a' they cud get their hands on. Some o' these thieves lucked respectable, an' ithers the vilest an' lowest-luckin' specimens you cud imagine. Many o' them staggerin' wi' drink, as weel as staggerin' onther their loads. It was the day o' their lives, an' weel they tuck advantage o' it. Boys an' girls micht be seen dividin' boxes o' sweets an' making exchanges o' ither things; an' ithers were offerin' valuable goold watches an' jewellery for shillin's an' sixpences. Weemen were merchin' aboot in furs an' fancy hats, an' yin I saw had a lang fur coat on an' a gent's tall hat, as prood as a peacock. Lawrence's fancy shap got a terrible wreckin', an' was a favourite wi' the young folk. Thoosands o' toys, photographs an' pictures were pitched oot, an' rockin'-horses were lyin' iverywhaur. Yin o' these withoot a heid was carried in triumph an' finally auctioned by a wee lad in front o' the hotel. Twa auld weemen for aboot ten minutes foucht an' scouled for a pair o' Tyler's boots, an' wi' the row the boots fell on the street, an' wur boned by anither woman, wha made aff wi' them as fast as she cud. I sa' yin wean, aboot six years auld wi' yin o' these carpet-sweeper things wheelin' it alang like a wheel-barrow, an' anither youngster sittin' on the box. At last the pile ootside was that big a match was pit tae it, an' the flames riz nearly the heicht o' the hoose. Mair stuff was thrown oot o' the windows on this tae a' was consumed. The hooses here were noo set on fire, an' continued tae burn far intae the nicht. Shootin' frae the Post Office by the Feiners was noo in full force as weel as frae the heid o' the street by the sodjers, an' we wur atween the fires frae that tae the siege was raised. Ither hooses were fired, an' micht burn awa' for the fire brigade daurna mak' an appearance. A priest was reported tae hae been shot in the street, an' numerous ither casualties talked aboot. Some o' the clergy movin' aboot compelled the looters tae lay doon their loads, an' yin auld wife was said tae remark tae yin o' them 'Wasn't the Lord good tae me this mornin'?' Snipin' frae the taps o' the hooses was noo common on baith sides an' the whud o' bullets heerd aff the walls, an' some wundas smashed, yin o' these in oor hotel, the bullet lodgin' in the wud work.

That nicht there was heavy firin' a' roon', an' snipin' conteenued, ivery noo an' then a bullet hittin' a skelp again a back return close tae oor window. Went tae bed at eleven o'clock, but got up at twa, owing tae the heavy firin' o' machine-guns an' artillery. Lucked oot at the edge o' the blind at the front daur, an' numbers o' drunk men an' weemen passed.

Wednesday mornin' at eicht o'clock, heavy firin' o' guns, an' tremendous noise. Heard the sodjers had blown up Liberty Hall, an' that the Feiners were in possession o' the Imperial an' Metropole Hotel. Believe they had been in possession o' these frae the first, but we had nae chance o' hearin' ony news frae the ootside. The day passed as usual, wannerin' aboot, an' no' much excitement.

At nicht we a' gathered into the smoke-room for a social an' kept the home fires burnin' up tae yin o'clock. Some ither fires started doon the street. We were niver sure when oor time wud come. An' aboot this there was a guid dale o' anxiety; maist o' us lyin' doon wi' oor claes an' boots on. This day the military tuck possession o' the hoose, an' an officer an' three or fower men wur in constant attendance day an' nicht.

Thursday was juist like the day afore. The time passin' in wanderin' aboot up an' doon the stairs oor o' yin place intae anither. Smokin' by the men, an' readin' by some o' the weemen 'at cud get a book, for a paper wasna tae be had for love or money. This mornin' the sodjer 'at had de'ed, an' the twa wounded men were ta'en awa' in an ambulance. The doctor 'at had been attentin' them was a civilian doctor on temporary military duty, an' his hoose had been ta'en possession o' by the Sinn Feiners, an' his wife an' wean put oot, as weel as a' his valuable X-ray apparatus destroyed.

Friday. Yin o' oor besieged this mornin' spied a bullet ootside the daur, which was allooed tae be apened an't the trophy secured. This was the first, later on they wur picked up in hunners on the street. Efther dinner a fearfu' volume o' firin' o' a' kinds o' guns an' artillery frae the tap o' the street, doon nixt the Post Office. It was juist the soun' o' thunner, if you were up whaur they mak' it. Luckin' oot o' the wundows side-wyes, we cud see it on fire, the roof doon, an' the flames risin' heeeh abune it. Hoose noo burnin' four daurs frae the hotel. Snipers blazin' awa' frae oor roof.

I should here remark 'at owin' tae the siege meat was gettin' rether scarce, an' we advised oor guid manageress tae reduce the rations, sae we had a wee bit o' Irish stew for denner, an' a wee soda bun an' three biscuits – ivery yin for tay. For breakfast we had parritch an' treacle for first coorse, an' a wee bit o' bacon wi' tay; an' we were a' weel pleased an' setisfied. Notice came frae the military tae keep frae the windows as troops had orders tae shoot ony yin luckin' oot. It wasna needed, as nane o' us was likely tae venture; though, takin' a side-glance, troops cud be seen merchin' at the tap o' the street, an' the Post Office bleezin' awa'. The Feiners reported tae be scattered a' ower the city. Nine o'clock p.m., very quate, an' venthured tae luck oot at Post Office. The hale inside bleezin' yellow an' naethin' but the bare walls stan'in'. This nicht we had a sing sang in the smoke-room tae the accompaniment o' the big guns an' ither martial music. By a special privilege the bar was apened for fifteen minutes for lemonade tae keep the singers frae haein' dry thrapples.[5]

The instrumentalists didna need refreshments, I was yin o' the singers. By this time there was a great scarcity o' tabacca an' cigarettes, an' as for matches you had tae licht six or eicht smokes, tae the last man burnt his fingers. I was that far reduced

I had tae keep a lot o' 'dottle' damped in the bottom o' the pipe, an' tak' chance o' yin o' the officers drappin' a 'butt' sae 'at I cud stick it in the pipe an' hae a wheen draws. This was sairer on some o' us nor the licht diet. Snipin' as usual.

The Surrender

Saturday. Riz at 6 o'clock by the nicht porter. Thoucht we had tae lee the hotel in a hurry. Reported soldiers goin' tae bombard house opposite, where sniper was suspected. Previous tae this the YMCA an' some ither buildin's near had been enthered by the Feiners, an' snipin' indulged in. It stapped efther half-a-dizen holes had been made by bomb shells. Man wi' white flag passed; broucht in, an' reported message frae manager Royal Bank, whaur he said the Feiners were on yin side o' the hoose an' the hoose on the ither side in flames. Heerd aboot capture o' Connolly an' ither rebels, an' Sir Roger Casement at Kinsale. Heavy firin' frae nixt Parnell monument. Yin o' the officers went across the street tae the Royal Liver Office, whaur six weemen an' twa weans had been withoot food since Munday, wi' some soup an' bread, an' was cheered tae the echo when he came back empty handed. Onther the circumstances he deserved the Victoria Cross, as he micht easy been pinned by a sniper. Reported large number o' hooses burnin' a' ower the city. Food in hospitals short, an' thoosan's in want a' ower the city. This efthernoon the men folk were noticed 'at they micht hae tae lee the hotel for a short time tae a thorough search wud be made for ony Feiners 'at micht be lurkin' aboot; an' preparations were duly made for this, but tae oor great delicht an' astonishment the news came in 'at the Feiners had surrendered in a body oncondeetionally, an' except for a few snipers the hale thing had collapsed. Maybe there wa rejoicin'. The relief o' Ladysmith was naethin' tae it,[6] an' in response tae an urgent appeal frae the Scotch section, the bar was apened for fifteen minutes, an' the lemonade was enjoyed tae a wonnerfu' extent. It was michty, an' iverybody was toasted on baith sides an' through the middle: an' noo 'at was a' ower nane o' us wud a missed it for onythin'. This nicht five biscuits for tay; we were as yet on war rations. Post Office fire broke oot afresh an' numerous explosions, supposed tae come frae the Sinn Feiners' ammunition, wi' which it was said tae be weel stocked. The hale city lucked like a sea o' fire, an' the sky lit up like daylicht. There was noo yin an' anither venthured ootside, wanderin' up an' doon, pickin' up bullets, bits o' shells, an' ither things 'at micht be kept as souvenirs in the days tae come. An' aboot eicht o'clock a body o' aboot fifty prisoners wa merched up the street in cherge o' sodjers an' lined alang the fitpad. They carried their guns, which they were ordered tae lay doon. Then their ither accoutrements, an' their names were ta'en doon in a book. In a short time efther anither lot, this time aboot twa or three hunner, were merched up, an' the same thing gaed through, an' when a' was completed the hale lot were merched awa' tae some place tae the mornin'. In a short time the streets were covered wi' a' kinds o' folk pickin' up relics, an' sae on; an' amang these some pistols an' revolvers drapped by the prisoners, an' some documents, very interestin'; an' this went on tae ten o'clock. I didna go in for ony lootin', but managed tae pick up a piece o' the Post Office, bits o' shells an' bullets, an' a hale lot o' love letters an' telegrams oot o' the Post Office 'at wur fleein' aboot the street. Some o' the ithers picked up letters o' the leaders an' reports o' their work on Monday, drapped on the street in the dark, as they laid doon their airms. That nicht there was a wee bit o' a dance for the young folk, an' I managed tae pick up a wheen o' cigarettes, but nae tabacca.

Sunday's Joy

Sunday mornin' broucht great joy an' some loaves frae a bakery. I may say 'at these were tae be shared wi' a hoose nixt daur. I toul the mistress o' the hotel if she cud juist raise twa wee fishes we wud be complete; an' she said she had twa boxes o' sardines. Efther breakfast, some o' the prisoners ta'en the nicht afore were merched past frae places unknown. They were maistly young lads juist in ordinary clothin', an' twa weemen. Heard a number o' the ithers had been shot by court-martial, but heeded naethin'. General ower-flow o' the population, an' in a short time the street was crooded. In a wheen minutes weemen came past frae yin o' the streets carryin' a' kinds o' provisions frae shaps, an' the lootin' commenced again. A sodjer wi' rifle at present cudna turn them. Naethin' but weemen were allooed through, an' a man, an auld sodjer, at oor daur was turned, an' was in a very bad wye. He said he hadna tasted meat for twa days, an' declared a woman juist past had sixteen hams in the hoose carried frae the shaps in Moore Street. At last the military cleared the street o' the hale lot. Aboot this time a Catholic clergyman, in his robe, came up tae the daur wi' a man an' a great hamper o' breed an' asked if we wanted any. He was only supplyin' the hotels. He was taul' we did, an' we got twa mair loaves, for he said there wud be nae bakin' this week. We gave him a hearty Sunday mornin' cheer, an' he replied wi' a 'Guid bliss you.' It was very nice, an' the father's kindness was, I needna tell you, appreciated. Denner at half-past twa an' efthernoon tay at fower for the ladies, and ginger-ale for the men. By this time the lemonade was a' done. At 5 o'clock the Sinn Fein flag still standin' on the front wall o' the Imperial Hotel, shot doon by a sodjer. Saw the rifle ta'en frae Pearce, yin o' the leaders; an' got a wee scrap o' the white flag o' surrender, as a keepsake. Aboot this time twenty mair prisoners passed the head o' the street, an great firin' was heard ayont the Park, showin' there was aye some resistance.[7] A milk-cart appeared at the Parnell monument, an' a' the jugs in the street were shortly at it. Heard for the first time o' the surrender o' Kut. Had the pleesure o' meetin' a young officer frae Belfast, an' promised as soon as I got hame tae inform his folk he was weel. Heard we were likely tae get a train nixt day. Guid nicht's rest.

On Monday had a richt guid substantial breakfast, an' ivery yin was makin' ready for the road: but we wurna sure aboot the time o' the train. Hooaniver, tae mak' sure, we left the hotel an' got tae the station aboot 11 o'clock, tae be in time, an' waited there tae half-past three afore the train started, an' we were, you may guess, a' relieved as we steamed awa', an' when we got as far as Drogheda wur kin'ly trated tae tay an' breed an' butter by kind ladies at the station.

Noo, tae go back tae the hotel. I canna tell you the name for certain reasons, but I'll say this much, it's in the hands o' yin o' the cleverest ladies I hae met, an' she got through what was tae hir the crisis o' a life time, an' the same may be said for ivery member o' the staff. It was a pleesure tae be wi' them, an' if at ony time ony o' you tak' a notion o' seein' the ruins o' Dublin, I'll be gled tae mak' you acquaint wi' the name o' the hoose an' the lady at'll luck efther you.

Am juist tellin' you some o' the things I came across, an' cud tell you a heap mair, but daurna. It was a very risky, an' at times a very dangerous experiment, but as true as my name's Bab, for a hunner pun' I wudna missed it.

Bab M'Keen

PS – I hae noo been permitted tae mention 'at the name o' oor hotel was the Granville, in Sackville Street, under the efficient management o' Miss Stephens.

BALLYMENA OBSERVER, *12 May*

On luckin' ower my remarks o' last week on what I come through in Dublin, I see some things left oot 'at micht been interestin' tae some o' you had I had time an' space at my disposal tae gie an accoont o' them. But it was juist a crush tae get onythin' intae prent o' a private nature, public metters haein' the first call. Hooaniver, as things ir settlin' doon, an' yer a' awaur o' the extent o' the Sinn Fein Rebellion, am maybe at liberty tae recall some things I may hae left oot in last week's letter.

Maist iverybody had their ain experiences on that Easter Monday in Dublin, an' sometimes even them in the same hoose thegither had knowledge o' some things 'at the ithers kent naethin' aboot, an' the daein's in yin pairt o' the city, owin' tae the absence o' newspapers, were kent naethin' o' in ither pairts. O' coorse, as time went on an' the reporters got preein' aboot they picked up bits here an' there, 'at got intae some papers ootside Dublin, for wi' the exception o' yin – the *Irish Times* – a' the ithers were wrecked an' oot o' the rinnin'. Noo, I didna see in yin o' them an accoont o' the shootin' o' the three Lancers 'at were broucht intae oor hotel, an' that was really the first encoonter wi' a force o' the military.

There was yin thing aboot that I micht mak' mantion o', an' that was 'at the young Canadian lieutenant wha had been wounded in France, was set upon by twa Feiners, an' shot yin o' them in self-defence wi' his revolver, an' immediately efther lifted yin o' the wounded sodjers on his shouthers an' tried taw get intae a hotel 'at was shut in his face, an' then got intae oor yin wi' his helpless burden, an' styed there tae him an' the rest o' us wur relieved, takin' his pairt in the military duty in the place. It was him 'at carried the bread an' soup tae the femishin' femily across the street on the Friday afore the Surrender. As memory comes back, I think it's only fair tae add this tae the ither remarks already published.

I think I didna tell you aboot Daisy faintin'. She was yin o' the waitresses, a very nice wee lass 'at ivery body liked, an' yin evenin' juist efther tay yin o' the big guns at the heid o' the street was let aff at the Post Office wi' a soun' like the brustin' o' a plenet 'at frichtened the hale o' us an' afore you cud wink doon draps Daisy in a deid faint, onther the table. It was for wha wud get tae hir first, but a young lad o' activity crossed the tape an' carried hir ootside, whaur she soon recovered.

An' there's anither thing worth mentionin' 'at has juist got intae the paper. By an' by as the censorship relaxes weel ken a' aboot it. At a place ca'd Swords aboot fifty o' the rebels surrendered, an' when they heerd o' their leader's order tae lay doon their airms they sent a message tae the military authorities statin' 'at they wur prepared tae surrender, but 'at they wud like an escort sent, as it wud be ondignified for them tae merch in under the guard o' twa pleecemen. The authorities supplied them wi' an escort o' twunty men, an' the rebels, their dignity served, come in withoot further trouble. At the surrender o' the first lot o' rebels in Sackville Street, I heerd a man sayin' 'Well, am ___ but I wud rether be shot nor stand that exhibition.'

An' I said afore, we had some military in the hoose, an' am no' at liberty tae say much aboot them; but frae the time they came in it gied us great confidence. They wur a nice lot o' men frae the captain doon, an' only 'at you sa' the uniform wud niver a kent they wur there. Am toul' the captain was a parteecularly cliver man an' he lucked it; an' yin sargin', a young fellow wha had seen a guid dale o' service, had got a patch o' stickin' plaster on his forehead frae the scratch o' a passin' bullet 'at nearly sent him hame. He was a regular favourite wi' the folk, an' a' the appearance o' makin' a future officer. On the Sunday mornin' o' the lootin' o' the bacon shaps in Moore Street, he was stationed opposite oor daur, in the middle o' the street, wi' a cherged rifle tae keep the weemen frae passin', an' there he was on yin knee, the rifle at present, cryin' oot at them on baith sides an' some stapped while ithers went on; but he tholed an' didna fire for am sure he kent the folk wur hungry.[8] At last he was relieved, an' a row o' sodjers, sidey by sidey, merched doon the street an' cleared it o' a' the folk 'at wur on it.

Tuesday evenin' an' nicht, the time o' the wreckin' o' the shaps, was a time o' amazement an' amusement. Yin cudna help wonnerin' at the coolness an' shamelessness o' respectable luckin' folk passin' by in dizens loaded wi' a' kin's o' articles frae the shaps 'at wur bein' robbed by the ruffians doon the street. Some o' the loads that bulky an' heavy the folk cudna carry them, an' spillin' them ower the street tae be picked up by ithers followin'. Articles o' goold an' silver, pictures an' paintin's trailed alang the street by the cords they had been hung by. Valuable sets o' furs, offered for maybe a penny, an' a bargain struck at that. I hear the police ir noo makin' a search for some o' these things in the back streets, but the owners'll niver be foun' noo for them if they're recovered frae these thieves an' robbers. But the ordinary folk in Dublin werena a' sympathisin' wi' the destruction gaun on. I heard yin auld woman at a corner sayin' 'May the Lord forgie them,' an' a man beside hir, 'Oh, why didn't the Lord lay His han' on them afore they did this.'

An' in the midst o' a' this there was some amusement for the spectators. Here was an auld lad aboot 60 or 70 wi' a beautiful dust coat an' a tall white hat gaun aboot smokin' a fine cigar wi' a label prominent on it, comin' tae grief when somebody come ahint him an' blocked the tile doon ower his nose.[9] A youngster got up as Charlie Chaplin an' a very guid imitation, was collectin' happens for showin' Charlie's big feet an' peculiar walk, an' when he had done yin place he was wheeled awa' in great style in a stolen pram tae anither daur, whaur he gied anither rehearsal.

I think I made mention last week 'at efther the surrendered Sinn Feiners had laid doon their airms an' wur merchin' awa, a number o' the visitors went ower the street luckin' for relics, an' sae on. At this time some private documents an' ither curiosities wur picked up, an' as these wur exhibited ithers went oot on the search tae, but yin o' the men oot o' oor place went ower near the line o' sodjers an' got arrested, an' his watch an' money taen frae him, but got them a' returned later wi' a warnin' tae keep hissel oor o' that lest waur micht befa' him. Yin o' the hotel servants had a similar experience, but he had nae watch an' little money. He was sent hame wi' only a bunch o' keys in his pocket. In anither pairt o' the city a man was lifted for the same thing an' kept in the Castle a' nicht, an' the only relic he has is the memory o' that lock up.

I heerd o' a couple 'at intended gettin' merriet, 'at wur held up, like the rest o' us, only in anither hotel, an' the refugees there tuck a great interest in twa, sae much sae 'at they subscribed amang them for a nice weddin' present whun a' wud be ower. Yin nicht in the smoke room they commenced takin' a reel oot o' the forthcomin' bridegroom, sayin' she michtna tak' him efther a'. Tae their surprise he assured them it wud be a' richt, an' produced a legal agreement, drawn up showin' the amoont o' the fortune she had, an' sae much disgusted his frien's 'at they resolved they'd withdraw the weddin' present, an' spent the money on a champagne supper. This is a true story an' can be vooched for. An' juist yin ither an' I'll stap. On Tuesday some o' the Sinn Feiners entered a baker's shap an' commandeered eicht shillin' worth o' breid, for which they left a memorandum receipt, sayin' they wud pye the amoont when they wun. An' that item am feered 'll noo be a lang time or it's settled.

Crowds on central O'Connell Street. This photo was reportedly taken just after the rebellion began and before looting started. We may be sceptical of such 'on-the-spot' photography from nearly 100 years ago, but the evidence seems to support the truth of this claim, particularly the large number of people on the street, mostly congregating in one area, with others pointing towards the same area. Also, despite being Dublin's busiest street, there is no moving traffic visible, while a tram at the North Earl Street junction was described as having been 'disabled by the rebels', and many photos taken after the Rising show a burnt-out tram in the same location. *Unless otherwise indicated, all images are from the author's collection*

Another, closer, view of the crowd on O'Connell Street before looting began. The Cable Shoe Co. was soon emptied of goods, and both it and the Munster & Leinster Bank were later gutted by fire.

A Lancer's horse lies dead on O'Connell Street. This may be the horse whose tail Wilmot Irwin's brother clipped for a souvenir – see page 208. The Lancers in the picture have just passed the multi-windowed Gresham Hotel. The building with the arched doorway on the right is the Granville Hotel, where Bab M'Keen was confined during the rebellion.

Tea and bayonets. Out of the line of fire, British soldiers take advantage of the hospitality shown by some residents, and enjoy a cup of tea, served on a tray.
'We have just sent out a tray full of bread and jam sandwiches, and big jugs of tea' – see Lady Chance's account, page 150.

Carisbrooke House, the home of William Russell Lane-Joynt and mentioned in the accounts by Andrew Bonaparte-Wyse and Margaret Mitchell. Bullet holes are clearly visible in the windows and British soldiers are on the steps. It was near here that St John Ambulance Brigade Corps Superintendent Holden Stodart was killed – see accounts by P.J. Cassidy and Thekla Bowser.

A shop on Grafton Street, that had been broken into and looted. This is Knowles & Sons, fruit growers and florists, 27 Grafton Street – see page 252.

An example of the type of barricade thrown up by the rebels when the Rising began – this one is on St Stephen's Green, and contains carts and motor cars commandeered from passers-by. Lady Chance mentions 'a barricade of motors across the street' (page 142).

Soldiers behind a barricade on Lower Merrion Street, made of benches from inside Merrion Square: 'They are taking all the seats out of the Square and making a sandbagged barricade across Lr Merrion Street' – see Lady Chance's account, page 148. The soldiers are looking in the direction of Merrion Street and along the west side of Merrion Square. Lady Chance's house is less than 100 metres away. To the right of the barricade is Clare Street, home of young Michael O'Beirne – see page 158.

A military convoy moving through the streets of Dublin. While possibly posed for the camera, this picture gives an idea of the potential danger of moving through a hostile neighbourhood.

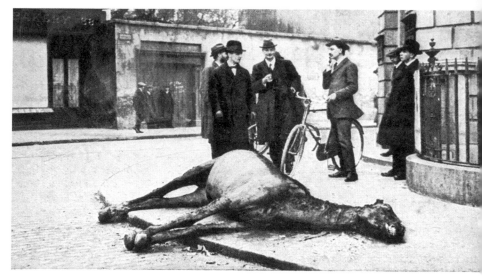

A dead horse on the corner of St Stephen's Green and Merrion Row. Bonaparte-Wyse (page 134) writes: 'We next went ... to the corner of Merrion Row & Stephen's Green – more firing going on with rifle & machine gun, but nothing to see except a dead horse lying at the street corner in a pool of blood.' In an account not featured in this anthology, St John Ervine wrote: 'A cab came down the east side of the Green, and the [rebel] sentries challenged the driver; but he would not stop, though they called "Halt!" a dozen times. Then they fired on him. The horse went down instantly ...' (St John G. Ervine, 'The Story of the Irish Rebellion', *The Century Magazine*, November 1916)

The funeral of an RIC man killed during the Rising.

An army guard at Clontarf Railway Bridge. This is the kind of post that would have been occupied by Mrs Le Peton's 'dear boy' – see page 114.

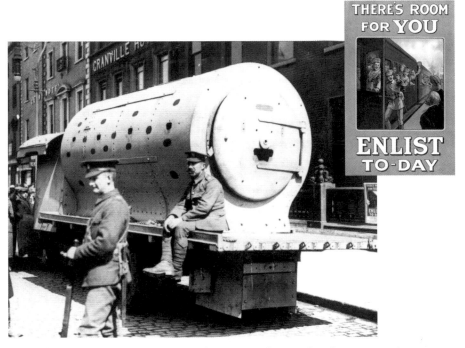

Several rudimentary armoured cars were designed and constructed at speed by the military during the Rising. In action by Wednesday, they proved very useful in suppressing the rebels. This one, made from four locomotive boilers, is parked outside the Granville Hotel on Sackville Street. (Note the recruiting poster on the railings behind.)

Left: The rebels' 'Irish Republic' flag flies from the GPO, while Nelson looks on from his pillar in the background. This photo was taken from the Metropole Hotel next door, the top windows of which were level with the GPO's balustrade. Joseph Plunkett, one of the seven signatories of the Proclamation, stayed in an upper room of the Metropole the night before the Rising began, and the building was occupied by rebels on Wednesday. The hotel was utterly destroyed by the end of the week.

Below: Henry Cameron Lyster finished his account of the rebellion in Enniscorthy with: 'Col. French arrived in a motor car, accompanied by Col. Jameson Davis. Etchingham and the five other Sinn Fein leaders put on their full dress uniform and went and had themselves photographed. They then surrendered to Col. French …' (see page 287). *Back row:* Una Brennan, Michael de Lacey, Eileen Hegarty; *front row:* Seamus Rafter, Robert Brennan, Seamus Doyle, Sean R. Etchingham.

O'Connell Street under fire during the rebellion. The Parnell monument and Nelson's pillar can easily be made out, and the GPO's portico is just visible to the right of the pillar. This is the view that Joseph Holloway would have had from Cavendish Row, where he went 'to stop … till the trouble was over' (page 275). *Courtesy of Mercier Archives*

A view of the GPO after the Rising. The flagpole which bore the rebels' 'Irish Republic' flag can be seen leaning over the parapet. 'The fluttering of the flag grows feebler. … at 9.51 p.m. [Friday] the staff supporting it begins to waver, and in a second falls out towards the street.' See *Irish Life* civilian's account, page 246.

Kelly's Gunpowder Office on O'Connell Bridge shows signs of the damage inflicted upon it.

'The *Helga* gunboat, which had been brought up the River Liffey, was demolishing, with its guns, Liberty Hall … After every shot, dust and smoke rose in the air' (page 55). The destruction of Liberty Hall is mentioned in many of the accounts. *Courtesy of Mercier Archives*

A view of the devastation in O'Connell Street, as seen from the top of Nelson's Pillar.

Searching for firewood among the ruins. There was also a lively demand for souvenirs, with items such as bullets, documents and pieces of shrapnel much sought after.

The rebellion seems to have had a happy outcome for these girls at least, heading home with firewood gathered from the ruins.
Courtesy of Mercier Archives

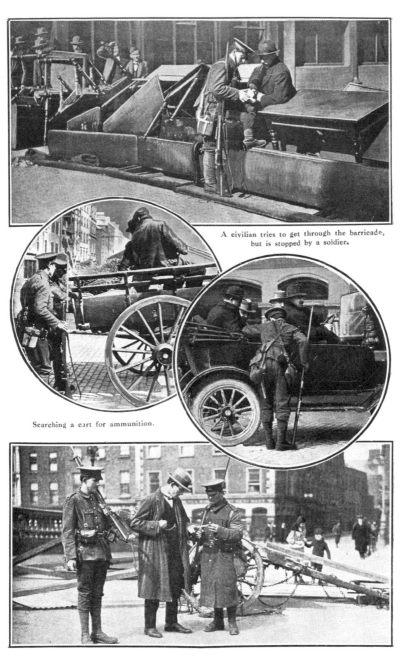

A civilian tries to get through the barricade, but is stopped by a soldier.

Searching a cart for ammunition.

Examining passports. Circle on right: Searching a motor-car.

STREET SCENES IN DUBLIN.

A sample of the sort of checkpoints set up by the military authorities.

Women carry sacks of flour away from 'a depot established by the military authorities for the relief of the civil population in Dublin'. This picture was taken on the Liffey's Butt Bridge, at the junction of George's Quay and Tara Street.

Soldiers distributing bread because of food shortages experienced during the Rising. L&NWR, written on the baskets, stands for the London and North Western Railway, which ran cross-channel steamers between Dublin and Holyhead.

A newspaper seller carries on business as usual, despite the destruction all around. Both the cart and the barrel on the left are stamped 'GPO'.

A branch of the Dublin Savings Bank announces that it 'will open when law & order is fully restored'. This is probably the branch at 12 Lower Abbey Street, just one block from O'Connell Street – all the buildings in the block numbered 1–9 were destroyed in the rebellion.

Nuns from
the Sisters
of Charity
distributing
bread after
the Rising.

'IT WAS A CREEPY BUSINESS DRIVING THROUGH THE DESERTED STREETS'

Sir Henry Robinson was a member of the privy council of Ireland, and an inspector with the Local Government Board for Ireland. In his published memoirs is included a chapter on Easter 1916, which, among other things, gives an interesting look behind the scenes at official arrangements to secure and safeguard the city's food supplies.[1]

With this atmosphere of unrest and sinister rumours, with vast numbers of people drilling and marching through the country, Easter of 1916 came upon us. The people scattered to the holiday resorts or came to Dublin to enjoy themselves at the race meetings, though at the same time they were full of stories of the audacity of the Sinn Feiners, and their open preparations for a rising, and full of indignation at the supineness of Dublin Castle in allowing these demonstrations of force to take place and doing nothing to assert itself, nothing to put down this foolish but dangerous pretence at establishing an Irish Republic. 'Humiliating,' they said it was, 'for if the Government were in earnest and worth its salt, the whole movement would crumple up and could be extinguished within a week. It was a ridiculous but dangerous masquerade'; but at the same time, outside the Sinn Feiners themselves, I do not think that there was a living soul in Ireland who was prepared for what was to follow in two days' time.

Mr Birrell had arranged to visit North Mayo that Easter, and I had journeyed to Mallaranny to await his joining me on Tuesday.[2] The hotel was full of Easter holiday-makers, and most of them had to return to Dublin on Tuesday by the 7 a.m. train or by the Limited Mail at 12.40. To everyone's surprise no night mail had come through, and hence there was no morning train to return. The manageress of the hotel could only inform her guests in blank dismay that all communication with Dublin was cut off, by wire, by post, and by rail, and that the station-master could not say when there would be trains up or down, and that the food supply for the hotel had not arrived. She could throw no light whatever upon the business, and the guests were in despair. Many of them had important engagements in Dublin, and one man, I remember, a bank manager, kept impressing upon everybody that, whatever happened, he must get back, as he had a meeting of his directors next morning, and that this sort of thing could not be endured. Some of the people tried to hire cars, but no petrol was obtainable. A supply would have come down by the train if it had arrived, but there was not a pint to be had in the village. Even then no one would credit the idea of a rebellion: the prevailing impression was that a railway bridge had been broken or blown up by the Sinn Feiners, 'who really ought to be put down'; and it was quite late in the evening when a vague rumour reached the hotel of a rising in Dublin. Although nobody credited it, great uneasiness prevailed. The bank manager, however, insisted that the fact, if confirmed, made it all the more urgent that no obstacles should be put in the way of his proceeding *at once* to Dublin.

I had a little Calthorpe coupe with me which I used as a runabout for short distances, and I thought I ought to chance it over the 198 miles to Dublin, as I believed my wife was alone in the house. I had a little petrol in the tank, and Vesey Stoney of Rosturk Castle gave me enough to take me on to Balla, where I spent the night and where I was lucky enough to get my tank filled. No one at Balla had any definite news about what had happened, and it was not until I got to Castlerea and called on The O'Conor Don that I learnt the true facts. He told me that on the previous day he had started for Dublin in his motor in company with the parish priest. They had heard vague rumours of a rising at Mullingar, but when they got to Maynooth they found a company of soldiers helping the police, who turned them back, saying that if they got into Dublin their car would certainly be taken by the rebels, and that they would be shot ruthlessly if they made any resistance. They said that the rebels held the Post Office and had occupied the workhouses and some large buildings all over the city, and that firing was going on at every corner. The rebels had omitted to cut the telephones, and troops were coming up from the Curragh, and the officer told The O'Conor Don that there were probably enough of them on the way, with guns and equipment, *en route* for France, who would be stopped and who would probably be able to crush the rising in a comparatively short time. He said that an enormous number of people had been killed, and that the firing was getting worse every moment. The O'Conor Don had then returned home, and he advised me to abandon any attempt to get to Dublin, but to stay with him for the time being. I knew the country lanes round Dublin so well that I felt if I could get as far as Maynooth I would be able to make my way home all right. So The O'Conor Don provided me with sandwiches and drink, and I pushed on via Longford and Mullingar, passing many young men on cycles making their way up to Dublin whom I deemed to be Sinn Feiners answering the call to arms. Outside Mullingar two of them got off their cycles when they heard me coming and tried to stop me, no doubt to take my car. I went full speed ahead and they side-stepped in time. Fortunately they had no revolvers. After that I was unmolested, but when I reached Maynooth I was warned by the military that things were going very badly, and that it was certain death to go into the city with the car. I therefore branched off to the south and skirted the Dublin Mountains to Glencullen; thence I dropped down to Foxrock and found my wife and daughter-in-law sitting on the steps listening to the booming of the big guns over Dublin.

A letter was awaiting me from Nathan[3] enclosing a pass through the city and a warrant from the Lord Lieutenant appointing me chairman of a committee which was charged with the arrangements for securing and safeguarding the food supplies of the city, for all the shops had run out, and there was neither bread, meat, butter, nor milk obtainable, and the people were looting.

The committee consisted of Colonel Edgeworth Johnstone, the Chief Commissioner of Police; Colonel Taylor, of the RASC, Sir Horace Plunkett, Mr Leonard, and one or two others; and as I was given authority to add anyone I wished, I appointed Mr Ponsonby of Kilcooley, Charles O'Connor and Mr Lane as additional members. Captain R. Kelly was secretary, and a more efficient person I have seldom met. The success of the committee's operations was largely due to his foresight. We held our meetings in the Lower Castle Yard and the business of getting there was not without an excitement of its own, as the streets were closed to the public and were held by very young English soldiers who were being sniped from the rooftops and in rather a nervy state, ready to loose off their rifles on the smallest provocation. The rebels were known to use motor-cars for their raids, and were quite expected to come up within range of the troops and fire upon them and then make off. A full car was therefore always looked upon with suspicion, and if one did not stop when signalled to do so the troops were not going to take any chances.

Horace Plunkett was driving in to the meeting, and when he was coming down Merrion Square West the troops at Nassau Street corner raised their hands and signalled him to stop. Horace Plunkett, however, took out his pass, held it aloft, waved it, and proceeded on his way; and like Rudyard Kipling's "arf-trained recruitie' who 'wonders to find he is frequent deceased', Plunkett wondered to find his car riddled with bullets, one of his passengers shot in the back and another through the arm![4] Two of the Food Committee were therefore *hors de combat* after the first meeting, and another member, Mr Leonard, was shot through the ear and foot, but it was a rebel bullet in this instance and not a friendly British one that did the damage, so it must have been a great solace to him to know that he was not the victim of a regrettable mistake.

I took very good care to be always alone in my car when going to the meetings, and as it was too small to seem dangerous, I never got touched. But it was a creepy business driving through the deserted streets; occasionally I would hear a distant report and a sharp smack on a house near by and would see where the bullet had struck by a red brick crumbling to powder. Once I found myself passing a house in Baggot Street where a brisk engagement suddenly opened over my head between some rebels on a house-top and some troops on Baggot Street Bridge. I crouched close under the wall, afraid to go either forward or back; there was no reason to fear the rebels' shots, as they would have had to lean far over the parapet of the roof to have got at me, but the soldiers were shooting wildly, and if they had depressed their aim too much they might have made things unpleasant. They kept waving me away, but I had no desire to run the gauntlet across the open, so I waited under the wall until the engagement was over.

Before our committee met, I went to see Nathan in his office to congratulate him upon having held the Castle, as he and Colonel Johnstone between them had successfully guarded all possible means of ingress and egress the moment news of the rising reached them. They had thereby baffled the rebels, one of whose first objectives had been the occupation of the seat of government. Johnstone, as he always is in times of danger and tribulation, was cool as a cucumber, but Nathan was naturally terribly upset at not having foreseen the eventuality of the rebellion, and told me he had placed his resignation in the hands of the Prime Minister. I did not imagine that they would let him go at such a juncture, and neither, I think, did he; and he was much hurt at the acceptance of his resignation by wire the next day. I then went to see Birrell to ask his support and approval in the allocation of two private funds we controlled, to carry on the administration and to prevent famine in the city, which we proposed to do by commandeering food in all parts of the country and getting it sent up by motor lorries, train or sea.

'My dear man,' said Birrell, 'you may count on my approval,

but I'm afraid my support won't help you much. I shall probably be in the Clock Tower tomorrow.'

He was very sad over the tragic termination of his work and his political career. Ten of the best years of his life wasted.

There was no post or telegraph or other way of communicating with the Treasury, so I had to chance it about the purchase of food; but as matters turned out, we recovered from the butchers, grocers and bakers practically all the money we paid for the herds of cattle we bought and slaughtered, and the groceries and foodstuffs which we bought from the country and distributed to the retailers, so that the losses on the financial transactions of the committee were almost inappreciable.

Lord Wimborne[5] was at the Viceregal Lodge at the time the rebellion broke out, and I believe that he showed great initiative and courage in the emergency, and that it was owing to his arrangements by wireless and telephones that the military at the Curragh were apprised of what was going on in sufficient time to strike in at a critical moment during the outbreak. If the rebels had not stupidly omitted to secure the telephones, they would have been able to cause the Government and the military serious embarrassment, which would have rendered the suppression of the rebellion a much longer and more difficult business than it was.

Wimborne was not saddled with any of the responsibility for the occurrence of the Sinn Fein rising during his Viceroyalty. He would have had a very good answer in the fact that he never was given any opportunity of exercising any responsibilities in regard to the Sinn Fein movement, for although the maintenance of order was nominally vested in the Lord Lieutenant-General and General Governor of Ireland, the suppression of political associations would be in the hands of the Chief Secretary and the Cabinet. There was therefore no question of his resignation until the necessity for a military Lord Lieutenant became apparent later on.

Birrell and Nathan took their departure while martial law was still being administered by Sir John Maxwell, and the strongholds of the rebels were rapidly crumbling under the big guns.

'WHEN I SAW HIM HE HAD LESS THAN TWENTY MINUTES TO LIVE'

Describing himself as 'a Dubliner – a member of the Loyalist minority group', Wilmot Irwin published his memoirs of 'the years of Revolution 1916–1924' in the late 1960s. Although present in O'Connell Street at the very start of the 1916 rebellion, Irwin quickly returned home to the north Dublin suburb of Glasnevin, and that is where the rest of his account is based.[1]

I

There was nothing particularly outstanding that Easter weekend that I can recall, beyond the fact that the newspapers devoted a lot of space to a small British army besieged in Kut-el-Amara in Mesopotamia under General Townshend. The efforts of a relieving force to reach the garrison was the main centre of the news. Would this army be in time? Actually it was not, and Kut-el-Amara fell during the Easter Rising. It was indeed, the first news we had of the outside world after an orgy of bloodshed and arson. But on Easter Monday, the events stand out crystal clear in my mind. It was the beginning of a new world and a different age. My childhood of happy illusion was at an end. War thrust its ugly snout into dearly familiar surroundings, a shock which still lingers after all the years and started off like a snowball the sense of disillusionment with which I survey people and things of all kinds today.

As I was the youngest of the family, my father was still my companion in off-duty hours and times. The Bank Holiday programme was simple in the extreme. It was a ritual which had gone on for years and seemed then as if it would go on for ever. A trip on a tram into the city, alighting at the Pillar. A walk through Sackville Street (now O'Connell Street) and Westmoreland Street to the top of Grafton Street, adjoining St Stephen's Green. Return by the left-hand side of the streets to the Pillar, still window-shopping, then a Glasnevin tram and home.

After midday dinner there was usually, if fine, a trip to Howth, Dalkey or Dun Laoghaire (Kingstown as it then was). Possibly a ritual which was identical with many other Dubliners. Fairyhouse races was then only a name for me! My father, although fond of horses and indeed all animals, was definitely not a racing man. Maybe it was just as well! I speak for years of disillusionment.

My father was a short thick-set man wearing a square-cut beard, turning grey at the time. I recall this particular Easter morning in the clearest detail as if it happened yesterday – possibly by reason of its subsequent implication.

We followed our usual routine proceeding on the left-hand side of the street from Nelson Pillar where we dismounted from the Glasnevin-Rialto tram about 11 a.m. and walked towards Grafton Street. We were both interested in books and pictures and, at that time, Grafton Street was a kind of Mecca. We lingered quite a time at Combridge's Picture Shop in Grafton Street as pictures of military interest were on display at the time. Then we passed slowly along to Sibley's book shop at the corner of the street opposite to St Stephen's Green. It was then getting towards midday and I noticed casually the fine young Metropolitan Policeman on point duty at the junction of South King Street and Stephen's Green. Though I did not know it then it was Constable Michael Lahiff, 125 B, aged twenty-eight years. When I saw him he had less than twenty minutes to live. Everything seemed normal and in order as we turned to go home. Just as we neared the end of Grafton Street, a column of Citizen Army volunteers with shouldered rifles swung along towards the Green. We paid little attention to them, as parades of armed and semi-uniformed men of unofficial armies were all too common during the regime of the benignant Augustine Birrell – an ideal exponent of the 'Wait and see' Asquith tradition. I should say they were at least a company strong. This was the rebel column which seized Stephen's Green and one of whom put three bullets into the hapless pointsman, who later died in the Meath Hospital. I cannot recall hearing any shots at the time, but then we were probably in Westmoreland Street and nearing the Quays. We were brought to a halt at O'Connell Bridge on the quays to allow a British military convoy to pass along towards the Phoenix Park. It consisted of five open lorries containing ammunition destined for the Magazine situated there and was escorted by horse troopers of the composite Fifth Lancer Regiment. They carried their lances in slings and the escort numbered forty or fifty men with a couple of officers riding ahead.

This column was ambushed minutes later at Charles Street near the Four Courts. They parked the lorries with their precious cargo and defended it successfully for three days with the loss of one officer killed and the other wounded. The only trophy the rebels obtained was a solitary lance dropped by a trooper when they took to their rifles. What a haul that ammunition would have been!

Yet still neither my father nor I suspected anything was amiss until we got near to Eason's shop in Sackville Street near the General Post Office. Our first intimation of trouble was the sight of a small crowd congregated on the roadway outside the Post Office. We passed Eason's bookshop. At the Metropole Hotel alongside, two porters were holding the glass panelled door to restrain a man who was trying to gain entry. I cannot tell whether he was a volunteer or not, as many of the insurgents wore civilian clothing, but he was certainly not armed, as far as I could see.

But our interest quickly switched to the Post Office by the sound of crashing and tinkling glass. A shower of broken glass in fragments swept across the pathway to avoid which we had to walk out into the road. I glimpsed a white-faced tensed volunteer in the slouched hat of the Citizen Army smash away the panes of one of the windows as if his very life depended on it, with the butt end of his rifle. I knew immediately what that meant. A few years before I had been taken by my father to see a popular play of the time, *An Englishman's Home*. Its theme was the mythical invasion of England by a foreign aggressor and I could recall how the British territorials had smashed the windows of the home in question to repel the attack of the foreign invaders in order to avoid glass splinters during the forthcoming attack. My father looked grave and worried.

'This looks bad,' he said quietly, 'I think we had better get home right away.'

I was only too glad to comply with his direction. In fact I

would have climbed on the first tram I saw at the Pillar – a Phoenix Park car – but my father restrained me.

'No hurry,' he declared laconically, 'we'll wait for the right one. It'll be along in a moment or two.'

As we waited, I looked back towards the Pillar and noted a khaki-clad British Officer apparently on leave quietly watching the scene of destruction, with a further little knot of sightseers close-by. There was a tense atmosphere about the broad familiar street which sent an involuntary cold shiver down my spine. I was not sorry when our tramcar arrived. My father hardly opened his mouth during the short journey to Lindsay Road. I think even then he knew it was the end of an era.

II

Staying with us at the time was the husband of one of my sisters, a subaltern in a British Line Regiment, lately returned on sick leave from the Ypres Salient, where the average life of an officer was ten days.

He had survived since the previous August but had then gone down with a bad bout of trench fever. He still looked pale and unwell, although actually off the sick list and now convalescent. He was awaiting the report of a medical board within the next few days to see if he was fit to return to active service.

His pale face brightened up when he heard our exciting news and he called out excitedly to one of my brothers, who happened to be home at the time. The other I suspect, was at Fairyhouse Races with a great many other people including a good number of the garrison officers.

'Come along!' he called, 'Let's go down and see the fun! We should be just in time!'

My sister tried to detain him, but I suppose after his experience at the battle of Hooge and elsewhere this local business seemed like a picnic.[2] A minor war on his own doorstep tickled him immensely. My brother was likewise eager and the two of them set off. By this time the trams had ceased running and many had returned to the 'stables' at Phibsborough near Dalymount Park Football ground – so they were obliged to walk.

At Rutland Square (now Parnell Square) near the Abbey Presbyterian Church a squadron of Lancers caught them up riding in columns of fours. An officer riding ahead, glimpsing the uniformed officer with my brother, turned and grinned encouragingly as if this indeed was child's play. He was very soon to change his mind. As the cavalry started to deploy just beyond the Parnell monument, a single shot rang out followed by a ragged volley. A horse trooper clattered to the ground, the former dead. Looking back I have no hesitation in stating that this shot heralded the break-up of the British Empire.

The cavalry halted for a time. Further shots rang out from the Post Office and as the mounted men were only providing targets for the insurgent rifle-men, the order to retire was given and the cavalry returned to the Marlborough Barracks without further incident. This particular instance of the futility of the Birrell regime is more than apparent. It is a glaring instance of ineptitude in high places, sending a cavalry column against rifle-men snugly entrenched in an improvised fortress with barricades and barbed wire. This was no 'stupid riot' but full scale rebellion. Sackville Street and the whole centre of town was left to the mercy of the insurgents, and certain low elements of the population were quick to seize their opportunity to loot and plunder under the guns of the volunteers, who now and then made half-hearted attempts to restrain their rapacity, but in the very nature of the rising, they dare not go too far, since they looked for popular support. After the Declaration of Independence had been posted up, a Stop Press edition of *Irish War News* was rushed out by the insurgents. It contained the message:

'The Republican forces hold the lines taken at twelve noon and nowhere despite fierce and almost continuous attacks of the British troops have the lines been broken through.'

This was something of an exaggeration since the repulse of the sorties by the Lancers was the only actual attempt made by the authorities to regain control of the situation – possibly due to the attractions of Fairyhouse Races!

There was a tense atmosphere at home during and after dinner. To relieve the tedium, and in consequence of rumours which we heard, my parents and I set out for a favourite walk along the Cabra Road and thence by Charleville Road to the North Circular Road on the return. The rumours proved to be only too true. Barricades had been erected on the railway bridges and the adjacent houses, both on the North Circular Road and Cabra Road and were occupied by armed volunteers, many of them in uniform. A volunteer officer bestrode a horse and was an object of much curiosity of knots of curious sightseers, who conversed in low tones. Some cast fearful glances around as if momentarily anticipating the arrival of police or military, but nothing happened and we drifted homeward. It was only afterwards that we heard that the Dublin Metropolitan Police, being an unarmed body of men at the time, had been confined to barracks, but unfortunately that did not prevent three of the force being shot dead and seven other members wounded, most of them with deliberation. But by far the worst tragedy of that fateful Easter Monday was the ambush of the Dublin Volunteer Training Corps (associated with the British forces), a collection of elderly men who undertook guard duties and the like in an emergency. From their red brassards with 'GR' engraved thereon they were known as the 'Gorgeous Wrecks'. They had been out in a route march to Ticknock that morning carrying rifles, but had no ammunition. They were fired on in Haddington Road on their way back to Headquarters at Beggar's Bush Barracks, five being killed and as many more wounded. Most of the dead were married men with families.

But, of course, we did not get this news until later in the week. That evening an uneasy silence settled in the neighbourhood. Towards nightfall only the hardier folk were abroad. One of my brothers penetrated into Sackville Street, and seeing the dead horse in the middle of the street, bent over it, and with a pocket scissors, clipped off part of its tail. His son still has that unique souvenir. A volunteer suddenly challenged him as he stood up.

'What are you doing there?' he demanded.

'Nothing,' grunted my brother, as he sloped back to the sidewalk. He was to get an even more interesting souvenir the following day.

My schoolmate, Paddy Donnelly, had to walk from Kingstown (now Dun Laoghaire) to Drumcondra, along the railway line and arrived in the city in due course. With the exception of Trinity College and the Bank of Ireland, most of the public buildings in the centre of the city were in the hands of the insurgents. Things were quiet enough as they passed by the GPO with its armed vigilant garrison. On the steps of a closed convenience in Sackville Street, a bowler-hatted citizen was urinating quite openly. He shouted aloud as they passed by.

'Now we have a republic we can do what we like!'

Nobody made any comment. It did seem a fitting commentary on the situation at the time. That night the citizens of Dublin were lulled to sleep by desultory firing, an exchange of fusillades between insurgents and military pickets. The volunteers' fusillades could be clearly distinguished by the heavy reports of their somewhat antiquated rifles with which most of them were armed.

III

Tuesday morning we awakened to the same desultory shooting. Later in the day a dairyman told me an abortive attempt had been made by the insurgents to blow up Nelson Pillar at about seven in the morning. Bombs were placed at the base, and there was an explosion but apparently the explosion did no damage beyond breaking a few windows.

To resume, from our back wall, we had a view of Mountjoy Prison which was not assailed by the Volunteers although they now had complete control of most of the inner city, excepting the barracks. The troops were immobilised in the barracks and evidently waiting for reinforcements before coming to grips in earnest with the insurgents. We had, however, not long to wait for action. At midday on Tuesday we sat down to a somewhat meagre dinner. Foodstuffs were getting scarce as most of the shops – particularly the larger ones – had closed and put up their shutters possibly for fear of looters, who were now making merry in the areas held by the volunteers, largely, of course, because these were the slum areas of the city, where, as ever in the slum areas of any city, the rights of the individual come before most of the Commandments with particular reference to the Seventh.

The looters took everything, from grand pianos out of Cramer's in Sackville Street to clothing, boots and shoes from True Form and many other shops in the central areas. One old woman, busily sorting through a pile of discarded new shoes, seeking her particular size, was heard to exclaim angrily: 'The bloody robbers. They've only left odd ones!' No doubt she looked a picture of outraged virtue.

Most of the family were home with the exception of my two brothers, when we had a taste of real war. Reinforcements including artillery had arrived from the Curragh, and round two o'clock in the afternoon the first counter-offensive against the insurgents was launched. A fieldgun was placed in position near the cattle-market on the North Circular Road and opened fire with shrapnel. We had just finished our meal when we heard the whistle and whine of the first shells. My father was very quiet. He spoke in quiet, even tones.

'Just sit quietly,' he advised, 'we must hope for the best.'

A few more shell-bursts rang out followed by the rat-tat of machine-gun fire. That soon ceased. The battle of the Phibsborough barricades was over and the insurgents were in full retreat across the open fields of Finglas and Glasnevin, as we later learned.

When the firing began, both my brothers were in Phibsboro', one of them in the vicinity of Dunphy's corner, (now Doyle's) near Dalymount Park. The first shell was an 'over' and scattered shrapnel around the corner, greatly to the consternation of the passers-by. My brother – a keen souvenir-hunter, stooped and picked up pieces of the metal, almost while they were red-hot. They are still in the possession of his son, along with the horse-hair from the tail of the first slaughtered Lancer's horse, and sundry military passes of the period. My older brother actually witnessed the latter portion of the battle. Shortly after, as the first shell whistled overhead, he noticed one of the volunteers – apparently an officer – making for his home with his uniform cap under his arm and his green uniform covered by a civilian water-proof. Evidently he had enough. My brother passed onward and saw Dublin Fusiliers from the Curragh garrison advance in single file along the roadway. Men detached themselves and with fixed bayonets charged the houses where the Volunteers were sheltering. The barricades in both Cabra and North Circular Roads had been shattered by shell-fire and a few of the defenders killed. The infantry were not opposed. Volunteers poured from the houses with upraised hands at bayonet point to the accompaniment of curses and jeers from the few sightseers. Nothing succeeds like success and the Irish People are not unique in that they like to climb on the band wagon and support the apparent winning side. The military cordon was beginning to close in, but the Glasnevin district was still isolated from their operations. How else can I explain the following incident which took place about five o'clock that same afternoon.

Lindsay Road consists of two long rows of semi-detached houses backing on to the Whitworth Road and Canal which in turn is overlooked by the great chimneys of Mountjoy Prison fronting the North Circular Road. I was looking out of a top bedroom bay window – an excellent point of vantage – to where my brother-in-law in his khaki uniform had gathered with a group of men, some of whom belonged to the Veteran's Training Corps, comrades of whom had been so roughly handled at Beggar's Bush Barracks the previous day, though at the time we knew nothing about it, no papers being published except the insurgents' news-sheets which naturally took an optimistic view of their position, speaking of 'bloody repulses' of English troops, unmindful of the fact that few risings have succeeded from static positions – the Brussels rising of 1830 being one of the few exceptions. I afterwards learned that the subject of their conversation at the time was to persuade my brother-in-law to organise a force of loyalists, some of whom possessed revolvers and rifles, to protect the district from looters. As I looked I heard a loud report and a bullet clanged off the railings just beside them. I never saw a group break up more quickly in my life. My brother-in-law retired promptly to the house and the others literally flew homewards. In about two minutes the street was deserted. There were no more talks regarding Vigilantes or such. It was obvious that Volunteer snipers were alert in the district although the shot might have come from a too vigilant sentry posted on the Prison wall, but strange that he should not recognise a British military uniform at a distance of considerably less than a quarter mile.

That night we sat indoors conversing in low tones, listening now to the rattle of machine-guns as the cordons commenced to close in on the centre of the city. The rifle shots of the Volunteers were still, however, clearly distinguishable. The night passed with sporadic shooting throughout, and now a sinister red glare glowered over the city. Afterwards we learned it was Lawrence's Photographic & Toy Stores, where looters had set alight fireworks and rockets found there. The Citizen Army men and Volunteers in the Post Office must have enjoyed the display, as they took no action, but it was an unpleasant prophetic warning to them of things to come.

IV

Wednesday morning we were fully wakened from a troubled sleep to the sound of cannonade. It came from the direction of the east city where the gunboat *Helga* bombarded Liberty Hall, the headquarters of the Larkin Volunteers, otherwise Citizen Army. The building was eventually destroyed but the garrison escaped without casualties. Kelly's Corner on South Circular Road was bombarded during the day but as time advanced one could not distinguish artillery fire in the general fusillades of machine-guns and rifles. It was evident to us, hapless listeners, confined mostly to our homes, that the military were now fully engaged in an offensive against the insurgents, although looting still continued in the central parts of the city where the volunteers awaited full scale attack. This was heralded by the arrival of reinforcements from Britain, the 178th Infantry Brigade consisting of the 5th, 6th, 7th and 8th Battalions of the Sherwood Foresters (Notts and Derby Regiment). These raw troops suffered very heavy casualties, as nearly two hundred officers and men were killed while fighting their way to Trinity College, the base from which the attack on the General Post and surrounding buildings was to be launched in due course. Of course we knew nothing of this operation at the time as we were entirely isolated in our own district. The food situation in this district was now deteriorating. The few shops open were now sold out, but a local mill-store was able to supply flour. The nuns at Cabra Convent worked overtime in baking bread and anybody willing to undertake the hazards of the journey were able to purchase a loaf or two regardless of sect or religion, but, of course, such supplies could not go far. Dairy men, however, still got through with supplies of milk and it was amusing to see well-dressed citizens, who normally would not even carry a parcel, staggering home under a sack of flour and bag of potatoes, but to show open mirth on such occasions was not advisable, as tempers generally were getting short as tension grew. One did not know what was going to happen next. To me, at the time, the city had undergone a horrible transformation. It may be grand for poets and patriots to declaim the glories of Easter Week, but how many of them lived through [it], and what proportion were born and bred in the city?

Glares and smoke in the sky spoke eloquently of fires in the city. At nightfall it was specially noticeable. With the increasing tempo of the sounds of conflict, fewer people attempted to make their way into the city. As yet there were no signs of Crown forces. Rumours of all kinds filled the air.

V

It was Thursday when troops of the Staffordshire regiment arrived to set up a military post at the North City Mill at Cross Gun's Bridge. Very young territorials they were, with somewhat shoddy equipment, although their rifles were of the current Lee-Enfield pattern. They would not let anybody pass beyond the bridge without a pass, and these were not easy to obtain. The pass was a roughly scribbled page from an officer's note-book signed with his name and rank – usually a 2nd Lieutenant. People were friendly to the soldiers and brought them tea and bread from their own scanty hoards. It appeared that these young recruits had very little training and some even confided that they had not had any musketry practice. In the main the Volunteers were better trained than the army which fought them, although, of course, not as numerous or as well-equipped. The Citizen Army in fact contained many time-expired veterans of the British regular army who had fought in the Boer and other wars. They had been trained, too, by a British ex-regular officer, Captain White, son of the famous general, who had distinguished himself greatly in the Boer War. Posters were placarded in the district by order of the British Command which told people to remain indoors as far as possible, so as not to hinder the operations of the troops. It also enumerated the forces at the disposal of the Commander-in-Chief, General Sir John Maxwell, who had lately defended the Suez Canal from Turkish invaders, and clearly stated they were ample to deal with the rising.

Rumours also reached us this day of the capture of Casement and some of his associates. We also heard rumours of a great fight at Ashbourne in the adjacent County Meath. It was evident now from the intensity of the firing and the glare in the sky over the city that the attack on the General Post Office and other central buildings in the possession of the insurgents had begun. The heavy boom of artillery with the almost continuous rattle of machine-guns reached the highest pitch of intensity and at night, the glares of fires were brighter than ever. We tried to settle down to sleep that night wondering when our ordeal was really going to end. My father had a conversation on the state of affairs with one neighbour, a retired District Inspector of the Royal Irish Constabulary, who lived next door. He was a handsome grey-haired old man with an erect military carriage.

He had risen from the rank of constable. He was talking of the military operations against the insurgents.

'The Government will come to some arrangement with them,' he declared, somewhat to the surprise of my father, who was Unionist to the core and could not think of any arrangement but surrender.

Reflecting years later, I decided there was much to commend the ex-District Inspector's opinion. It would have saved a lot of bloodshed and turmoil. But the spirit of compromise with rebellion was not at all widely prevalent then in the average Dublin citizen. All around one heard nothing but condemnation of the Sinn Feiners in the strongest possible terms. Even then this antagonistic feeling had not reached its zenith. That was engendered by the sight of the ruined city centre.

The fusillades had continued throughout the night and continued during the morning interspersed with cannonade still directed at the centre of the city. The British Commander-in-Chief had now cordoned off the Sackville Street area and was forming another cordon round the Four Courts, despite the fierce resistance of the Volunteers entrenched and barricaded in North King Street. In fact it was not until the following day (Saturday), that resistance here was overcome. Casualties on both sides in this area were heavy and afterwards there were charges that the troops concerned had committed acts of private vengeance. As many of the volunteers were not wearing uniform it is more than probable that some innocent persons suffered.

In the Glasnevin area, where we lived, everything was quiet except for occasional sniping. My brother-in-law – still wearing his uniform – went into the garden of the house next door for a game of croquet during the morning and had a very narrow escape. A bullet whistled by his head, presumably from the Whitworth Road area where snipers had been very active and indeed continued up to the surrender and beyond. Needless to say, the croquet game was discontinued and everybody trooped indoors once more. Despite the nearby military pickets, the streets were still unsafe. Curiously enough, it was on this day on the eve of the surrender that the Republican volunteers were addressed in a very confident manner by James Connolly despite the terrific bombardment which was now making things impossible in the General Post Office and the immediate vicinity. He told them among other things:

'The British Army ... are afraid to advance or storm any positions held by our forces. The slaughter they suffered in the first few days has totally unnerved them, and they dare not attempt again an infantry attack on our positions ... Courage, boys, we are winning ...'

Certainly it must have taken courage and endurance of a high order to pen such a document in the prevailing circumstances. It proves conclusively I think, that Connolly was the mainspring and backbone of the rising. Like Bismarck, a man of blood and iron.

The food situation at home was now slowly improving. More shops opened in the neighbourhood now that the immediate fears of looters from the slum areas had subsided, and bakers bread – a great luxury – commenced to arrive in small quantities from parts of the country which were not affected by unrest – mostly northern areas. The loaves sold for double the usual price. It was, however, still impossible to get into town from any suburb, since British troops now ringed the entire city with pickets at all vantage points. Only a pass signed by a military officer would avail.

It was now evident to us, although we were in the dark about the progress of military operations, that the final embers of the insurrection were in process of being crushed. The almost incessant machine-gun fire and the whine and explosions of artillery told their own tale in eloquent terms. It was only afterwards that I learned that the cavalry-guarded convoy my father and I had seen shortly before they were attacked, were relieved from their besieged positions in Charles Street by improvised armoured lorries built by Messrs Guinness at Kingsbridge at the request of the High Command! That night the sky over the city glared more fiercely than ever. Building after building in the vicinity was committed to the flames. The conflagration started by the looters at Lawrence's shop was completed by British artillery. The Republic was coming into being in an agony of flame and turmoil.

VII [*sic*; the numbering matches the original source]
The artillery fire seemed to have intensified during the night and one could clearly hear the fall of masonry after the explosions. It was evident to us hapless listeners that events were reaching a climax. Nothing could live in that crescendo of shell fire. Some time after midday the roar of cannonade died down and then finally ceased, although stray shots were still clearly discernible. Rumours began to multiply and soon later in the afternoon, reports were spread that the rising had ended and that the surviving insurgents had surrendered. Rumour said that they had suffered frightful casualties, although I heard no expressions of sympathy or sorrow on that score. Anybody I spoke to in

the district still roundly condemned those who had wantonly turned the city into a battleground. Perhaps it was only natural.

Although the rising to all intents and purposes had ended, snipers were still busy in the streets, and military pickets were most active in rounding up insurgents who had escaped the military cordons. In these chases through the streets the citizens remained passive while volunteers were apprehended.

I witnessed one such raid myself on the following Saturday morning. A commandeered mineral water firm's lorry containing six or seven soldiers of assorted regiments with a single Metropolitan policeman drove up to the door of a known Sinn Feiner and neighbour. A pioneer with an axe forced the door. Riflemen and the constable raced into the house and emerged a few minutes later with the prisoner, an elderly man with a grizzled moustache, the father of a young family. He was hoisted none too gently on to the lorry in full view of curious neighbours. It was then I had my first revulsion of feeling. All along I had been dead against the rebels but the sight of a neighbour under the armed guard of an old Bill type of Connaught Ranger was too much for me.

'It's a damn shame to exhibit him like this!' I exclaimed hotly to a man beside me. He said nothing for a moment. He glowered at the Metropolitan policeman.

'H'm,' he muttered, 'they ran into their holes quick enough when the firing started. But they're out now!'

VIII

Although the rising had now ended by the Sunday following, stray shots could be heard now and then. The pall and glare in the sky over the city had almost completely disappeared as the

Fire Brigade had now become fully operational in the streets, and the main fighting had ceased and the military had taken control. The last fires were extinguished during the day, but the smoky pall continued for a time. The smell of burning wood was discernible in the air.

It was that Sunday afternoon, I witnessed another stirring spectacle, a mobile cavalry column with two eighteen pounders passing along the Finglas Road to deal with the insurgents, who had ambushed the Constabulary force under County Inspector Gray at Ashbourne. A neighbour who was a salesman with a leading Dublin firm, who was usually the most taciturn of men, uttered an outburst which surprised me.

'They're going out to shoot those bastards!' he hissed. 'They should crucify them!' Although his opinion was uttered in stentorian tones, nobody made a rejoinder. A few years later such an outburst would have cost him his life.

It was still difficult to get into town and only those with the most urgent business were granted passes to do so. One of these, a connection by marriage, an elderly man, who held an important post with a wine firm, wished to get into his office. He was permitted to go into the city, but at the Parnell monument, when in sight of his office in Upper Sackville Street, was stopped by a private of the Royal Irish Regiment on sentry duty.

'Nobody permitted to pass here,' he declared gruffly.

'But I have a pass!' protested the manager, displaying the hastily written sheet signed by an officer giving rank and regiment. The soldier glanced at it.

'I have my orders,' he said, still gruffly. He seemed to soften. He glanced around him as if to make sure nobody was within earshot.

'I'll tell you what I'll do, sir,' he declared. 'I'll turn away a little piece and you make a quick dash for your office. It'll be all right if I fire a shot over your head?'

My friend the office manager refused the offer. As he himself used to say: 'I was afraid he might fire a shot under my hat instead!'

So, for refusing the soldier's 'kindly' offer, he had to wait for another day or two before he reached his goal.

I myself did not get into town until the Wednesday following. The sight of Lower Sackville Street with the odour of burnt wood and debris of all kinds was enough to make angels weep. All the old familiar landmarks were gone. The General Post Office, Elvery's Elephant House, the DBC Restaurant, the Metropole Hotel, the Coliseum Theatre, where I had spent many enjoyable evenings, and the old Waxworks Exhibition in Henry Street, so often a haunt in winter months, were all gone in dust and debris. Nothing but piles of broken masonry and rubble guarded jointly by rifle-carrying Veteran's Training Corps and Metropolitan policemen. It was more depressing than walking through a graveyard. I think it was the sight of the city centre in ruins which impelled citizens to hoot and jeer the long strings of insurgent prisoners, heavily guarded by military with fixed bayonets, on their way to North Wall for internment in England. They were lucky – unlike their leaders, fifteen in all, who were executed after trial by Courts Martial. The rank and file lived to fight another day and to some purpose, too.

IX

It was very melancholy living in Glasnevin in those days imme-diately after the rising as funeral corteges followed one another in quick succession. Horse-drawn vehicles followed by lines of carriages and cabs. The horses were plumed. Black for married deceased and white plumes for the young and single. Funerals have lost a great deal of their pomp and dignity with the passing of the horse and the introduction of the motor hearse.

I have often speculated to myself and sometimes discussed with contemporaries what would have been the course of events if the rising had, in fact, been successful and the British garrison had evacuated the country as they did five or six years later. I have come to a somewhat startling conclusion after long thought and study. I believe that James Connolly and his worker associates would eventually have taken complete control and that the gentle Pearse and the literary Plunketts and MacDonagh would have been thrust aside or even eliminated to make way for the first communist government of the twentieth century. After all, such a course of events would have followed the set pattern of revolution throughout the centuries. The moderates have ever gone to the wall until an orgy of bloodshed and violence has exhausted itself. Who knows that if the rising of 1916 had succeeded in the first instance, the Plough and the Stars might have replaced the Tricolour as the national flag of Ireland? Just think that over.

'SACKVILLE STREET PRESENTED A BEWILDERING ASPECT'

The Office of Irish Life published a magazine supplement called The Record of the Irish Rebellion of 1916 within two months of the end of the Rising. It contained a lot of pictures of the people involved and the devastated buildings, as well as photographs and transcriptions of some of the documents and orders issued by the rebels. It also included several personal accounts of the rebellion, including this article, titled: 'Impressions of the Street Fighting by a Civilian Eyewitness'.

The identity of the eyewitness is unknown, but this civilian left behind a fascinating account of events as witnessed from an enviable, but very dangerous, vantage point atop a building on the south side of O'Connell Bridge, with a view encompassing the GPO to the left and Liberty Hall to the right. With the amount of sniping going on, they were extremely lucky not to have come under direct fire, particularly from the rebel side, as the Volunteers were very conscious of army spotters operating from such prime observation points.

At Lansdowne Road
On Easter Monday I caught the 12.20 p.m. train to the city, and, engrossed in the perusal of a magazine, I took little notice of my surroundings until the train came to a standstill at the disused station at Sandymount. I looked up from my book, and

listened eagerly for the familiar 'Tickets, please!' which, from past experiences, have become associated with this station. Instinctively I fumbled in my pocket for my ticket. A minute passed; two minutes passed; three minutes passed without any indication that a check was in progress. What was the matter? I rose from my seat and thrust my head through the carriage window. Some of the passengers had alighted. I too got out. The guard approached. 'What's up?' simultaneously asked half-a-dozen travellers. 'We are not going any further; that's all I know,' replied the official. Feeling anything but satisfied, I set out along the railway line in the direction of Lansdowne Road. There another train en route for Dublin was held up. I ran up the platform. 'The Sinn Feiners have taken possession of the city and occupy Westland Row Railway Station,' a porter explained. 'Look,' he added, pointing towards the far end of the Rugby Football Ground adjoining the railway line, 'see them ripping up the tracks.' I looked and saw about a dozen men in their shirt sleeves working feverishly with pick and shovel apparently uprooting the steel rails. I gazed for a few moments in astonishment, and mediated whether I should return home or push on into the city. Personal safety prompted me to return home, but a thrill of adventure rushed through my veins, and, regardless of risk, I decided to proceed at once to Dublin.

The nearer I approached the city the more animated the scene became. Knots of people stood here and there discussing the rumours they had heard. I endeavoured to obtain some definite information, but nobody knew anything, except what they had heard from others. The stoppage of the trams at Lower Mount Street Bridge, a couple of reports from a rifle, and the groups of people hurrying along, all combined to convince me that something was seriously amiss. At length I reached Westland Row Station.

The Scene at Westland Row

It would appear that at twelve o'clock (noon) the Stationmaster at Westland Row saw a squad of armed Volunteers marching along the 'arrival' platform. He ran towards them and asked what business brought them there. For reply, a Volunteer swung around and pointed a rifle (without a bayonet) at the official's chin, and covered him thus while the general body proceeded towards the signal boxes, and there cut off all communication. Another party closed and barricaded the entrances to the station. Here occurred a rather amusing incident. An old lady, who had apparently set out from her home to take the train to Kingstown, became rather indignantly excited on seeing an armed Sinn Feiner on guard inside the entrance. In a loud tone of voice she questioned the sentinel as to 'what he and the likes of him meant,' but failed to elicit a reply. Before turning away in disgust she yelled that she would like to 'bate' him herself, he with his 'tuppence ha'penny rifle'.

In Sackville Street

Sackville Street presented a bewildering aspect a little after one o'clock. Ambulances rushed hither and thither. Clusters of people now stood in the street, and, in a moment, dashed wildly down the side streets, to reappear disconnectedly and cautiously in the course of quarter of an hour. The cackling of firearms in the neighbourhood filled the air. Police and military were ominously conspicuously absent.

An eyewitness tells me that at about one o'clock a squad

of Sinn Feiners marched over O'Connell Bridge, and, after deliberately smashing with the butts of their rifles the lower windows of Messrs Kelly and Sons, Gunpowder Office, Bachelor's Walk, scrambled into that establishment. The broken glass lay scattered on the footpath. Subsequently an RIC constable in uniform, from the Phoenix Park Depot, while passing this building, stopped for a moment to survey the scene. Suddenly the point of a bayonet was thrust through the window blind, which had been drawn down. The policeman fell back in amazement and took to his heels in flight.

A little later I saw a motor car dash suddenly from Prince's Street into Sackville Street. A volley from the General Post Office at once rang out, and a party of Sinn Feiners rushed to arrest its flight. A woman throwing herself recklessly on the ground, just in front of the car, caused the driver to apply the brakes and swerve to avoid the prostrate body. At once several spectators and Sinn Feiners close at hand, jumped into the car, the driver of which made a desperate though fruitless attempt to throw off his captors. The car was stopped and then driven back into Prince's Street.

In Dame Street

At three o'clock I made my way along Dame Street, which is almost deserted. Outside the City Hall I see small knots of people. The gates of the Lower Castle Yard are closed. The footpath outside Mason's, the photographers, is heavily smeared with blood, and the windows of the adjoining shop are riddled with bullet holes. The door of the City Hall is open, but, so far as I can see, there is no one inside the Main Hall. The *Evening Mail* offices are closed.

Suddenly reports of two shots ring out overhead. I look up. The barrels of half-a-dozen rifles are protruding over the parapet of Messrs Henry and James', the windows of which have been ruthlessly smashed.

Sackville Street Again

I walk back along the quay to Sackville Street and take up a position of vantage at the O'Connell Bridge corner of D'Olier Street. Crowds of people are again pacing the thoroughfares in view. At intervals detachments of armed Sinn Feiners march from Liberty Hall to the General Post Office, via Lower Abbey Street. Now and then carts containing provisions and what seems to be cases of ammunition, guarded by armed escorts disappear down Prince's Street. The hoisting over the General Post Office of a flag bearing the words 'Irish Republic' is greeted with a storm of cheers from a small sympathetic portion of the crowd in Sackville Street.

Looting Begins

As dusk comes on, the unruly element of the crowd in the street begins to assert itself, and as darkness envelopes the city this element grows bolder and bolder. Free from the supervision of the police, the riotous spirit of the mob grows violent. At length, the sound of shattering glass commingles with the shouts and cheers. Smoke is seen to rise from the vicinity of Sackville Place. The Fire Brigade arrives on the scene, and in a quarter of an hour conquers the flames.

About nine o'clock the underworld of Dublin slum-land starts on a campaign of wholesale looting. Men, women, and children run along with boxes of boots and shoes under their arms. The shattering of glass on the opposite (GPO) side of the street next attracts my attention. Manfield's boot establishment is the subject of attack. For over a quarter of an hour the sound of breaking glass fills the air. Someone turns on the electric light in the shop, and thus reveals a disgraceful scene of violence and destruction. Not a single pane of glass on the ground floor of this fine shop is left intact. The mob pours in and out, bearing away boots and shoes, openly and daringly. Old women and tiny mites join in the raid on the premises.

It is now almost eleven o'clock. The dimensions of the mob become smaller and smaller, but the remaining dregs are bent on further destruction and robbery. Lemon's sweet shop and the adjoining houses are ruthlessly looted. The stock of bicycles in the New Hudson establishment in Bachelor's Walk is raided and soon cleared out.

A Battle?

Suddenly, about one o'clock, a crackling of rifles rings out seemingly from the direction of Cork Hill. A continuous rattle of the discharge of firearms echoes and re-echoes through the streets for over half-an-hour, and, at length, gives way to an ominous silence. Thenceforth the calm stillness of the night is periodically broken by the rifle reports.

As I turn in for a few hours of sleep I feel that great events are pending. What is the meaning of all that I have seen and heard? Rebellion? Impossible – too true! At the moment the city is no longer under British rule; this night, at least, the Republican flag floats over its centre.

TUESDAY

At dawn on Tuesday morning Sackville Street presents a desolate spectacle. The roadway is littered with scraps of paper and broken boot boxes. Paper packing, shop fittings, and broken furniture are strewn along the pavements. Stragglers of the looting mob hang round on the prowl for fresh booty.

The 'Irish Republican' flag still floats over the General Post Office. The recruiting posters have been torn off the walls and the fragments scattered over the street.

In the early morning knots of people begin to gather. Young women and men on their way to work stand together in groups and look upon the disgusting scenes of plunder. 'Business as usual' is today an axiom of problematical truthfulness. Every establishment within view is closed. The employees pace the streets in expectation of adventure.

The destructive propensities of the rougher element once more begin to materialise. At ten o'clock Messrs Frewen and Ryan's emporium, near the Sackville Picture House, is subjected to a riotous attack. Women and children are the chief perpetrators of this outrage; they emerge from the shop with bundles of collars, hats and caps. Hard hats and silk hats are kicked like footballs around the street. The better class of people look on, but make no effort to check the looting mob.

The Sacking of Lawrence's
Thence the crowd transfer their attentions to Lawrence's, Upper Sackville Street. Bare-footed boys and scantily-dressed girls soon possess the toys of the rich. And how they enjoy themselves! One little urchin, seated on a tricycle horse and

carrying an air-gun slung over his shoulder, pedals hilariously over O'Connell Bridge. He looks a picture of happiness. Other mites run joyously along with bundles of the choicest toys – tennis bats, teddy bears, footballs, miniature bagatelle sets, beautiful dolls – large and small.

Battle at Cork Hill

At half-past twelve a torrenade [*sic*] of firing is in progress in the vicinity of College Green. This outburst, however, proves to be but the precursor of some violent and prolonged exchanges at Cork Hill. Round after round, volley after volley, peal forth until it seems that a regular battle is being fought. At two o'clock the battle is at its height, and during the next hour and a half rifles crack, maxim guns spit, bullets whistle, and guns bark.

At 12.45 p.m., Mr Sheehy Skeffington walks hastily from the General Post Office to O'Connell Bridge. He is dressed in private attire and wears knickerbocker trousers. In one hand he carries some papers and in the other a brush. He pastes one of the papers on the Smith-O'Brien monument, around which a crowd gathers, eager to read the proclamation. A copy of the notice is given hereunder:

Sheehy-Skeffington's Manifesto

'When there are no regular police on the streets, it becomes the duty of the citizens to police the streets themselves and to prevent such spasmodic looting as has taken place in a few streets. Civilians (men and women) who are willing to co-operate to this end are asked to attend at Westmoreland Chambers (over Eden Bros) at five o'clock this (Tuesday) afternoon – Francis Sheehy Skeffington.'

The above is typed upon a slip of paper, eight inches by four. The typist was apparently inexperienced, for over half a dozen amended technical mistakes appear on the manifesto.

Retreat

At three o'clock, during a lull in the fighting at Cork Hill, seven or eight Volunteers rush across the Metal Bridge, along Bachelor's Walk, and up Sackville Street, to join their fellow-insurrectionists in the General Post Office. Three clusters of people, obviously bearing wounded men, also cross this bridge and enter Liffey Street, en route, no doubt, for Jervis Street Hospital.

Lawrence's on Fire

At 3.30 p.m., the firing at Cork Hill ceases. Clouds of smoke begin to rise from Lawrence's toy shop. The Fire Brigade is called out. Hundreds of spectators line up the opposite side of the street and watch the efforts of the Brigade to conquer the flames. The doomed building belches forth volumes of smoke until after six o'clock, and despite the torrents of water poured into it, it is practically gutted.

Casualties

Meanwhile a couple of tragic incidents occur outside Liberty Hall. During the day hundreds have passed this building without molestation. At four o'clock two shots ring out, and two men, who seem to have escaped from the building, collapse on the ground – shot. One man is killed outright; the other, slightly wounded, rises to his feet, and, bandaging his head with his handkerchief, makes good his escape into Marlborough Street.

Reinforcements

A little after seven o'clock Sinn Fein reinforcements, amounting to about twenty men, proceed from Liberty Hall, via Lower Abbey Street, to the General Post Office. This party receives a few insignificant cheers as it crosses Sackville Street. After its entry, a huge crowd collects around the General Post Office, to be stampeded by a volley in the air from the ground floor windows.

At Night

With the approach of darkness an ominous silence comes over the city. People parade up and down Sackville Street just as under normal circumstances. The exit of a Volunteer, lowered by a sheet from a window on the first floor of Kelly's ammunition office, Bachelor's Walk, and his return with a pick-axe attracts little attention. The people in the street thin out as midnight draws near. A cornet-player strives to earn a few coppers by playing Irish national airs. About eleven o'clock a party of women singing music-hall songs walks up along Burgh Quay. They enter the wooden structure known as the 'Coffee Palace', near O'Connell Bridge.[1] An unruly concert is begun, and lasts for half-an-hour. The women reappear in the street. One lassie causes general amusement by exclaiming in a loud voice, 'Come on, Mattie; come on. Are ye afraid, Mattie?' Mattie walks up to her. Despite his low stature and bandy legs, he is not 'afraid'. 'Mattie, me bhoy!' she exclaims, throwing her arms around him. 'Thanks be t'God I lived to see the grand green flag flyin' over the JPO [*sic*].' I then lose sight of them both in the crowd.

Thenceforth the stillness of the night is broken by occasional rifle reports and an almost continuous sound of shattering glass.

WEDNESDAY

Bombardment of Liberty Hall

At seven o'clock on Wednesday morning reports of rapid firing come from the direction of Butt Bridge and Tara Street. A maxim gun has been put in action and is peppering away at Liberty Hall. The windows are riddled with bullet holes, and puffs of brick-dust fly off the walls. Bang! A field gun has been fired. A hole is burst in the side of the ill-fated building. When the cloud of smoke and dust subsides the green flag over the roof is gone. At eight o'clock the bombardment is at its height. Shell after shell is poured into the building, the face of which is crumbling away under the merciless spray of machine-gun bullets.[2]

A Miraculous Escape

Suddenly, amid the roar of the field gun and the whizz of the maxim's bullets, a Sinn Feiner emerges from a side door and dashes wildly up Eden Quay. A machine gun is turned upon him. Bullets hit the pavement in front of him and behind him; they strike the roadway and the walls of the buildings along his route, and still he runs on *and* on. I hold my breath, as I watch his mad career. Will he escape? He will – he won't. 'My God!' I exclaim, as a bullet raises a spark from the pavement at his toe. A hundred yards in nine seconds – a record! Nonsense; this man does the distance in five, and disappears into Marlborough Street, his breath in his fist, his heart in his mouth, but – safe!

Charge!

At 8.20 a.m. the bombardment ceases. Liberty Hall, riddled

through and through, is like a sieve. The pathway and roadway around it are littered with broken bricks and fragments of plaster.

From a side door in the Custom House, facing Liberty Hall, soldiers dash recklessly to the shattered building. About twenty others follow and disappear into the ruins. They search for fugitives in the buildings and on the roofs around. At 9.30 a.m. the ambulance arrives and makes three or four journeys with wounded. The reign of Liberty Hall is at an end at last!

Sackville Street

About nine o'clock small clusters of people begin to gather in the vicinity of Sackville Street, but stampede wildly at ten o'clock, when a machine-gun begins to speak from the direction of Trinity College, down Westmoreland Street. The bullets pepper the windows of Messrs Hopkins and Hopkins' well-known jewellery establishment. The bombardment is ultimately concentrated upon Messrs Reis' establishment at the corner of Lower Abbey Street, over which a wireless apparatus was erected during the night. A communication cable is stretched taut across Sackville Street between this building and the General Post Office. Just now I feel a flutter of excitement. The house, on the roof of which I am seated, is heavily peppered by Sinn Fein snipers. The panes of glass are successively pierced, and to my alarm, a couple of bullets whizz over the parapet behind which I am making these observations. Forthwith, I descend through a skylight, and by skilfully arranging two looking-glasses I make a large periscope, by the aid of which I can see into the streets below without endangering my personal safety.

Running the Gauntlet

At ten minutes after ten o'clock seven Sinn Feiners successively dash from the GPO to Lower Abbey Street. One by one they run the gauntlet across the bullet-swept street. None of them appear to be hit.

'No Man's Land'

Sackville Street has now become a veritable 'no man's land'. It is swept through and across by bullets. Now and then a Sinn Fein sniper replies from a roof or window. The re-echoing din of discharging firearms is almost deafening.

At 11.50 a.m. the firing unexpectedly ceases as three young women bearing aloft a Red Cross flag traverse Sackville Street from the GPO to Lower Abbey Street. They enter the Hibernian Bank, which also flies the Red Cross flag. The firing is resumed as they disappear from view.

Hair-breadth Escapes

Suddenly, at 12.30 p.m., the machine-gun and rifle fire become intensified. Bullets jump and dance off the O'Connell monument, and emit sparks from the paving stones in the street. A handful of Sinn Feiners in single file are dashing across to the GPO. Bullets hop here and there around them, but on they run. My heart jumps within me as the last man, who has around him the mattress off a bed, stumbles and falls. The mattress unfolds itself on the street. The man jumps up and dashes along with seemingly renewed vigour. Despite the intensity of the fire directed at them all the Sinn Feiners reach their destination in apparent safety.

A Casualty

Stealthily, amid the roar and din, a man emerges from some houses in O'Connell Street, near Hopkins', and proceeds across to the O'Connell monument. At once a volley is directed at him. Just as he comes abreast of the monument he wriggles and falls to the ground. Immediately a man wearing what seems to be the uniform of the St John Ambulance Corps rushes from Westmoreland Street. The firing subsides. The Ambulance man divests the injured man of coat and vest, and is seen folding a bandage, with which he binds the injured man's wound. He then helps his unfortunate comrade to stand erect, and linked together both stagger forward. No sooner do they emerge from the cover provided by the monument than a couple of shots ring out and both fall. In a subsequent lull in the firing they are removed by the ambulance. It is now one o'clock.

Military Take Possession

At two o'clock soldiers take possession of the block of buildings in which I am located. I notice other detachments creeping along the roof of the Ballast Office. The military also occupy the triangular block bordered by Westmoreland Street, D'Olier Street and College Street.

The Sinn Fein snipers again pepper this building. Whizz-bang! Two bullets crash through the window over my head and break the upper glass of my periscope. Chips of glass strike my face. I collapse off my seat with fright, but happily am uninjured. The bullets bury themselves in the plaster wall. It is some time before I recover my usual equanimity. Regaining courage and crouching beneath the level of the window sill, I peep through a corner of the window.

Bombardment of Kelly's Gunpowder Office

Bang! A field gun has been fired from Westmoreland Street. The house trembles beneath me. I shiver. My attention is at once centred on Kelly's gunpowder office, Bachelor's Walk, which in a moment is clouded by a cloak of smoke and dust. The bullets from the rifles and machine-guns whizz and whistle, they pepper the walls and windows of this establishment. Bang! The house trembles again. A hole is bored clean through Kelly's wall. More smoke and dust! Thenceforth the noise of the maxims and rifles is punctuated by the roar of the field gun. Kelly's is riddled through and through, and, at half-past four o'clock, when the firing subsides, it is practically demolished.

Amazing Recklessness

The bombardment has no sooner ceased than an old woman huddles out of a lane near Bachelor's Walk, and, standing in the midst of bricks and mortar scattered on the pavement outside Kelly's ruined establishment, gazes fixedly at the ruins. The shouts of soldiers awake her from her evident lethargy. She looks aimlessly around her and, responding to the warning calls, waves her hand feebly and toddles off across O'Connell Bridge and up Westmoreland Street.

'Familiarity ———'

I have now grown accustomed to the discharge of firearms. Thoughts of danger no longer fill my mind. The crackling of rifles, the rapid 'pat-pat-pat-pat' of the machine-guns and the thunderous bang of the field gun have become almost part of my life. But – our stock of provisions is running out. Privation seems to stare me and my fellow-residents in the face. I sit down to what promises to be my last square meal for some days, at least with the spectre of hunger around me. What odds! The Irish stew on the plate before me tastes delicious; the enjoyment of it drowns my loathsome thoughts of famine and starvation.

A Heartrending Incident

At ten o'clock tonight, by the aid of the arc lamp in the street, I behold a sad and sorrowful incident. An old man helping himself along with a walking-stick emerges from the shade of Hopkins'. Shouts of 'Go back!' interspersed with the crackling of rifles, echo through the streets. As the old man steps on to the footpath on O'Connell Bridge he stops and stares around. He jumps nervously as half-a-dozen bullets raise sparks from the pavement at his feet. He steps feebly on to the roadway and proceeds diagonally across the bridge. The bullets whistle around him. He is hit. He twitches violently as he falls. With a wriggle he lies dead.

THURSDAY

The Fire Demon

Thursday morning dawns amid an ominous silence, but the occasional discharge of firearms rings out periodically. Sackville Street is 'no man's land' more than ever. About 9 a.m. rifle reports become more alarmingly loud and rapid in Lower Abbey Street. At ten o'clock a field gun barks in that district. Volumes of smoke begin to rise from Wynn's Hotel. A fire of large proportions is soon in progress. Smoke towers in the sky and huge flames flicker and leap above the block of buildings. The fire is spreading. An inferno of flame is eating its way into

Sackville Street. The military regard the task of rooting out Sinn Fein snipers as inexpedient and hopeless, except at the cost of an appalling sacrifice of soldiers' lives. Snipers here and there on the roofs could decimate a regiment without giving an opening for effective retaliation. Life is more valuable than property – let property suffer. The fire demon is let loose to hunt human mice from their haunts or to bring upon them infernal destruction.

A Casualty

At half-past eleven o'clock a man waving his hands excitedly suddenly emerges from the GPO and seems rather to stagger than walk into Sackville Street. A well-placed shot finds its mark; the man collapses in the street. Immediately a couple of men bearing aloft a Red Cross flag rush from the GPO to help their fallen comrade. The rules of warfare are respected, the hail of lead is summarily stopped. The two men half drag, half carry, their human burden into Prince's street, and – the rifles open fire again.

Wild Dash for Safety

The conflagration in Abbey Street continues unabated. So far as I can judge, no effort is made to confine its dimensions. Life in the entire block of buildings bounded by Lower Abbey Street, Marlborough Street, Eden Quay and Sackville St is in imminent danger of ruthless extermination. Overawed, as it were, by the grand stupendous, though tragic, spectacle, the soldiers and Sinn Feiners dally in their discharges of firearms. The crackling of rifles is replaced by the roar of flames, the hissing of steam, the creaking of steel joists, and the crackling of burning wood. Suddenly from Reis' corner of Lower Abbey Street ten Sinn Feiners rush across Sackville Street to escape from the flames. From one terror they rush into another. The machine-guns and rifles play upon them. A sickening feeling comes over me as I watch their wild dash for safety. Bullets hop and leap around them. But fortune again favours the frantic brave. They reach the GPO.

At one o'clock the communication cord across Sackville Street collapses.

Devouring Flames

Meanwhile the devouring flames have eaten their way along the buildings bordering Sackville Street. Almost half the block is now a holocaust, a mass of flame and smoke. The grandeur of the spectacle is indescribable. The burning of almost a modern Rome is being enacted before my eyes. At three o'clock the flames have eaten their way over to the Eden Quay houses, from which non-combatant fugitives are beginning to come forth. Men, women and children run along Eden Quay towards the Custom House for safety. The flames and smoke have almost enveloped all the houses on this side of the block, and judging from the sudden cessation of the bombardment, I conclude that the order 'Cease fire' has been given to the military. How ironical! Cease fire, indeed! Yes, gunfire and rifle-fire; but the devilish flames consuming the ill-fated buildings seem only to laugh and flicker on their career of destruction.

A Touching Incident

At a quarter to four o'clock a soldier pluckily steals his way from Butt Bridge to the burning block and knocks at the doors of the buildings on Eden Quay. From some there is no response. In others, men, women, and children, timorous and trembling, hear the welcome knock, and, burdened with bundles of clothing, run along the quay. Three young women from a house already being licked by the flames fall upon their knees and fervently kiss the hand of their deliverer. This soldier is now joined by a comrade with a megaphone, who bellows, 'Come out! Come out!' After taking these precautions to ensure the escape of innocent non-combatants, both return to their headquarters. The rifle-fire is again resumed.

DBC on Fire

The blaze gradually creeps its way up along the upper stories of the DBC Restaurant, and at 4.30 p.m. the dome is on fire. The flames kissing the ball on the dome's summit are singularly impressive. Standing high above the lower plane of flame and smoke it is thrown out in relief by a background of clouds. A scene of greater grandeur I have never before witnessed, not even in the realms of cinematography. It is only outshone by the avalanche of flame and smoke that crashes to the ground when the dome collapses at five o'clock.

The GPO

The monotony of gazing continually at the sea of flame is relieved at 5.45 p.m. by the report of a field gun. A puff of smoke rises from the northern side of the GPO. 'The attack has begun! The attack has begun!' I whisper to myself. I watch and listen for over an hour without noticing any further developments. I fall into a kind of lethargy from standing motionless in anxious expectancy. At seven o'clock five or six Sinn Feiners run the gauntlet as before from Lower Abbey Street to the GPO. The scene already described in this connection is repeated. All are blessed by miraculous good luck, and reach their destination unharmed.

Magnificent Scenes

Thenceforth my attention is directed to the seething mass of burning buildings, the heat from which I perceptibly feel upon my face. At 7.30 p.m. the front of the Waverley Hotel falls with a maddening roar. A vast cloud of smoke, glistening with burning embers, oozes into the street, and ascending leaves beneath a mass of smouldering bricks. This scene of superb, though dolorous, magnificence is repeated as other buildings similarly collapse, and at nine o'clock the climax is reached by the dismemberment of Messrs Hopkins' jewellery establishment, which crushes in its downfall thousands of pounds worth of gold and silver.

Baffles Adequate Description

The brilliancy of the spectacle before me in the depths of the night baffles all adequate description. Imagine the scene. The roar and crackling of inflammable material; the leaping and flickering of the immense tongues of bright, seething flame, the mountains of variegated smoke rising high into the clouds, and the sad, sickening thoughts loitering in your mind, of the homes destroyed, the hopes shattered, the employment lost, through the devastation caused by the devilish flames. Add to that the din caused by hundreds of firearms. Picture it all, expand it in your mind to extravagant limits, and you will have some idea of the awful, terrific, stupendous scene I witness just before I retire for a few hours' sleep.

FRIDAY

Desolately Desolate

Elsewhere I have described the scene before me as being desolate. The houses on the opposite bank of the Liffey are one mass of smouldering brick, exuding a thick, heavy smoke. There is not a living individual in sight. The dead body of the old man shot the night before last still lies stretched across the tram tracks on the bridge. Bricks and plaster from the burned buildings that collapsed during the night are scattered half-way across Sackville Street. The skeletons of the buildings still standing tower high over the heaps of debris. Steel girders twisted beyond all recognition, hang helplessly from wall to wall. The opposite (GPO) side of the street makes a striking contrast with its ruined *vis-à-vis*. Although portions have been battered by field and maxim gunfire, and some of the shops wrecked by the looting mob, it is as yet untouched by incendiary flames, and so it looks comparatively majestic and stately. Over the GPO the green republican flag still flies, and, fluttering in the breeze, seems to smile at the hordes of military, slowly but surely closing in upon it.

The Calm Preceding the Storm

The morning passes in comparative quietude. When I say comparative quietude I mean that the din of the rifles and maxim and field guns is less pronounced than has now become usual. Acute acoustic disturbances are now a feature of life in the city. I have a strange foreboding that this is the calm preceding the storm about to sweep over the GPO.

The military are active. Soldiers in twos and threes creep

furtively over O'Connell Bridge and reconnoitre in the lanes and by-ways in the vicinity. A couple daringly ventures into the open street in an unsuccessful endeavour to draw the fire of Sinn Fein snipers.

The rumblings of a bombardment in the direction of the Four Courts fall upon my ears. The thundering of the field gun pulsates through the echoes of crackling rifles and machine guns.

Attack on the GPO

The GPO has long since seemed to be the chief stronghold of the rebels. I have come to regard it as the centre of all their activities, the heart of the entire rebellion. The finale of the attack upon it would, I expected, be the central lily in a wreath of thrilling experiences. I pictured in my mind that hundreds of khaki-clad soldiers would march upon it amid a bombardment of unique magnitude, excelling anything I had hitherto witnessed. I had dreamt of the building being brilliantly illuminated by the quivering flashes made by pelting bullets, rebounding off the granite walls, and the murderous tongues of leaping flame from Sinn Fein rifles, dealing death and destruction upon the attacking troops. All the thrilling events I had witnessed would, I thought, fade into comparative insignificance.

At 4.20 p.m. I am sadly disillusioned in my expectations. A field gun barks in the direction of Earl Street. A column of smoke rises from the upper portion of the GPO. Another bang! The column of smoke is augmented. 'Now for it,' I say to myself. I look and listen in expectancy. The machine guns spit spasmodically, but nothing further occurs to satisfy my hunger for excitement except the piercing bark of a dog limply running across Sackville Street!

Fire!

At a quarter to five the dimensions of the column of smoke rising from the GPO assumes dangerously large proportions. Some Sinn Feiners with a hose on the roof endeavour to cope with the onslaught of the flames. At frequent intervals their frantic efforts to overcome the fire demon are interrupted by well-directed bullets from a maxim gun. The consuming flames creep ever onward, and at ten minutes to five o'clock break through the roof and leap upward into the sky. In less than an hour the entire building is a boiling, frizzling, seething pot of smoke and flame. The ebullition grows and grows, and seems to bubble over as heaps of glowing debris crash over the granite walls and through the flame-eaten windows.

Flag Still Flies

And high above the doomed building the Republican flag flutters excitedly in the stifling atmosphere of dust-laden smoke. The leaping flames lick and kiss the pole on which it hangs. With the aid of a powerful field-glass I see the white letters of the words 'Irish Republic' on its surface gradually scorch a deep brown hue. Now and then it is buried in an upheaval of thousands of fragments of burning paper belched as it were from a volcano's crater. Jeeringly *it seems to defy* the flames beneath and the hail of lead sweeping about it from the maxims and rifles around. Fanned by the hot ascending air it seems to raise its arms to heaven in an hysteria of sorrow. And all the time the building at its feet is being consumed by the ravishing flames. During four days and nights it has flown above the building proudly and defiantly; it now begins to hang its head as if in shame. At nine o'clock the General Post Office is reduced to ruins. Its four granite walls look like the bones of a skeleton skull. Its core is nothing but smouldering debris. The fluttering of the flag grows feebler. In the dimness of the night I see it gives an occasional flicker, as if revived by the gust of air. At length at 9.51 p.m. the staff supporting it begins to waver, and in a second falls out towards the street. The Sinn Fein fortress is no more; it has met with an ignominious end.

SATURDAY

The Hotel Metropole

Loud reports of distant shooting continue from dawn on Saturday morning, but affairs in Sackville Street are relatively quiet. At 9.30 a.m. the military resume operations in this locality by spraying the Hotel Metropole with machine-gun fire. Immediately the roar of a field-gun echoes through the street. A shell crashes through the upper storey of the hotel, which, after a severe bombardment, takes fire a little after noon. Fanned by a gentle breeze, the harrowing scenes already described are here re-enacted, the furious flames eating their way through Eason's and Manfield's establishments and across to the opposite side of Middle Abbey Street. At 2.15 p.m. the Hotel Metropole collapses.

Searching the Ruins

Meanwhile, throughout the morning the soldiers are busy searching the ruins in Lower Sackville Street. Officers with loaded revolvers disappear cautiously into the gaping walls of the ruined buildings. Barricades of sandbags and borrowed furniture are erected across the quays at Liffey Street and Marlborough Street.

Cease Fire!

At a quarter to four o'clock the order 'Cease fire!' is passed round to the military in my vicinity, and at four o'clock the deserted thoroughfares enjoy a period of respite from the almost ceaseless echoes of the discharge of firearms. Just now the Fire Brigade comes rattling along to make an effort to conquer the flames. Throughout the entire conflagration in Lower Sackville Street the Brigade has been singularly conspicuous by its absence, which fact, no doubt, has been due to the exigencies of the military situation. Two pumping engines are placed in position on O'Connell Bridge, and lines of hose are laid along the footpaths to the mouth of Middle Abbey Street. Red-shirted Brigadiers, in steel helmets, run here and there undeterred by the magnitude of the task before them. They look peculiarly picturesque in their unique surroundings.

A Dastardly Outrage

Suddenly, at 4.15 p.m., the reports of a number of rifle shots ring out. The hard-working Brigadiers scurry to take shelter in archways and doorways. The rifles continue to cackle. The firemen scour the buildings with their eyes in an obvious endeavour to trace the perpetrators of this dastardly outrage. Suddenly they are seen to rush collectively to their horse-drawn and motor-driven vehicles. They drive off, leaving their mission of mercy as yet unfinished. The promiscuous 'potting' continues until 5.30 p.m.

Surrender

A little after seven o'clock I am startled by the sound of marching footsteps. Over fifty Sinn Feiners, with white flags borne aloft at both extremities, are marching from the direction of Nelson's Pillar. A military officer with an armed guard crosses O'Connell Bridge to meet them. The lately contending forces meet under the flag of truce at O'Connell's monument. The Sinn Feiners – an ill-sorted collection of uniformed and privately-dressed individuals comprising youths of fourteen and fifteen and old grey-headed men – proceed to discard their military equipment. A parley takes place between the military and the volunteer officers, after which the Sinn Feiners re-don their equipment and take up their arms. The order 'about turn' having been given, they retrace their footsteps up the street.

A Priest

A priest is the first non-combatant to enter Sackville Street since the enactment of the scenes of horror described above. I recognise him as Father Brendan O'Brien, ODC. He is accompanied by a military escort. The body of the old man lying on the bridge receives his ministrations. The soldiers by his side remove their hats as he imparts his benediction. He then proceeds along Sackville Street.

Fire Brigade Resumes Work

At 8.30 p.m., under the cover of darkness, the Fire Brigade resumes its effort to confine the flames to the building already being devoured. The fire has now spread along Middle Abbey Street and threatens to consume the entire block.

Final Surrender

At 9.0 p.m., the Sinn Feiners in this locality surrender finally. They are disarmed and formed into column of fours in Sackville

Street. A large military escort accompany the captives along Westmoreland Street, obviously en route for Dublin Castle.

SUNDAY

Next day all is quiet. The rebellion has practically been squashed. Crowds of people flock to see Dublin's finest thoroughfare in ruins. Only those who have secured permits are allowed to enter the street proper. The photographic reproductions that have appeared in the public Press give adequate pictures of the scene of destruction.

At 9.0 o'clock on Sunday night two batches of captured Sinn Feiners, amounting in all to about five hundred men, are marched along the quay right under my window. Although it is dusk I seem to recognise some of the faces as being familiar. Poor devils! They did their best, and – a poor best at that.

'THE LOOTERS WERE WORKING WITH FRENZIED ENERGY'

The following is another article, titled 'The Looters', from the magazine supplement, A Record of the Irish Rebellion of 1916, *published by the Office of Irish Life in Dublin in 1916, 'while the ruins of the city are still smouldering'.*

The looters were mostly young lads and women, although there was a sprinkling of men amongst them. It was curious to observe the different demeanour of the men and women looters. The men did their looting in a furtive, hang-dog way and cleared off the moment they had as much booty as they could carry. The women flaunted their spoil: they seemed to be totally without shame or any remnant of moral sense; to have thrown off the conventional trammels of civilization and to have relapsed in an instant into the savage state. Moreover, the looters were by no means confined to the submerged slum population. A remarkable proportion were well dressed and belonged to the wage-earning working class, or perhaps to classes still more 'respectable'. The shops which came in for the most attention were boot shops, drapery establishments, tobacconists and sweet shops, in which almost invariably the goods were temptingly displayed in the windows without any shutters or blind. In very few cases was there any looting for food, and those only late in the week.

In Sackville Street on Wednesday evening the scene was of the weirdest description. An immense crowd of sightseers was promenading up and down the centre of the street under a blaze of electric light. All along the east side of the street the looters were working with frenzied energy. Every now and then the shouts from the shops would be drowned by the crash of glass as another window was hammered in. At the Earl Street corner, Noblett's sweet shop, which had been looted the day before, was empty save for one thin-faced, unwholesome-looking youth who was working furiously to remove the brass handle from the door. What on earth will he do with it when he gets it? Further on a little girl of twelve or so is tottering under the weight of a huge circular office chair. A passer-by knocks against it and is rewarded with a string of the most appalling blasphemy. A fresh-faced youth is crossing the street with an armful of boots. He is brandishing a pair of white satin shoes and shouting hysterically 'God save Ireland.'

Meanwhile the crowd move up and down in the centre, silent, dejected, and disapproving, but no one of them interferes by word or deed, while dominating all on the other side of the street is the sinister menace of the Sinn Fein fortress with barricaded windows and levelled guns.

On Wednesday the Brunswick Street[1] and Westland Row neighbourhood saw a repetition of the scenes of Sackville Street. I saw one of the priests of the Westland Row Church make a valiant effort to save some of the shops opposite the station; but it was quite useless, the crowd had got far beyond the control of moral suasion. The mob here, as everywhere, was quite good-tempered, but of course they had everything their own way. As I listened to the jokes and chaff of the looters I could not help thinking of the delighted purring of a cat who has just captured a mouse, and how easily a little opposition would turn her into a spitting fury. There was no want of ludicrous incidents. As I came round from Brunswick Street into Westland Row I met a tall old man, I should say of eighty, with a very long white beard and a most patriarchal appearance; he was supporting himself with a stick in his right hand, and under his left arm he was carrying home a large glass cylinder full of coloured sweets, obviously from the looted sweet-shop in Westland Row. I hope he didn't make himself sick.

On Thursday morning, the top of Grafton Street was the scene of operations. During the night of Wednesday the corner sweet-shop was raided, but on Thursday morning, shortly after eight o'clock, as I was passing through, the work was being started methodically and in real earnest. I found afterwards, however, that the looters were unable to get further down the street than Knowles' fruit-shop. The street here makes a bend which brings it within view of the roof of Trinity College, and I was told that a rifle volley definitely put an end to the industry as far as Grafton Street was concerned.

On the same Thursday I think the most impudent looting that I observed took place in Dorset Street, on the North side, where Baker's, a very extensive drapery establishment, was looted in broad daylight. In all the other cases the loot was carried away, one could not tell where; here one could see where it went. Of course there were raiding parties from Hill Street and the neighbouring slums; but the bulk of the stuff went into the houses beside the shop. Hardwicke Street and the lanes off it got a good proportion, but I do not think that there was a single one of the tenement houses in the crescent facing St George's Church which was not stuffed full of Baker's goods. I doubt if the women in those houses ever worked so hard before in their lives. In the middle of the proceedings Father Dempsey, of Berkeley Road Church, arrived on the scene. Father Dempsey is a big man, and on this occasion an angry man, a fact which he made no attempt to conceal. In about five minutes the women were flying helter-skelter, abandoning their booty. About a dozen young lads, most of whom had been looting enthusiastically the moment before, were converted in an instant into equally enthusiastic defenders of law and order. They collected the stolen goods off the street and threw them back into the house, and collected loose timber and made a sort of barricade to the windows. I shall never forget the ludicrous face of pain and bewilderment of one old harpy in a cape covered with black beads. She was returning for more spoil, and was making her way through the window, evidently unaware of the fresh development, when she was received by one of the youthful defenders with a jab from the end of a curtain pole. Then she looked round and saw the priest and fled incontinently, amid the laughter of the crowd. It looked as if the place was saved, but I had my doubts. The priest obviously could not stay there all night, the boys would soon get tired of their new amusement, the barricade was flimsy, and above all I observed that a stout young woman at the upper window, with a broad, rather good-humoured face, who had been showering down parcels of goods on to the street, and who was obviously hugely enjoying her role of Lady Bountiful, made no attempt to leave her post, but sat fanning herself with some broad white feathers and waiting for the fun to begin again. Next morning I passed the shop again. It was cleared out, lock, stock and barrel. They had even stolen the timber of the boys' barricade.

'THOSE AWFUL DAYS WHEN THE RIOTERS LET LOOSE THEIR VIOLENCE UPON THE CITY'

Thekla Bowser was the author of a seminal book on Voluntary Aid Detachment (VAD) work carried out during the First World War. Published in 1917, the book devoted an entire chapter to VAD work in Ireland during the rebellion, and while not an eyewitness herself, Ms Bowser's publication gives a valuable overall account of the extraordinary work carried out by civilians whose sole aim was to help those who needed help.[1]

Chapter XIII – VAD Work in the Sinn Fein Riots
The Sinn Fein Riots gave a sad but unique opportunity to Ambulance and Red Cross workers in Ireland of showing how they could cope with an emergency. The mischief, it is true, had been brewing for a long while, but few people realised that it could ever come to anything serious, and practically all the work that was done for the wounded was arranged on the spur of the moment.

Of all the magnificent pieces of work carried out by VAD members during this devastating war, there has been nothing to surpass that which was accomplished in Dublin during those awful days when the rioters let loose their violence upon the city and its inhabitants.

From St Patrick's Day, Friday, March 17th, 1916, up to

Easter Monday, April 24th, the fire smouldered, with flashes of flame here and there, which gave an indication of what might be expected when the general outbreak occurred. On Easter Monday at noon the storm burst in Dublin, and for the following six days the city and suburbs were the scene of grave loss of life and destruction of property.

Dr Lumsden issued a detailed report of the work done by Ambulance and Red Cross workers during the rebellion.[2] The members, he said, lost no opportunity of rendering First Aid to soldiers, civilians and rebels alike. The general efficiency of the various detachments was fiercely tested and not found wanting. Members performed duty in all the zones where fighting took place, and it is sad to say that some of them were killed and injured in the course of their work.

The wounded were collected by men and nurses, who went on foot and in Ambulance wagons, rendering First Aid and taking patients to Hospital under circumstances of great danger and difficulty.

The first move towards the organisation of First Aid work in the rebellion was made by the late Corps Superintendent Holden Stodart, who on Easter Monday telephoned to the Military offering help. Two days later this heroic officer was killed, and his death made an impression throughout the Red Cross workers in Ireland which will not fade.

Mr Stodart, who was only thirty-three, was one of the strongest supporters of the St John Ambulance Brigade in Dublin, and since the outbreak of the war had rendered valuable service as a Superintendent of the Brigade. To the work he devoted himself with the wholehearted enthusiasm that characterised everything he did.

When the rebellion broke out in Dublin he was the senior St John Ambulance officer then in the city, and the Military authorities were only too thankful to accept the help which he offered. His was an arduous task, for he organised bodies of Ambulance workers to take duty at the various Hospitals. Despite obstacles that might have seemed insurmountable to another man, he gathered his forces and placed them where their services were most needed. Once the organisation was complete, he settled down to carry on his own work under his superior officer, who had by then arrived on the spot.

The St John Ambulance Brigade since the rebellion has awarded medals and certificates to a number of the officers who distinguished themselves in the work of the riots, but at present the Chapter-General of the Order of St John of Jerusalem has no power to award posthumous honours.

In the report which was issued of the work, it is well said that those who knew Mr Stodart best are content to think that 'Better than martial woe, or the burden of civic sorrow. Better than praise to-day, or the statue we build tomorrow. Better than honour and glory, from history's iron pen. Is the thought of duty done, and the love of fellow men.'

The War Office has decided to place the officers and men of the Red Cross and St John Ambulance Brigade working during the riots in the same position with regard to pensions and compassionate allowances as the equivalent ranks in the Army and in pursuance of this liberal policy the widow and child of Mr H. Stodart have been granted the pension and allowance of a Lieutenant killed in action.

It was whilst Mr Stodart was proceeding with a stretcher party to the relief of a wounded soldier that he was shot, and instantaneously died. His heroic death and noble example will ever be remembered amongst those who serve under the white eight-pointed star of the Ancient Knights of St John.

Pembroke Red Cross VAD

It chanced that on the Monday of the outbreak a member of a BRCS[3] VA Detachment passed the Royal City of Dublin Hospital[4] when the first of the wounded GR Volunteers arrived. He sent a message to assemble his detachment, and they immediately took up duty in the various Hospitals. Some of them took in wounded men on stretchers under circumstances of great danger.

Mr Dickson of this detachment was specially mentioned for his good work in connection with the running of the Rathmines ambulance. On Wednesday the 24th it ran from Portobello Military Hospital to Beggars' Bush Barracks, being in danger of being shot at all the journey. During that night he made five journeys with the Ambulance, and in the following two days he made several journeys and assisted in evacuating some of the cases, and also in taking drugs and necessities to the small Hospital at Beggars' Bush.

Difficulties of the Work

Imagine the conditions under which the work was carried out. The tram and train service had ceased; postal and telegraph facilities no longer existed. The telephone service was completely controlled by the military, and all the usual ways and means of communication were cut off; yet obstacles were surmounted by the VAD members.

One of them was repulsed by the insurgents at two places,

but succeeded in getting through at the third; another was twice fired at whilst driving a Motor Ambulance, and a third walked twelve miles out of his direct route in order to get through to his destination.

Richmond Hospital was the centre of the area where fierce fighting took place. As the danger increased, the beds were placed on the floor to avoid bullets fired from the housetops. In the middle of the week food ran short at the Hospital, and Miss Hezlett, the Lady Superintendent, co-operated in the organisation of an expedition to obtain more. On a white sheet the words 'Richmond Hospital Supplies' were marked with black type, and Dr Pollock and two students, bearing this banner, took out a borrowed horse and cart. In spite of having to go through some hot firing they returned safely with supplies.

At the Rotunda Hospital food almost gave out, and extreme economy had to be practised. Eventually, when a gallant friend sent down food on a van, the driver was fired at, but luckily got through unhurt.

Gas was cut off on Tuesday morning, and the electricity on Wednesday. Working in semi-darkness added enormously to the difficulty of the situation. The nursing staff, however, maintained a wonderful degree of calmness under the stress of work, whilst there was an accompaniment of roaring cannon and spitting bullets.

Ambulance Patrol

On Easter Tuesday it was decided to start an Ambulance patrol with its headquarters in Harcourt Street Railway Station. Day by day the cars ran the gauntlet of bullet-swept streets, being frequently struck by shots. Dangers, always present by day, increased a hundredfold by night. The darkened streets had to be negotiated without the aid of lights. The voluntary drivers were wonderful in the way they kept up a high speed and yet managed to take their load of wounded men through in safety.

Glass was everywhere. Tram wires, coiled in big loops, lay about, and in one place a huge length of telephone wire coiled itself round the wheels of a car. In the daytime the drivers had to memorise the danger spots where houses and walls were down, so that they should not run amuck at night. Many a time the drivers were asked to go and fetch wounded men across a dangerous area, and in every case they just 'cranked up' their cars and went without a word.

When the ordinary cars could get no further there was an armoured motor car which carried stretchers right into the thick of the fight. It would turn broadside so as to give the stretcher-bearers as much shelter as possible from the snipers.

The bearers would lie down and wriggle along the streets, pulling the stretchers after them. It is never easy to load a stretcher with a wounded man, but add to the difficulties pitch darkness and the fact that you must yourself lie on the ground and it becomes apparently impossible. But the impossible was achieved again and again by these gallant men, who did their duty as simply and as courageously as those other Red Cross men who are working on foreign battlefields against a common foe. These bearers often had to walk half a mile under cross fire.

Gallant Conduct

Amongst so many instances of gallantry and conspicuous courage it is difficult to mention any names in particular. For instance, Mr Henry Olds was informed that a wounded man was lying on O'Connell Bridge. He hastened there and found that a blind man had been seriously wounded.

First Aid was applied, but whilst he was putting on the bandage he was himself shot in the shoulder. This, however, did not prevent him completing his work, and he managed to bring the man to a place of safety before he became unconscious himself.

On Wednesday work was allotted to a great number of St John officers and men who wished to assist, a room being placed at the disposal of the Brigade in the City of Dublin Hospital, Baggot Street.

Corrig Castle Red Cross Hospital

Dr Reginald Peacocke, Assistant County Director of the County of Dublin branch of the BRCS, speaks highly of the work done by the VAD members, especially at Corrig Castle Red Cross Hospital.[5]

There was a continuous procession at the Hospital of refugees, amongst them being two stokers from HMS *Tara*, who had been liberated by the Duke of Westminster's armoured car expedition, and who were passing through Kingstown on their way home, but were unable to proceed.

Owing to the great difficulty in procuring food, bread had to be baked and butter churned on the premises, some of the VAD members being on duty for fourteen hours a day, whilst the Matron, Miss Harris, Commandant, was on duty for three days and three nights continuously.

The British Red Cross branches of the City and County of Dublin took a large share in the work. Mrs Heppell-Marr, Assistant County Director of the City of Dublin Branch, was at her post at 29 Fitzwilliam Street, each day, and many members of the BRCS Detachments took their share in carrying the wounded in under fire. The offices at 29 Fitzwilliam Street were converted into a temporary hospital, the VAD members collecting supplies from the public. This Hospital contained fifty beds.

Another hospital, with twenty-five beds, was set up at 32, Fitzwilliam Square.

Refugee Women and Children

All kinds of duties were taken over by the Detachments, whilst isolated members helped refugee women and children, gave assistance at the BRCS Dressing Stations, carried bales of dressings on stretchers to the various Hospitals, fed the starving poor and rendered First Aid to civilians.

One Detachment started a Canteen for soldiers; another kept a Canteen going at the munition works throughout the riots.

Women Stretcher-Bearers

In pre-war days many were the discussions as to whether women could or should do stretcher work. The women VAD members in Ireland settled the question once and for all because an enormous amount of stretcher work was carried out by them most successfully.

There were not nearly enough men to do this work, and the women showed not only their knowledge of how to do it, but their complete indifference to danger when it became a matter of duty that they should go out and rescue wounded people in the shell-swept streets. They made regular tours in the city, and rendered First Aid to the wounded before they brought them into the Hospitals.

Filling Gaps

All sorts of gaps were filled by the devoted members of VA Detachments during that terrible week in Dublin. At the Castle Hospital it was found that there was exceeding difficulty in getting the laundry work done. VAD members volunteered to do it, and everything went well. Washing, cooking, kitchen work – it did not matter what it was, what kind of labour was required; it was all cheerfully and capably undertaken by VAD members.

Ella Webb, MD

Dr Ella Webb, Lady District Superintendent of SJAB, and member of the Joint VAD Committee for Ireland, rendered splendid service during the rebellion, for she organised hospitals, and cycled through the firing line continuously.[6] She visited the City Hospitals day by day, ascertaining their needs and giving all possible assistance. She and Dr Lumsden were both awarded silver medals by the Chapter-General of the Order of St John of Jerusalem for their services during the week of the riot.

Dr Webb, in the report which she issued later, remarks that she was particularly struck with the two great lessons which the VAD members had learned; the first was to be plucky, resourceful and competent, and the second was to obey. She says: 'I was particularly struck with the way in which members took their orders to devote themselves to dull, arduous and uninteresting work with the same cheerfulness as to nursing in the wards.'

Dr John Lumsden, MD

Dr John Lumsden, MD, Knight of Grace of the Order of St John of Jerusalem, Deputy Commissioner of the St John Ambulance Brigade, Director General of the Joint VAD Committee for Ireland, showed extraordinary courage throughout the rebellion. He was always in the thick of the fight.

An eyewitness, speaking of his work, said: 'His conduct was simply magnificent. He is the bravest man I ever saw. He coolly and calmly knelt in the middle of the road attending to the wounded soldiers, while bullets were fired from the houses on both sides. He helped the men into the Ambulance wagons himself, sent them off, and waited until they returned, and during all the time he was under a heavy cross fire.'

He was under fire for several hours together. Day by day the Ambulance cars ran the gauntlet of bullet-swept streets. The dangers increased a hundred-fold by night, when the streets, shrouded in darkness and encumbered by obstacles, had to be negotiated without the aid of lights. Ambulances were frequently struck by shots whilst on their journeys.

In one house where six or seven wounded soldiers were found the men managed under these conditions to get the wounded loaded on to the stretchers and into the armoured cars in safety. Two bearers had very narrow escapes, bullets passing through their clothing; one stretcher handle had its end knocked off. Several bullets struck the armoured car as it left.

Another typical feature was the extreme care and correct handling given by the stretcher-bearers amidst the most nerve-trying conditions.

Their first thought was for the comfort of the patient, and the best method of ensuring his safe and comfortable transport.

The Military casualties during the insurrection amounted to some five hundred, and the civilian losses in killed and wounded amounted to more than a thousand, so some idea may be formed of the emergencies under which the Ambulance men and women of Dublin worked during that week.

Nursing Detachments

The chief piece of work undertaken by the Nursing Divisions was the transformation of the War Hospital Supply Depot in Merrion Square into a temporary Hospital. This was carried out in the amazingly short time of three hours.

Dr Ella Webb sent out messages at noon to members to report themselves, and at 2 p.m. girls began to arrive, though in many cases their journeys had been hazardous. At five o'clock that afternoon an amputation was being done in the improvised operating theatre, and quite half of the thirty beds were already full.

Dr Webb says in her report: 'As this work entailed the carrying in by hand of all mattresses, beds, bedding, and utensils from the neighbouring houses, and the clearing away of large, heavy work tables with which the rooms were originally filled, it is a performance of which the VAD members have every right to be proud.'

Auxiliary Hospitals

Seven auxiliary hospitals were equipped by other detachments. In one case a Hospital was helped by a band of ladies who organised an all-day working party for dressings, etc., and a food supply party. Large quantities of both food and dressings were provided.

Too much praise cannot be given to the ladies of the Red Cross branches of the City and County of Dublin for the work which they performed during the rebellion, and it is impossible here to mention the individual acts of gallantry which were done by many members.

A great many temporary hospitals were equipped and made absolutely ready for the reception of patients, which happily were never used, as the rebellion was quickly quelled by the authorities.

Kingstown Men's Detachment
This detachment was mobilised, and on Thursday, April 27th, twelve of them left Kingstown and marched into Ballsbridge, and reported to the MO in command of the RAMC there. On the following day they returned to Kingstown, and did excellent work at Corrig Castle Hospital.

Many military and naval refugees arrived at the hospital, which added considerably to the work of the staff, as they all had to be fed and housed, the majority of them remaining about ten days. A number of soldiers were brought in on Tuesday, including an RAMC Captain who had been wounded, and a number of men suffering from vaccination fever. Shortly afterwards there arrived five Queen Alexandra nurses on their way to King George V Hospital. In fact, there was a continuous procession of refugees, both Military and civilian.

There was such terrible difficulty in procuring bread that the kitchen was turned into a bakery, and even butter was churned on the premises. Some of the VAD members were on duty day and night.

Canteens

Canteens were opened in various places so that the soldiers on duty might be fed, and these were for the most part entirely run by VAD members. Of one lady who was in charge of a canteen, it is recorded that she never went off duty for eleven days, taking only snatches of sleep in a chair.

Smart Work

The Misses J. and R. Fitzpatrick first reported to the military authorities the seizure by the Sinn Feiners of various points of vantage. During the whole of the rebellion they worked in the hottest and most dangerous fighting zone. They warned the incoming soldiers and troops and acted as guides to them.

They gave first aid to any number of wounded military and civilians, and they carried the wounded from under fire to places of safety. They provided food for the soldiers in the trenches on the canal bank, and elsewhere, and all the time they were passing to and fro, their garden being under a severe cross fire from troops and rebels.

A Dramatic Incident

It was on the Wednesday evening following Easter Monday that the Sherwood Foresters marched towards Dublin into the death trap that awaited them in the neighbourhood of Northumberland Road. Into the inferno the Lady Superintendent and nurses of Sir Patrick Dun's Nursing Home bravely set forth at about four o'clock in the afternoon.[7] They were the first on the scene, and they improvised stretchers out of quilts.

The resident medical staff of the hospital were also gallantly engaged in this rescue work, and between them they carried seventy-nine wounded men, including soldiers and rebels, into the home. This work went on from four in the afternoon until midnight. Men and women alike rendered aid under fire with the utmost coolness and courage.

A soldier who had been for many months in the trenches in France and happened to be in Dublin on leave during the riots told me that he had never seen hotter fire than that which swept the streets of the Irish capital.

Sir Patrick Dun's Hospital became full to overflowing with wounded, and its approaches were so constantly swept with rifle fire that it was found necessary to throw open the maternity hospital for the treatment of casualties. In all some forty bullet wounds of a shocking nature were treated at the hospital, twelve of them proving fatal.

The priests attached to St Andrew's Church, close by, were constantly in the thick of the danger, ministering to the wounded and dying.

It is satisfactory to know that the Sinn Feiners always respected the sign of the Red Cross and never deliberately fired upon an ambulance or a hospital.

Enough has been said to give some slight notion of the magnificence of the work which was carried out by each and every detachment in the district where the riots took place. Instances of personal courage there were without number, and although we can only mention a few here as being typical of all the others, we are glad to know that their services have been recognised by the War Office and by the authorities of the Red Cross societies.

Terrible indeed it was that such an occasion should ever arise; but since the thing happened one can only be thankful that there was already prepared a body of men and women, efficiently trained, capable and willing, who could deal with the emergency.

Of doctors and regular trained nurses there could not have possibly been anything like enough to cope with the situation, and there can be no doubt that the work of the VA Detachments in Ireland proves how invaluable they are to a country whether it be at war or enjoying peace.

One can scarcely dare to imagine what would have happened to those hundreds of wounded men and women in the streets of Dublin during that awful week had there not been this devoted band of voluntary workers who had trained themselves in the principles of first aid, of stretcher-bearing, and of elementary nursing.

The work which was done by the VA Detachments in the Sinn Fein riots alone must prove to the whole world how necessary it is that patriotic men and women should identify themselves with the Voluntary Aid Detachment movement, learning not only the principles of how to render help under such circumstances, but perhaps the even more important matters of discipline, and of carrying out any bit of work which comes to hand and which is an infinitesimal fragment in the design of mercy which was pictured for the world by the pioneers of Red Cross work.

'MOST OF THEM WERE STARVED, HUNGRY-LOOKING POOR FELLOWS'

Joseph Holloway (1861–1944) is best described as a devotee of the arts, especially the theatre (and particularly The Abbey). An ordinary man, he left behind an extraordinary journal, covering decades, in which he daily noted the events he experienced and the people he met. The full journal, which he called Impressions of a Dublin Playgoer, *fills 221 volumes and 100,000 pages with over 25 million words, and is now housed in the National Library of Ireland. For most of his life, Holloway lived in 21 Northumberland Road, just two doors from No. 25 in one direction, and 100 metres from Mount Street Bridge in the other. And while he was lucky to leave the Mount Street Bridge area just before the terrible battle began, he ended up being an all-too-close eyewitness to the death and destruction on O'Connell Street, when he went to stay at 5 Cavendish Row 'till the trouble was over'. The extracts from his journal which cover the Rising are reproduced here.*[1]

Easter Monday, April 24

An eventful day in the history of English misrule in Ireland. I was in blissful ignorance of anything unusual happening in the city till I went out after dinner at 2 o'clock to attend the matinee of *Shall Us* at the Empire. Just as Ellen the maid called me to dinner, some trams stopped opposite the house as if there was a breakdown on the line, and the end one of the string of cars reversed the trolly, and the passengers got off, and it moved off towards Ballsbridge as I went into dinner, and I thought no more about it. All trams were cleared ere I had finished my dinner.

When it was time to go into town, I started to walk in. At Mount Street Bridge and down towards Grand Canal Street end, knots of people had collected and were chattering earnestly and excitedly, and a man inquired of a woman as he passed, 'Is there anything up?'

And she said, 'It is them Sinn Feiners, or whatever you call them, are about.'

All down Mount Street people collected in groups, and I began to notice no trams passed and many people with children and baskets of eatables passed me walking from the city. Dark, threatening, ominous clouds hovered all around in the sky, and something oppressive was in the air, and I couldn't tell what. Very few cars or motors were to be seen about, and most people chatted in groups along the way. Somehow I soon felt something unusual was happening, and, as I passed along Merrion Square, a series of noises resembling the falling of corrugated iron from a great height lasted for about a minute and then ceased, and I thought for the time being it was something falling over at the new science building. Now and again as I walked along Nassau Street, I heard the same strange sounds. I knew by this time that there was something out of the common in the air. At the printseller Howe's window in Nassau Street as I passed, a man with two ladies looked in at a bas-relief of a nude infant marked 7/6, and he was saying, 'I would think it worth 7/6 if it were real.'

At Grafton Street corner and all down towards O'Connell

Street and up Grafton Street, crowds spoke excitedly, yet I walked on towards Dame Street. An odd soldier could be seen about, but never a policeman, and it was not till I came to George's Street corner did I enquire what was happening in the city. And a youth said, 'Firing is going on in many places, but you are safe where you are.' Then he added, 'I know as I am one of them.'

I went on and found the Empire² doors closed, and a few in front talking. I asked a man at corner of lane, [*sic*] 'Will there be any matinee?' and he said he didn't know. There was one advertised for 2.30, but it was that now and no doors open. So I went down the laneway, and at Essex Street corner I saw three of the actresses chatting to people at the corner in an excited state. From Anglesea Street I went on to the quays and found them deserted. No trams, no cars, and but few people about.

I passed a hoarding and read a Proclamation pasted up which caught my eye at once. It had a Gaelic heading and went on to state that Ireland was now under Republican Government, and they hoped with God's help, etc., etc., to do justly to their own countrypeople. It was signed by seven names including T.J. Clarke (who headed the list), Thomas MacDonagh, Joseph Plunkett, P.H. Pearse of St Enda's, James Connolly and two others in Gaelic characters. It was a long and floridly worded document full of high hopes.

Having read it, I went on towards O'Connell Bridge and saw great crowds up the street especially near the GPO, and as occasional shots were to be heard I did not venture up, but went round by Marlborough Street. Seeing Ervine and O'Donovan outside the Abbey chatting, I went over to them. (I had previously met Mr Mannix and his wife and the bell porter and pit-entrance keeper of the Abbey near the Metal Bridge, and they it was who first told me of some of the happenings of the day. The Abbey was closed for matinees. They said the GPO had been captured early that morning and companies of Volunteers were entrenched in Stephen's Green and Westland Row Railway Station was in their hands also. Some soldiers – Lancers – had been shot on O'Connell Street and their horses as well. All the windows of the GPO were smashed, and Kelly's gunshop broken into and looted. The police had been called off the streets and one shot dead at the entrance to the Castle.) Ervine and O'Donovan told me more or less the same thing over again. As we spoke, two men passed up old Abbey Street leisurely, one with a pair of new ladies' boots under each arm, and the other with two boot boxes under his. On seeing them, we surmised looting was going on. (Afterwards I heard it was Tyler's at the corner of Earl Street and also Noblett's.) Down Abbey Street towards Earl Street, rushes took place every now and then, and I decided to face home …

It was rumoured that the mysterious stranger who was taken in Kerry was Sir Roger Casement, and that a cruiser full of Germans had been sunk off the coast …

Most of the Volunteers felt that the government intended suppressing them, and they thought it as well to take the bull by the horns, and take their oppressors unaware, and give a blow for Ireland before they died. No matter when for Erin dear they fell! They had been ridiculed as tin-pike soldiers, but they would show the world that they were boys with hearts undaunted in the cause of Ireland's liberty …

I met Charles Dawson, Jr, and a big friend of his with him. They were going in to see what has happened in the city. All sorts of rumours were about. The big one said, 'If they wanted to fight, why didn't they go out to fight Germans?'

I said, 'Because they are Irish!'

And he replied, 'Anyone with a stake in the country is against the Germans. If they got uppermost, they would take everything.'

I said, 'It is only fighting for one plunderer to keep off another.' Those who were ready to die today preferred to die on Irish soil for Ireland! Of course, he couldn't see it in that light, being an Imperialist …

I met Tom Nally and his sister-in-law going in towards town … Nally wondered what the fate of his play would be, and I added, 'Now two stirring events are taking place at the same time!'[3] I walked back with them into town and heard shots now and then as we went towards town … All was quiet and we walked as far as O'Connell Bridge, and then Nally said he'd like to see the Proclamation, and I took him on to read it. Quite a number were doing the same … A drunken soldier loitered about the quay, and a crowd rushed over the bridge. We parted at the corner of Westmoreland Street, they to go home by Great Brunswick Street, and I to go on to Eileen by Marlborough Street …[4]

As I came out of Eileen's, I met Jim Moran and wife … They had been all around and walked close to the GPO, and saw the muzzles of the guns pointing out, and mere youths of fifteen or sixteen behind each of them. They were also up at the Green. There was a barricade across at the Shelbourne, that gave them to understand that the hotel was in military hands. They spoke to a policeman at Store Street, and he said, 'We're not very likely going out with only batons to be shot.' At Stephen's Green a woman had asked one of the Volunteers, 'What are you doing there?' And he said simply, 'Defending Ireland!' ...

On parting I met Father Dinneen and a friend chatting at the corner of O'Connell Street, and while lamenting the course things had taken, Father said they were more or less driven to it by the action of the Government towards them ...

On parting I came home by Marlborough Street and found it strewn with boot boxes and boys and women in every direction with pairs of boots or boxes. A rush came up Earl Street into Marlborough Street and I went by, and I saw Mannix and his wife go towards the Abbey, which was all in darkness as I passed. The quays were quiet. I crossed Butt Bridge and looking towards O'Connell Bridge saw all the lights dancing gleefully in the water, long jagged swords of various colours, and I thought of the slaying of good Irish youth on the morrow.

Tuesday, April 25

I didn't sleep a wink all the night, and through the night and early morning shots were continually fired very close at hand. I counted over thirty at least, and some of them seemed right under the window. Ellen came up to tell me there was no gas in the stove or jets, and I concluded that the firing had been around the gasometer. Shots were fired from Haddington Road corner, and also from Schools at [Mount Street] bridge at a soldier in a motor going into Dublin.[5] In fact, Mr Cussin's house had been commandeered, and two machine guns mounted ready for action in the drawing room. The Armstrongs cleared away next door ...

There is an ominous silence over all things. Nothing to be heard save the occasional whiz past of a motor cycle or the footfalls of people walking past, with sounds of shooting emphasising the silence frequently. Poor brave fellows, it is sad to think that those who serve Cathleen ni Houlihan must give her themselves, must give her all.

Lawrence came in on his way from town and told me he had been out all the morning ... Nally's play has been postponed till next week. The military occupy the Shelbourne Hotel and are firing volley after volley into the Green on the Volunteers therein. The Countess Markievicz is with them in the Green. Lawrence saw one of the Volunteers lying dead near the railing inside the Green. Many of the shops in O'Connell Street are being looted by the populace. Sheehy-Skeffington has called on the citizens to form into a body of special constables and guard the people's property[6] ... Those entrenched in the Green commandeered all sorts of things – motors, etc. They ordered one old cabman to stop, and when he didn't shot his horse, and he soon fled away leaving all after him.

After dinner I left home and went over to 5 Cavendish Row to stop with Eileen till the trouble was over. ... All day excitement ran high in O'Connell Street, and several shops near the Pillar were looted, and Lawrence's set on fire. It was a day of dread and suspense.

Wednesday, April 26
This was a day full of dread happenings with firing kept up all during the night, and the terrible booming of cannon was to be heard shortly after eight with the whizzing, prolonged, weird, wave-like sounds of the machine guns coursing through the air. We afterwards heard it was a warship in the Liffey blowing up Liberty Hall, the headquarters of the Citizen Army. Early in the morning, O'Connell Street was cleared of all people,

and soldiers fired on anyone who crossed over by Parnell Monument and succeeded in taking down a poor woman at the foot of the Monument and also a man near the pathway. Two men rushed out and carried the woman off the street, and an ambulance removed the man. And as they did, I saw a man rush out and take a snapshot. A terrible fusillade of rifles was kept up each minute in the day almost, and the cannon boomed afar off, and the machine guns zigged out their cargoes of death and destruction frequently. The Republican flag floated over the GPO through it all, and, when darkness came on, the din of firing died down, and almost ceased altogether during the night. The sharp pong-pong of the rifles at intervals only made the dread silence after the din earlier in the day all the more terribly impressive. The sun shone out for the most part of the day, and the twitter of birds could be heard amid the noise of strife.

Thursday, April 27

The birds twittered in the eaves, and the sun came out early, and the bells tolled for 7 and 8 o'clock Mass, and shots were constantly being heard afar off. Things were fairly quiet till close on the stroke of twelve, and then came the most awful ten minutes of cannonading and shooting, I am sure the ears of human beings ever heard. Afterwards dead silence followed for a long time, with occasional volleys of shots to punctuate the silence. Scarcely anything was astir in the streets after the awful din – save a boy coming along past the Rotunda whistling shrilly, and a pigeon alighting on the roadway in search for a meal. ... Looking down the deserted O'Connell Street with the dead horse lying as it was shot under a Lancer on Monday last, one thought desolation had come on the city so gay and normal but a few days ago. It was awful to contemplate what was happening and which of your friends were in the thick of the fray.

I write this as I sit in the parlour at No. 5 Cavendish Row, from the window of which room I can command a view of O'Connell Street and can see the flag of the Irish Republic still floating over the GPO. Please God, out of all this carnage and destruction may come good, and that it may open the eyes of England to the fact that there must be something rotten in her government if this country can make such a thing possible in the twentieth century and in the midst of England's troubles abroad. That hundreds of young men were willing to sacrifice their young and valuable lives to drive this fact home is an arresting condemnation of power misapplied. They died, poor misguided youths, for an ideal; where, to my mind, they would be far more useful to the country alive. I always hated warfare and bloodshed, and never more than at the present moment, and was always against the use of arms in this country. But Carson's armed forces up north were the only thing that made the arming of the rest of the country possible, and the blind eye being given to Carson's seditious utterances and the persecution of the Irish Volunteers for the same cause clearly proved to the latter that there was one law for those who hated and another for those who loved their own land ...

At a quarter to three, an awful din filled the air all around, and, as Eileen went down to see about dinner, I noticed a company of soldiers scaling the rails of the Rotunda opposite, and by the aid of step-ladders reaching the roof of the new annex and vestibule, and I called down to Eileen, 'What is happening?'

And a sort of panic seized us all, and dinner was soon forgotten, and we all at last got into the doctor's study at the back of the house, as the safest retreat from the fusillade all round. Earlier the officer told me to get away from the window as he gave orders to his men to 'Fire up the street!' And from that forward the noise was terrifying, and the booming of cannons close by was the most appalling sound I ever heard, I think. For the rest of the day all was chaos, and poor Eileen almost became hysterical with fear every time William left the room in dread he might look out and get shot. We all spent an awful afternoon ...

A lull came with the dark, but during the night repeated dull booming shots were fired, as if they were blowing in the entrance of the GPO which seemed to withstand all attempts to shatter it.

Friday, April 28
... After a day of most awful noises – musketry, cannon, machine guns, etc., etc. – about five o'clock the roof of the GPO took fire, and then the shooting had begun in real earnest. Regiments of soldiers had been passing through Parnell Street during the afternoon on their way to surround the Henry Street block for fear of any of those taking part in the GPO escaping, so that when the place went on fire and they saw some of those in the building hasten away as if to make their escape behind, the military instantly set to work to set the whole block on fire, and succeeded in doing so, and a fire the like of which was never seen in Dublin before was the result. Some hours later, the roof of the GPO fell in with a crash, and a mighty cauldron of flame rushed up into the skies. All the while through the

smoke, every now and then, the little green flag still waved from its post defying the flames to demolish it. The firing, deafening and terrible, continued all the while, and from the Rotunda and the National Bank a continuous fusillade was kept up. The glare from the GPO lit up the heart of the city. Cannon went noisily rumbling along, and an armoured car hastened out of O'Connell Street and up Parnell Street towards Capel Street, and all was excitement and bustle with the military. We wondered what was really happening, and if any of those who were in the GPO escaped alive. The Rotunda had become the Military Headquarters for the time being, and Cavendish Row became within its area. I was almost maddened by depression. Just as darkness closed in, I saw that the little flag had disappeared, and the fire still burned fiercely within the grey stone shell of the ruined building. All of us thought that with the darkness would come some spell of restful silence, but, alas, no, such was not to be. Volunteers were discovered to be in the YMCA building near the top of O'Connell Street, who had been firing on the military, and a cannon was mounted at the corner of the street opposite and boomed away continually for some time amid continuously kept up rifle fire. It was a night of horror and noise. There was a great blaze afar, looking across the Rotunda.

Saturday, April 29

On looking out next morning, one could see the damage done by the cannon's thrilling booms ... Fierce fires raged up near the GPO in O'Connell Street, and an engine of the Fire Brigade passed the sentries on duty at Cavendish Row ... One old man on being put back said, 'Damn it all, man, you've beaten them. What more do you want?'

To a poor woman the sentry said, 'Get on the other side.' But she didn't know what he said and murmured, 'It's a lovely Saturday.'...

Later on as I went to bed, I looked out and saw the flame-tipped urn on top of the Parnell Statue silhouetted against the glowing sky. All the block from Middle Abbey Street to Liffey Street was ablaze it seemed. Towards evening a company of Volunteer prisoners arrived and took their stand beside the Parnell Statue to have their names taken down by an officer. They were twenty-two in all, some of them mere boys and most of them starved, hungry-looking poor fellows. One was a stout middle-aged man. None wore uniforms, but a sturdy little boy had on the cap of the Citizen Army ... Shortly after, another company of prisoners came marching down O'Connell Street, and, having laid down their arms in the middle of the street, ranged themselves along the Rotunda side of O'Connell Street in single file to have their names taken. Later on a big company of Volunteers bearing a flag in front came along in fine marching order, and, halt being called, they stood at ease, and, dropping all their guns and trappings, retired to the pathway this side of the Gresham Hotel. It was a most dramatic moment when they marched down the street. ... I wonder what they thought as they stood there in the street and saw all the destruction that had come in the city since last Monday at noon.

Wednesday, May 3
Pearse and MacDonagh were shot today.

'A GOOD DEAL OF PLAY-ACTING WAS KEPT UP BY THE SINN FEINERS'

Although later to become canon of St Patrick's Cathedral Dublin, in 1916 Henry Cameron Lyster was working in the parish of Enniscorthy. In his memoirs he gives an account of the Easter Rising as it affected his parish.[1]

Chapter XIV – The Rebellion of 1916
I must now turn to matters of more important public interest, and give an account of the events connected with the rebellion of 1916, and the subsequent troubles in Co. Wexford. As far as I know, no accurate account of these things has ever been written.

On Tuesday morning in Easter Week, we learned in Enniscorthy that there had been some rioting in Dublin the previous day, but none of us, I think, realised the seriousness of the situation.

It was Fair Day in Enniscorthy, and the town was full of people, amongst whom there was considerable excitement, but nothing out of the common happened. In the evening we held our annual Easter Vestry at St Mary's, and as I walked home about 9.30 p.m., the town was absolutely quiet, scarcely a soul stirring.

However, the next morning we learned that serious happenings had taken place in the night. There were two workmen doing a job to one of my outhouses, and when they came to work at 8 a.m. they told us that a large body of Sinn Fein troops had taken possession of the town during the night, and that District Inspector Heggart and eight members of the Royal Irish Constabulary were besieged in the Police barracks.

Immediately after breakfast I started to go down town. I met Mr F.R. West, sub-agent of the Bank of Ireland, who lived at Clonhaston, a short distance beyond the Rectory. He told me that it was quite impossible for the Bank to open, and that indeed it was not safe to go through the streets, as stray shots were constantly being fired.

The Sinn Feiners had cut down a big tree at the Cross Roads just beyond the Rectory, to block the road. The town was full of men in uniform, or rather of boys. At first no shops were open, but the Sinn Fein authorities issued an order that all the shops should open, except the public-houses. The sale of drink was strictly prohibited.

For four days we remained in complete isolation from the outside world. There were no trains, no newspapers, no letters, and the telegraph wires were all cut. It was before the days of wireless. We had not the least idea whether similar events had taken place in other parts of the country or not.

A good deal of play-acting was kept up by the Sinn Feiners. They marched through the streets, and they posted sentries at all the roads leading to the town. They had commandeered all the motor-cars in the place, and every few hours a car would come up to relieve [the] guard.

The rectory is outside the urban area, and if I went into the town, it was necessary for me to go to the Athenaeum, where the rebel head-quarters was, to get a permit before I could return home; but the rebel soldiers were always most respectful.

A detachment was sent round to search for arms. They came to my gate lodge and asked if there were any arms there. They were told that there were not. They then sent one of their number up to the house, but he never came into the house at all, and after a few minutes he went back and told the men at the Lodge that there were no arms in the Rectory. As a matter of fact, I had a shot gun.

At last, on Saturday afternoon, I got a letter from Father Fitzhenry Adm, [Roman Catholic parish administrator], asking me to attend a meeting of a Peace Committee at the Technical School at 6 p.m. I went down and found a committee assembled consisting of Father Fitzhenry, Father Rossiter, Messrs P. O'Neill, Chairman of the Urban Council, Henry Roche, P. Byrne, H.J. Buttle and Norman Davis. I may say that the following week we all figured in the *Daily Sketch* as 'The men who saved Enniscorthy'.

Mr O'Neill and Mr Roche told us that workmen of theirs had come into the town from Wexford and New Ross, and had informed them that Col. French, in command of a considerable force of British troops, was in Wexford, and that he intended attacking Enniscorthy on Sunday, if the town were not surrendered. The position was very serious, and we discussed at length what ought to be done. Mr Buttle suggested that we ought to get in touch with Col. French, and finally it was agreed that Father Fitzhenry, Mr O'Neill, and Mr Buttle should ask permission from the Sinn Fein authorities to go to Wexford to interview Col. French.

Father Fitzhenry and Mr O'Neill went over to the Athenaeum to see those in command there. They were absent for nearly an hour, and when they came back, they told us that they had had great difficulty in obtaining the permission they wanted. The Sinn Fein leaders said they wanted to fight French, not to interview him. They had, I believe, made certain military plans. The houses near the Bridge were to be occupied by Sinn Feiners, and as the British troops marched up the quay they were to be shot down. This was the plan that was so successfully carried out at Northumberland road in Dublin. But the Enniscorthy leaders forgot there was such a thing as artillery.

In the end the desired permission was given, and a motor car was procured to take the delegates to Wexford. When they reached Ferry Carrig Bridge, two miles from Wexford, they found it held by British troops, under the command of Major Warren. He told them that under no circumstances whatever could they be allowed to pass. He seemed to assume that they were rebels. They assured him that they were not, that they were unarmed men, and that all they wanted was to be taken to Col. French. At last, after three quarters of an hour's parley, Major Warren consented to accompany them to Col. French.

With Col. French was Col. H. Jameson Davis, who was an Enniscorthy man, and was Colonel of the National Volunteers in Co. Wexford. When the rebellion broke out in Dublin, Col. Davis, who was in London, hurried over to Wexford and called out the National Volunteers, who held Wexford against the Sinn Feiners for two days, until the arrival of the British troops.

Col. Davis told Col. French that he could vouch personally for all delegates, and that he might implicitly rely on everything that they said. The delegates said that they had come to ask him what would be the terms of peace, so that they might inform the leaders at Enniscorthy. He replied that of course he could accept no terms but the absolute and unconditional surrender of the Sinn Fein leaders. He told them that the Rebellion was over in Dublin, that the Post Office and Liberty Hall had been bombarded and destroyed, and that Pearse and the other rebel leaders had surrendered.

'I have a large force of troops here in Wexford,' said he, 'and I have a big gun posted on Bree Hill. If the town is not surrendered, I shall issue notice to the civilian inhabitants to withdraw, and I shall bombard the town.'

The delegates were greatly alarmed at this, and they hurried back to Enniscorthy to lay the situation before the Sinn Fein leaders, arriving about 2 a.m. They found the rebel leaders impossible to deal with. They said that they did not believe a word of what French said, that it was all bluff. The delegates did not know what to do. They knew very well that it was not bluff, and they decided to go back and interview Col. French a second time. It was very fortunate that Col. French, who was a Co. Wexford man and understood the people he was dealing with, was in command of the troops. Col. French shewed them a telegram he had received, in which Pearse acknowledged to defeat, and advised all his followers to surrender. He gave them a copy of this telegram, and also two safe-conducts for the rebel leaders which would enable them to go to Dublin and see for themselves what had taken place there.

Bearing these documents the delegates returned to Enniscorthy, and at 7.30 two of the leaders, Messrs Etchingham and Brennan, started in a motor-car for Dublin. At Camolin they met with a British out-post, to whom they shewed their safe-conducts. Two officers got into the car with them and accompanied them to Dublin.

Meanwhile, we had a very quiet day in Enniscorthy. The

evening before we had thought that it would not be possible to hold services in the various Churches. However, at 10 a.m. the Peace Committee met again at the Technical School, and the delegates told us of their adventures during the night. I told the sexton to ring the bell of S. Mary's as usual for the 11.30 a.m. service, and we had a fair congregation. It was strange that we should be praying for the King and the British Army, while the rebel sentries were on guard outside!

In the afternoon I went over to take service at the County Home, and on my return, I was challenged by the sentry to shew my permit. 'I expect this is the last time I shall have to challenge you, Sir,' he said, 'and a good job too.'

Evening service in S. Mary's was held as usual at 7 p.m. When my curate, the Rev. John Levis, and I came out, the streets were full of people standing about, and in a few minutes a motor car arrived, containing Etchingham and Brennan, who went into the Athenaeum. We stood in the street for some time, and then at my suggestion, we went up to the rectory for supper. After supper Mr Levis went down town again, and after a short time he returned to tell us that Etchingham had come out and addressed the people in the Market Square. He told them that their friends in Dublin had been beaten, that many had been killed, and that the rest had surrendered. In order to avoid bloodshed, he and the other leaders in Enniscorthy had agreed to surrender to Col. French the next day. Meanwhile he recommended all the Sinn Fein troops to disperse. A large number of motor cars had been commandeered, and these were all quickly filled and driven off to the mountains. They were found abandoned all over the country the next day.

Early next morning an armoured train came in from Wexford containing a party of the Royal Engineers, who quickly set themselves to repair the rails and telegraph wires that had been destroyed. They were rather afraid of the tunnel coming into the station, thinking that bombs might have been placed there, so they threw a powerful searchlight before them. Shortly afterwards a party of the South Irish Horse rode into the town, followed soon after by the Connaught Rangers.

About 1 p.m. Col. French arrived in a motor car, accompanied by Col. Jameson Davis. Etchingham and the five other Sinn Fein leaders put on their full dress uniform and went and had themselves photographed. They then surrendered to Col. French, and were placed in motor cars and conveyed to Waterford Gaol.

The Rebellion of 1916 in Co. Wexford was over, fortunately without any bloodshed.

'IT ALWAYS GIVES AN IRISHMAN OF THE LOWER CLASS IMMENSE PLEASURE TO CUT DOWN A TREE THAT DOES NOT BELONG TO HIM'

Moira O'Neill was the pseudonym of Agnes Shakespeare Higginson, an Irish poet and songwriter born into the Anglo-Irish ascendency, who lived in Ireland and Canada. At the time of the 1916 rebellion, she was living near Ferns, County Wexford, and an account of her experiences appeared in the June 1916 issue of Blackwood's Magazine.[1]

We have been 'held up,' as they say on the other side of the Atlantic. Every one knows the expression now, but not every one has had the experience.

It began here on Easter Tuesday, 25 April, and our first intimation of something being wrong was that we got no second post. There came instead a message from the post office that the Sinn Feiners had risen in Dublin, seized the General Post Office, and cut the wires. We do not believe implicitly everything that comes from the local post office. But my husband had started for Dublin by the early morning train, and I began to wonder how he would get either there or back; for they said the railway line was cut somewhere.

In the evening we went to a village concert for the help of

the Nursing Fund. After waiting a while, we were informed that there would be no concert, as the 'star' could not get down from Dublin, or even send a wire. 'All communication was cut off.' There was something distinctly ominous in those words; and we felt thoughtful as we drove home through the cold evening mist along the riverside.

The village we had left was quieter than usual at 7.30 p.m. Our own village nearer home was really unnaturally quiet. Lights everywhere, but no one visible: the people seemed to be all behind their own doors, which is just the place they generally avoid at that hour.

About nine o'clock we heard a motor-car at the door, and my husband got out of it. He had been to Dublin, and we could hardly believe the things he had actually seen and heard. Barricades at the street corners, rebels in green uniform and out of it firing at every soldier they could find in the streets, shooting them down and then shooting any one who went to help them – rebels entrenched in Stephen's Green and already hiding their heads from the soldiers who were firing at them from the roof of the Shelbourne Hotel. A wounded officer near Portobello Bridge was actually murdered, and no one dared to bring in his body from the street where it lay, for fear of being killed themselves. An everlasting disgrace to the city. But these Sinn Feiners cannot feel disgrace. They reverse every principle of civic decency, and their glory is in their shame. The only good news was that troops were being landed at Kingstown, and would march on Dublin straight.

We spent the night thinking of these things, and of our own position. We are here in Wexford, nine miles from Enniscorthy, which is about the most disloyal town in Ireland, where soldiers in uniform are hooted in the streets, where German victories are rejoiced in and magnified, and German atrocities are denied and ascribed to the malice of their British detractors. Enniscorthy is dominated by Vinegar Hill, the scene of the Irish rebellion of 1798, and a perpetual reminder of such savage cruelties and horrors as one might suppose the decent citizens of today would blush to remember. But quite the contrary! They have been loudly declaring for months past that they would make another stand on Vinegar Hill, that the 'glorious memories of '98' would be far excelled by the deeds they would do; and no one could possibly doubt that their intentions were serious. Only a few weeks ago two men were arrested in Dublin driving through Stephen's Green in a motor-car which was filled with rifles and bayonets, intended, as they plainly confessed, for Enniscorthy and Ferns. As Ferns is just five miles away, it seemed likely that our position would become an interesting one.

For five days after Easter Tuesday we could get no letters or papers. We knew that there was desperate street fighting going on in Dublin, and as British troops were there we knew that of course they would put down the rebels. But how soon? – that was the critical question. Would there be any troops to spare for Wexford? How many other risings of Sinn Feiners would take place between the four corners of Ireland? Had any German troops been landed on our sympathetic shores? These were the questions we debated among ourselves unceasingly, but there was no possibility of getting an answer to any of them.

On Thursday, April 27, came the expected news. The Sinn Feiners were up in Enniscorthy. They had seized the railway station, and held up a train, which was on its way from Wexford with 300 workmen for Kynoch's factory.[2] They had taken the 'Castle,' – no great feat – and had commandeered blankets, boots, tea, sugar, bacon, anything they needed, from the principal shops of the town. A lot of sugar was distributed among women in the poorest quarters, – a shrewd stroke for popularity. They held all the approaches to Enniscorthy, and barricaded them. Any one might come in, but no one could go out again without a 'pass'. They tried to take the police barracks, but the police held it against them. Now they had 'scouts' out, to watch for the soldiers coming, and were ready to cut the line and blow up the railway station at the first appearance of troops. It was impossible to find out how many there were of these rebels, but they were 'the full of Enniscorthy, anyway'; wearing green uniforms and big hats, carrying rifles and bayonets, and proclaiming the Irish Republic.

How long would they confine themselves to Enniscorthy? That was the point. They very soon sent out a detachment to Scarawalsh. Here there is a fine old bridge across the river Slaney, and it was said that they meant to blow up the bridge. But if so, they abandoned the idea, and built a barricade across the road instead, with some trees which they cut down. It always gives an Irishman of the lower class immense pleasure to cut down a tree that does not belong to him. Then began the raiding. Parties of Sinn Feiners went out to the country houses round Enniscorthy, held rifles to the heads of their owners, and demanded their guns and their motor-cars. They got them. As we heard of one house after another being held up in this way we became very thoughtful. For we did not intend to be held up if we could help it. We had no motor-car, but we had arms; and we kept watch both day and night. It was very tiring. Of course there was no possibility of concerting any plan of action with friends or loyal neighbours. No place is so isolated as a country house in a lonely spot. In the house with ourselves were my sister and our five children. I shall never forget those days of waiting and watching; waiting for the news from Dublin, watching for Sinn Feiners.

It was a week of absolutely lovely weather: sunshine and sweet air, apple blossom and cherry blossom everywhere, and this deadly anxiety day and night. We were quite aware of being watched ourselves, and we knew who were watching us.

The demeanour of the country people altered. In the beginning of the time they were carefully respectful. Then they began to look at us oddly, and to keep out of the way. On Saturday my husband went into the market-town, where there was a fair. He told me on his return that the excitement there was intense; but still the people held themselves in, and waited to see which side was going to come out on top. I was more ashamed of this than of anything else, except their shooting the unarmed soldiers in Dublin.

Before the end of the fair a Sinn Feiner on a bicycle came into the little town, an emissary from the precious Irish Republic in Enniscorthy. He informed the sergeant of police that the Sinn Feiners intended to march on the town that night and take it. The Sergeant told him to go about his business, and offered to give him a poke with his sword if he didn't take himself off. He did take himself off, a good deal disappointed; as he had expected to be arrested, and thought his arrest would serve for a signal to the townspeople to rise and join the Sinn Feiners.

This Sergeant is a brave and determined man. We knew of reasons why he was in real danger of the Sinn Feiners' vengeance, as in the course of his duty he had given them cause to fear him. That would be an interesting story, if one was at liberty to tell it. There were just four men in his Police Barracks; their windows were sand-bagged, and they were ready to defend the place. I think they would have defended it successfully too. The half-dozen police in the barracks at Enniscorthy held out most pluckily to the end, though they were in the thick of the rebels, were constantly sniped at, and were very short of food.

On that Saturday morning a motor drove up to our house, and its owner handed me a fine salmon which a kind friend had asked him to convey here. He said – 'I am taking a last drive in my motor, trying to get what provisions I can, – if I only have the luck to get home! They are sure to take my motor next.'

And they did, on the same evening.

I was very glad of the salmon, as my butcher had sent a message that he could supply no more meat, and from the Bakery came a letter explaining that 'Owing to the present disturbed state of the country it is impossible to get supplies. Consequently I am compelled to close down the Bakery for the present, and cannot undertake to deliver bread until the present difficulties are overcome.'

Both the butcher and the bakery's owner lived in Ferns, and they stood up to the Sinn Feiners like men, the butcher flatly refusing to kill any meat for them, even when they threatened to burn his house over his head. Ferns was full of the rabble for days; tramps and tinkers of all sorts joined them. Boys of fourteen and fifteen were given rifles and bayonets, and flourished them freely in the faces of respectable people, whether men or women; stopping them as they went in or out of the town, and making them go and ask for passes from the Provisional Government, as they called themselves. Robbery under arms was of daily occurrence, of course. The one thing they were really afraid of was the soldiers coming, and they seized every bicycle they could find, so as to be ready for instant flight, in emulation of their leaders in other people's motor-cars. Their leaders meantime took possession of the public-houses, and refused to sell drink to the townspeople; which caused some bitter feelings.

Naturally the rebels soon got out of hand, and a familiar sound began to be heard, of 'D'ye think I'm here to be takin' orders from the likes of you? Who are you, to be givin' me orders?'

A man who was leaving Ferns late in the evening, having provided himself with a 'pass' in the correct manner, asked for a light for his cart.

'Oh, don't trouble yourself, there's no more o' them rules now at all,' he was informed.

And like a true Home Ruler, no doubt he rejoiced in the summary abolition of all laws for the public safety.

How we longed in those days for the soldiers to come! Without papers or letters, and uncertain of what was happening in other places, hearing rumours and partly disbelieving them, knowing nothing about the safety of our relatives in different parts of Ireland, it was a wretched time indeed. There was a constantly repeated rumour of some incredible number of Germans having landed in Ireland, one day in the north, the next day in the south. No doubt the Sinn Feiners spread that, for they would hope it was true.

When Sunday came we remained unaware in our isolation here that the rebels had made an unconditional surrender in Dublin. Had we known it, we should have been saved some hours of a suspense that was growing almost intolerable. The raiders from Enniscorthy had been coming nearer every day; the last house from which they had taken a motor-car and searched for arms was less than three miles away. It seemed highly likely that they would come to us next, and probably choose the hour when we should all be away in church. My husband decided, therefore, to stay at home and take care of the place as best he could, while I went with my sister and the children to church; but our eldest boy stayed with his father. In the uniform of a Naval cadet he could not have gone out with us, as he would have been the mark for every rebel's insult and attack, and we had more than two miles to go to church. On the other hand, he was steady and a good shot, and I was glad of his being at home; though naturally I did not say so.

As we drove along the road where each Sunday morning we are accustomed to see familiar faces and exchange greetings, every door was shut, and not a creature was visible. It seemed like an uninhabited country until we got near the church gate. I think we were all thankful for the service, and as usually happens the Morning Psalms and the Litany uttered the thoughts that must have been in every mind –

'From all sedition, privy conspiracy, and rebellion, Good Lord, deliver us!'

After the service, it has been our habit since the war began to sing the first verse of the national anthem. It never before had such meaning for us as on that morning.

We drove home again through an empty country. Even at the cross-roads, where a public-house stands, and which I never before saw unattended by humanity, not a man was to be seen. But just beyond the cross-roads there is a deserted cottage, and glancing through its broken windows in passing I met several pairs of eyes looking out from the dirty gloom. They were eyes of men all sitting there quietly. The children went into fits of laughter at seeing them 'hiding in such a dirty place'. But I considered that they might have two reasons for being there: one good and the other bad.

It is hard for any one who has not lived in Ireland to understand how little liberty of action is permitted to the poor man, whether in town or country; but especially to the agricultural labourer. His father before him lived in bondage to the Land League, as he well remembers. He himself has been brought up in subjection to the Irish League, which is simply the Land League under another name. Of course he is supposed to obey his priest, and he is supposed to obey the law of the land; but the priest can be disobeyed nowadays without much fear of punishment, and as for the law of the land, it no longer even pretends to punish those who break it. But the Irish League will punish, and does punish severely; and it is the Irish League that he obeys. Now there are the Sinn Fein organisations, and the secret societies as well. He has been inveigled into one or other of these before he was twenty; probably he has signed a paper promising to 'come out' and bear arms whenever he is called upon, on pain of death, for the Irish Republic. I know of different men in this country who actually signed blank papers, not knowing what they were promising, but afraid to refuse the Sinn Feiners. The day of Rebellion came; they were called out, and had to go.

The first night they never left the rendezvous, but lay with others till morning, very wet, in a little wood. When morning came they received no orders, and so made off to their homes.

But they were called out again, and the second night they were not allowed to return. They had to be rebels; and of such reluctant material are rebels often made.

The men who remained at home were those whom we saw changing countenances from day to day. In another two days they would all have joined the force in Enniscorthy, from pure fear of remaining at home. The Sinn Fein leaders had an excellent idea of the way to influence waverers. They spread a report that there would be a Sinn Fein conscription throughout Ireland; any men who would not join were to be shot.

On Monday, May 1, we received authentic news that the rebel leaders in Dublin had made an unconditional surrender, and advised all others in the country to do the same. Then came the soldiers. We are not likely ever to forget the feelings with which we welcomed those soldiers. Few as they were, they brought back peace and order, and the reality of England's rule, to this divided and distracted County of Wexford. They did it without wasting one life or firing one shot. They came, and with them came a very heavy and persuasive gun, which the soldiers called 'Enniscorthy Emily'.[3] The sight of her was enough. She had no need to speak.

I shall not forget either the joy or relief on the faces of the country people at the very first tidings that the Rebellion was put down. It was impossible to mistake; their tongues can always deceive one, but not their faces. They had been absolutely terrorised by the Sinn Feiners; and if the Rebellion had lasted a week longer and these terrorised people had joined it, they would have been the most cruel of the lot. We are under no delusions about what would have happened.

It remains unaccountable how the leaders in Enniscorthy

controlled their following even for the short while that they did, and prevented them from getting drink. A severe penalty was denounced against any one who should give drink to a Sinn Feiner. But such an unnatural state of things could not have continued. Another mysterious thing is how the rebels escaped being shot by each other. Some indeed were wounded, but none killed; and considering the number of rifles and revolvers in hands which had never used weapons before, it seems little short of miraculous. Bayonets were given to boys of fourteen, who had the time of their lives, 'halting,' threatening, and driving people about. Of course in a very short while threatening would have become tame sport, and the real thing would have begun. As it was, the principal shopkeepers were held up by their own workpeople; in one case a well-known merchant was overpowered in his shop by two girls and a boy, who marched up to him with revolvers. Any worthless young woman who wanted some excitement put a Red Cross on her sleeve, called herself a Sinn Fein nurse, and rushed off with a raiding party, taking a revolver as a nursing outfit.

Two of these ministering angels were in Ferns when the scare was given that the soldiers were coming. They jumped into a stolen motor-car and were driven off at top speed by a Sinn Feiner, who knew as much about driving a motor as they knew about nursing. All went well until it was time to turn a corner at the foot of a steep hill. Here the motor, instead of turning the corner, charged straight into a cottage, and landed a damaged 'nurse' somewhere about the floor. She was soon recognised as a local dressmaker of small skill, and the opinion was expressed to me by a disgusted acquaintance that 'Her parents would have to be ashamed of her.'

Most of the raided motorcars were broken up very soon in much the same way, as there was no one who knew how to drive them; but every one was willing to try. I know of one that was returned to its owner after three days, with a letter of elaborate politeness and an illegible signature. All the notes of these days purported to be from the Provisional Government of the Irish Republic.

Here ends a trivial record of a time that finished in a fiasco, though it was intended to finish in blood. The things I have written of might have been treated very differently, and have made a more readable article. With a few touches of exaggeration it would be easy to give a more heroic and interesting aspect to our position, which was in reality humiliating and exasperating. Or again, one might take it from the ridiculous side, and turn it all into a bad joke, as nearly anything that happens in Ireland can be turned; call it a Rebellion *pour rire* in Wexford, with the fifteen-year-old warriors and the sham nurses, and the rest of it. Either of those methods would be a plausible *misrepresentation*, and at this time it is all-important that the simple truth should be told.

That truth is that the people of Ireland have acquired a profound contempt for the British government, which has so thoroughly deserved their contempt, which condones crime and disorder, refuses protection to the loyal and law-abiding subjects of the King, releases criminals from prison before half their time is served, and ostentatiously allies itself with their leaders. The old definition of a government's reason to exist, 'for the punishment of evil-doers, and for the praise of them that do well,' must be exactly reversed to fit the government we have had in Ireland, and which has brought us to this pass. Of course the people are not afraid to rebel. Why should they be? Is it likely that they have forgotten the lessons of 1911 – when a lowborn schemer called Larkin, posing as a Labour leader, and with the help of German money, raised such riots in Dublin that trade was paralysed and the streets became Pandemonium? What happened next? The brave policemen who, at the risk of their lives, had tried to keep order in the streets, were accused as murderers and put on trial; but the Citizen Army which was threatening to wreck the city was allowed to parade, to be drilled, and finally to be armed. The Citizen Army and the Sinn Feiners are one force now.

There was never any disguise about the objects of the Sinn Feiners. Indeed there was no necessity for any. In Ireland disloyalty is the chief recommendation to place and power; for loyal subjects do not command enough votes to make them of any importance to a British government anxious about its own tenure of office. When the Sinn Feiners avowed that their chief aim was to root out every sign of British domination in Ireland, they were only smiled upon and rather encouraged to proceed, especially as they became more numerous. Naturally their insolence increased. From the beginning of the war they have allied themselves with the Germans, cheered at their successes, helped their submarines, and maligned our Army. They have magnified the power of Germany to the ignorant country people, and persuaded them that the Huns have a peculiar tenderness for the Irish, and a special yearning to see Ireland 'free.' It is useless for any loyal person to try and open their eyes – to ask them, as I have repeatedly done, how they would like to have a German army landed here, and to see Ireland treated as Belgium has been?

'Ah, they would never do the like o' that here! Sure, they're not that sort o' people at all,' is the obstinate reply.

Is any one surprised at this? Let him remember that the ignorant and the unprincipled always believe whatever they wish to believe, that their invincible instinct is to join the side that is going to win, that as long as they can remember they have seen crime and outrage successful in Ireland, and loyalty penalised and discredited as if it were a crime.

Is it too late to ask of England now to show her strength, in which these rebels do not believe, to do justice and punish the wrong-doers who have openly boasted that she is afraid to punish them, to give us order and law, and save our beloved Ireland even now at the last hour?

Is it possible that the English people are still unaware that Germany is here, that her money has furnished the sinews of this Rebellion, that the Sinn Feiners were counting on German promises? – kept in the German fashion, as the event proved.

'CROCODILE TEARS BEING WEPT OVER THE POOR TRAITORS'

Although signed 'Dot', the following letter is contained in an envelope marked 'Geraldine on the Rebellion in Ireland, 1916', and addressed to 'Cecil Harmsworth Esq. MP, 28 Montague Square, London. w.'[1] The 1911 census lists just one Geraldine in Roebuck, Dundrum – Madeline Geraldine Thompson, but we can't be sure this is the same person. Cecil Harmsworth was a British businessman and politician.[2]

May 11 [1916]
Roebuck Hall, Co. Dublin
Telephone No. 33 Dundrum

My dearest Cecil

It did not occur to me that anybody would be anxious about *us*! Except for a little sniping at night, all is quiet, & we go in & out of Dublin unchallenged. Between this & Kingstown there were four lots of sentries to get through – & it was a work, literally of hours, to get on & off the Mail Boat. We had to see the boys off.

Here is a story –

A Cockney Johnny was heard to remark during the riots – 'This 'ere's a funny plyce. Ye gets cykes, oranges & bullets all out of the same 'ouse!' With Sinn Feiners parading the roofs & loyalists in the houses, there were many mistakes made.

When the enemy is – as often as not – dressed in civilian dress, & speaks the same language as yourself, you can imagine the muddle!

No ambitious man, in his senses, would take a billet in Ireland, in any capacity – & yet there have been one or two successes – why not a viceroy & chief secretary in one. A working viceroy in fact, like in India.

I hope Mum is all right.

People of all classes are sorry conscription was not extended to Ireland in spite of that Mr Redmond, who, by the way has very little power nowadays. The amazing number of professors who were in this Rebellion, & people in comfortable civil service, Guinness, & such like billets, is astonishing. And the crocodile tears being wept over the poor traitors who deserved all & more than they got. A very conservative estimate gives the killed & wounded in Dublin alone – of all sorts – military, police, civilians & Sinn Feiners at least 2,000.

In the new Republic, Pearse, shot for a traitor, was to be Provost of TCD!

Much love dear
Yours ever
Dot.

'GOD HAS KEEPING
OF A GOOD GIRL'S SOUL'

This final document is one of the most poignant included in the collection and is a moving reflection of the loss of civilian life as well as the distress caused to civilians caught up in the fighting of 1916. On 30 April 1916, Henry Dumbleton had the very unhappy job of writing to a woman to say that her daughter Bridget was dead. Henry was Works Manager with the Alliance and Dublin Consumers' Gas Company, of Sir John Rogerson's Quay, and Bridget appears to have been a servant in his home. She was shot dead in Henry's house on Thursday 27 April 1916. Neither her surname nor her mother's name are known.[1] This document powerfully illustrates the plight of the civilians caught up in the fighting of 1916: the helplessness of their situation, the fear they must have felt, and the chance that their experience of rebellion might well be fatal, even within their own home.

30th April 1916
Summerville
Clontarf

Dear Madam

It is with the deepest regret & sympathy I have to inform you that your daughter Bridget was shot by the military on Thursday morning last. This is the first possible occasion that I have been able to communicate with anybody either in or out of the city.

I cannot attempt to adequately express our sorrow which we feel except to say that we looked upon the dear girl as one of our own. We had no control over her removal from the house as the authorities took the matter in hands at once. However we would be obliged if you can come to Dublin at the earliest moment when the trouble is over & you can do so with safety, at the present it is not safe. It may be of some little consolation to you to know that she was shot by accident & in my house, also that she passed away peacefully & without knowing pain. I'll close this letter of sorrowful tidings with the knowledge that God has keeping of a good girl's soul.

Yours in sorrow,
H. Dumbleton
45, Sir John's Quay,
Dublin.

NOTES

INTRODUCTION

1 Notice issued by the authorities, 1916.

2 The accounts have been reproduced in their original form, including any quirks of grammar or punctuation, and using their original spellings, so there is some inconsistency in names like Stephen's/Stephens Green, Jacob's/Jacobs factory.

'THE STREETS ARE NOT EXACTLY HEALTH RESORTS'

1 National Library of Ireland (NLI) Manuscript (Ms) 36,172.

2 A terraced house in Sidney Street, in London's East End, was the scene of a famous, and fatal, gunfight between police and a gang of burglars on 3 January 1911.

3 Probably Jane Somerville, listed in the 1911 National Census as a hotel proprietress in 36 Kildare Street.

4 The siege of British Army troops in Kut-al-Amara ended on 29 April 1916, when General Charles Townshend unconditionally surrendered to the besieging Ottoman forces.

'AS HE LAY ON HIS BACK HE SPOUTED BLOOD LIKE A FOUNTAIN'

1 *The Salopian*, Vol XXXV, No. 12, 20 May 1916. The same issue contains the following notice: 'School Museum – Mr Ingrams and the Curator wish to thank: N. S. Norway for the gift of a Bomb and Piece of Morse apparatus from the Post Office burnt in the recent revolt in Dublin.' Unfortunately the school museum

no longer exists, and the donated bomb and Morse apparatus disappeared long ago.

2 These descriptions of summary executions are noteworthy, because accounts of incidents such as this, and the one immediately after, are extremely unusual in histories of the Rising. The second incident could possibly be dismissed as second-hand information, but Shute claims to have seen the 'postman's' execution himself.

'THE POOR DOG IS NEARLY OUT OF HER MIND'

1 Author's collection.
2 Under this date heading, Gloechler is describing things that happened on 25 and 26 April.
3 DBC = Dublin Bread Company, a café on O'Connell Street. The tallest building on the street, the DBC was occupied by rebels and eventually burned down and destroyed.
4 In 1916 Daylight Saving Time was introduced as a way of saving precious resources during wartime.
5 The US Consul-General was at 15 Merrion Square.
6 It was in fact Kevin O'Duffy's father, John, who was killed by a stray bullet during the Rising. John O'Duffy, 81, was a prominent dentist and a founder of the Dental Hospital in Dublin's Lincoln Place. His son, Kevin O'Duffy, was 'Dentist in Ordinary' to the Lord Lieutenant. The priest whose account of the Rising is reproduced in this anthology witnessed O'Duffy being shot on O'Connell Street – see page 87.
7 The three leaders shot on 3 May were Patrick Pearse, Thomas Clarke and Thomas MacDonagh. Clarke had a tobacconist's shop on Parnell Street.
8 When the rebels evacuated the GPO on Friday, they released their prisoners. Five days later (and four days after the surrender), two soldiers were found hiding in the ruins of the Coliseum Theatre on Henry Street. Apparently Sergeant Henry and Private Doyle

had found safety in the theatre, and there they remained, unaware that the rebellion was over, and without food, until discovered 'showing a dishevelled appearance [but] seemingly in good spirits'.

9   This may be an accidental reference to the same two soldiers.

10 The list of casualties in the *Sinn Fein Rebellion Handbook*, published by the *Weekly Irish Times* in 1916, has this entry: 'Mackenzie, Robert, provision merchant, was shot on Thursday, 27th April, at midday when sitting in his shop at the foot of Rutland square. Mr Mackenzie was one of the survivors of the *Lusitania* having had the remarkable experience of being rescued from that great disaster dryshod.'

'WAIT A MINUTE – HAVE A LOOK AT OUR CORPSE FIRST!'

1   *Those Days are Gone Away*, Hutchinson & Co., London, 1959. Unfortunately, from our point of view, the book is prefaced with the statement: 'Where proper names occur they are, in nearly every case, not those which the characters bore in life.'

2   In 1907 the Irish International Exhibition was held in Ballsbridge, just half a mile from the young Taaffe's house, on the site now occupied by Herbert Park. One of the permanent entertainments was the magic performed by the Indian Fakirs – 'a gang of depressed-looking, wizened men' – whose many daily performances were announced with the same florid speech again and again. Cousin William became obsessed with learning this speech, and later at home succeeded in repeating it, word- and tone-perfect, at a family performance.

3   *Embusqué* = a man who avoids military conscription by obtaining a government job.

4   The rebel was 20-year-old Gerald Keogh, returning to the GPO having delivered a dispatch to Stephen's Green. His body lay in an empty room for three days, before being buried in the college grounds, where it remained for two weeks.

5   OTC = the Officers' Training Corps of Dublin University (TCD).

6   The author has got this name slightly wrong. *George Rex* should be *Georgius Rex.*

'NOTWITHSTANDING THE SOUND OF MACHINE-GUNS AND CANNON, I WAS COMPLETELY ENGROSSED IN MY READING'

1   *The Years of my Pilgrimage – Random Reminiscences,* Edward Arnold & Co., London, 1924.

2   Ross was chairman of the committee, which dealt with the selection of Irish candidates for commissions in the British Army.

3   Oatlands was an eighteenth-century mansion in Mount Merrion, South Dublin, now home to Oatlands College, a boys' secondary school.

4   These were the Irish Volunteer Training Corps, referred to in many accounts as the GRs, because of the letters on the brassards they wore. GR = Georgius Rex (King George).

5   The legal Office of Master in Lunacy was formed around 1844 – its work involved hearing summonses, settling deeds, issuing orders, and administering the property of mentally disordered persons coming within its jurisdiction. http://discovery.nationalarchives. gov.uk/SearchUI/details?Uri=C679

6   VAD = Voluntary Aid Detachment.

7   Markievicz was actually second-in-command of the garrison, under Commandant Michael Mallin and it was he who surrendered the garrison.

8   George Wyndham was Chief Secretary for Ireland from 1900 to 1905.

9   Peter O'Brien, Lord Chief Justice of Ireland, 1889–1913.

10 Dublin Metropolitan Police Constable James O'Brien.

11 No longer will you give us your wonted jests.

'WITHIN THREE HOURS OF THE OUTBREAK OF FIGHTING, AN AMPUTATION WAS GOING ON'

1 *ESB Journal,* April 1966, Vol. VIII, No. 9.
2 According to the Journal, 'Mr Cassidy was awarded the Brigade's "VC", a gold medal for valour, for his courageous action under fire in rescuing the wounded man, Mr Michael Doyle.'

'ALL THAT MADE LIFE WORTHWHILE WAS BEING TAKEN FROM US FOREVER'

1 The 1911 census shows the Malcolm family, including then five-year-old John Eustace, sharing No. 24 Eden Quay. On census day there were only four children, ages five, four, two and one. By 1916 then, the older children would have been ten, nine, seven and six, while another four babies had been born into the family in the five years since 1911.
2 American poet John Greenleaf Whittier wrote a poem called 'Barbara Frietchie', which tells the legend of a woman in her nineties who leaned out her window to wave the Union flag in defiance of Confederate troops marching by. According to the poem, Confederate General Jackson was impressed and ashamed: '"Who touches a hair of yon grey head / Dies like a dog! March on!" he said ...'

'THE LITTLE WAR UP IN DUBLIN LEFT MAYO UNMOVED'

1 *The Years of the Shadow,* Constable and Company Ltd, London, 1919.
2 Tynan had previously lived in Shankill, south Dublin.
3 Grue = a shiver or shudder.

'HERE AND THERE YOU HAD TO STEP ASIDE TO AVOID A DEAD MAN'

1 The Gresham Hotel was closer to the top of Sackville Street than the Hammam.
2 Katharine Tynan Hinkson.
3 Now Parnell Street.

'THE CHIVALRY, THE MADNESS, THE INEVITABLE END'

1 Volunteers' accounts deny the oft-stated accusation that they were trying to blow up Nelson's Pillar. It seems that the rumour began because some rebels chose the safety of the pillar's solid base to test the quality of their home-made bombs.
2 Now the Olympia Theatre, Dame Street.
3 *Fons et origo* = source and origin.
4 A long-extinct ground sloth, the size of an elephant.

'THE PEOPLE WERE THOROUGHLY COWED'

1 *Struggle 1914–1920*, Ivor Nicholoson & Watson Ltd, London, 1935. Wrench's father was an Irish Land Commissioner and also sat on the Congested Districts Board. John Wrench wrote of him: 'I regret that [my father] identified himself so completely with the Unionist Party. I wish politically he could have been more detached. But no Englishman ever loved Ireland more than he did.'
2 Augustine Birrell was Chief Secretary for Ireland, resigning in the aftermath of the rebellion.

'HER DEAR BOY IS AT NORTH WALL WITH HIS MACHINE-GUN'

1 NLI Ms 24,553(2).
2 The 1911 census lists three families of Armstrongs on Pembroke

Road, but based on a later description of Mr Lane-Joynt's house (124 Pembroke Road) as 'a house immediately opposite the Armstrongs', the most likely reference is to the occupants of 73 Pembroke Road. In that case, Emmie is probably Emma Marjorie, daughter of Alice and Owen Armstrong. The writer also mentions Joan Armstrong further into the account, and the only Joan Armstrong on Pembroke Road in the 1911 census is also in No. 73 – but as a twelve-year-old domestic servant.

3   See account from *Irish Life* by 'A Civilian Eyewitness', pages 224– 5.

4   Arthur was Margaret's husband.

5   Most likely Jameson's Distillery in Marrowbone Lane.

6   The Irish Volunteer Training Corps, GR = Georgius Rex.

7   Francis H. Browning was a forty-seven-year-old barrister, living in 17 Herbert Park Road with his wife and family.

8   According to the 1911 census, Rose Le Peton and her husband, Alfred, lived in 4 Earlsfort Place with their three sons, Clive (19), Howard (16) and Desmond (13). In 1916 they would all have been of military age, so we can't say which of them was 'at North Wall with his machine-gun'. However, if we assume that the 'dear boy' was Mrs Le Peton's youngest son, then although he survived the Rising, he only had a few more months to live – the Commonwealth War Graves Commission lists two Le Peton casualties: one of them 2nd Lt Desmond A. Le Peton, who died 9 August 1916, aged 19. The other is Mrs Le Peton's oldest son, Lt Clive Alfred Le Peton, who died on 15 August 1917.

9   Several witness accounts talk of Sinn Féin machine guns, but there is no reliable evidence to show that the rebels actually possessed any, and it would be safe to assume that they didn't. One weapon that was used by a number of rebels (notably Countess Markievicz) was the Mauser C96 ('Broomhandle' or 'Peter the Painter'). This had a very high rate of fire of 1,000 rounds per

minute, so its sound could be mistaken for a machine gun.

10 *The Irish Times* commented that 'This regulation warns the citizen that the present military operations are not public entertainments, but a grim and dangerous business.'

11 This is probably Miss Wade's School for Young Ladies in 78 Morehampton Road, where the 1911 census lists Miss Georgina Constance Wade and her sister Miss Edith Octavia Wade as schoolmistresses.

'THE SOLDIERS HAVE COME AND WE REJOICE'

1 NLI Ms 46,627.

2 In 1916 Isabel P. Fleming was fifty-six and her mother, Elizabeth J. G. Fleming, was ninety-two.

3 Thirty-three-year-old Captain and Adjutant Frederick Christian Dietrichsen had marched with the troops from Dun Laoghaire (Kingstown). On the way, he was surprised to see his wife and children among the crowds of well-wishers – he had earlier sent them to Ireland to escape the growing threat of Zeppelin raids. He hugged them and continued on his way. Captain Dietrichsen was one of the first to fall when the rebels started shooting from 25 Northumberland Road. He is buried in Deans Grange Cemetery, Dublin.

4 Edward Carson was perhaps Northern Ireland's most famous Unionist politician, so 'Carson's Crowd' would refer to the anti-Home Rule movement.

'NOTHING TO SEE EXCEPT A DEAD HORSE LYING AT THE STREET CORNER'

1 NLI Ms 44,654 – both letters.

2 Maria was Bonaparte-Wyse's Russian-born wife.

3 Probably William Lucien, his eight-year-old son.

4 Possibly his daughters, Helen Victoria, 18, and Mary Alexandrine, 12.

5 'Boots' was the title given to a servant in a hotel who cleaned and blacked guests' boots and shoes.

6 Eoin MacNeill, Chief of Staff of the Irish Volunteers in 1916.

7 In this letter Ballsbridge is written in three different ways, Ball's Bridge, Ballsbridge and Balls Bridge. These have been left as in the original.

8 William Russell Lane-Joynt was a barrister, as well as a famous philatelist, Irish Revolver Champion and silver medallist in the 1908 Olympics (for shooting).

9 Officers' Training Corps.

10 Maurice Headlam wrote in 'Irish Reminiscences': 'I noticed that the dead horse was still lying outside my house, and, thinking that it would be a nuisance, I rang up the Zoo and asked them to take it away to feed the lions who might be getting short of food, which they gratefully did.'

11 The Report of the Royal Commission on the Rebellion in Ireland, 1916 – *'presented to both Houses of Parliament by Command of His Majesty'* on 26 June 1916.

'HEAR TRAMPING ON OUR ROOF AND SO DISCOVER THAT SOLDIERS ARE POSTED THERE'

1 Charles Deering McCormick Library of Special Collections, Northwestern University Library, Evanston, Illinois, USA. Call number I Irish D539.

2 Lady Chance was a daughter of William Martin Murphy, James Connolly's nemesis and pillar of the Dublin Lockout. She was romantically involved with Willie Beckett, father of Samuel, and it was to end that romance that she was married to Sir Arthur.

3 One of Sir Arthur Chance's sons befriended Noel Browne in school, the politician who as Minister for Health introduced the

controversial Mother and Child Scheme, and the Chance family paid his way through medical school in Trinity College Dublin.

4 At Arbour Hill, now known as St Brican's Military Hospital.

5 Charles Wisdom Hely was a magistrate, and one-time managing director of Helys Ltd, stationers and printers, for which role he garnered a mention in James Joyce's *Ulysses*, as a previous employer of Leopold Bloom.

6 Home of the Sheridan family.

7 Possibly a reference to an area of Dalkey nicknamed Khyber Pass.

8 It's possible these were looted goods.

9 Chance's twenty-four-year-old stepdaughter.

10 24 Lower Leeson Street.

11 It's most likely they were hearing the battle of Mount Street Bridge, the fiercest engagement of the rebellion – it was less than a kilometre away.

12 During the battle, the rebels occupied No. 1 Clanwilliam Place, from which the Wilson family were ejected. It was the first in a row of large three-storeyed houses directly facing the bridge, with commanding views over the approaches into the city. When the battle was over, Nos 1 and 2 were blazing, and Andrew and Janet Mathers of No. 2 sat on deckchairs in the garden, watching their house burn down.

13 Possibly the resumption of shelling in the O'Connell Street area.

14 It appears that this word, and another one in the same paragraph, have been deleted.

15 R. and A. Barrett, soap, chandlery and seed merchants, oil importers, etc. 20 Westland Row.

16 The Newmarket Dairy was at 5 Lower Merrion Street.

17 VAD = Voluntary Aid Detachment. The headquarters of the Irish War Hospital Supply Depot was at 40 Merrion Square, and was converted into a temporary hospital during the rebellion. See Thekla Bowser's account, from page 254.

18 Charles O'Connor, of 28 Fitzwilliam Place, was Solicitor-General and Master of the Rolls. He subsequently served in the Supreme Court under the Irish Free State.

19 For the view from Clare Street, see Michael O'Beirne's account, from page 158.

20 53 Merrion Square.

21 35 Merrion Square East.

22 Chance mentions this name twice, once as 'Lahmann's here beside us', and then as 'Lamans (here beside us)', and says the house was occupied by rebels. A business called Lahmann Agency was located in No. 2 Harcourt Place. Harcourt Place is now Lincoln Place/Fenian Street, and No. 2 is probably 36 or 37 Fenian Street.

23 See another description of this incident in Henry Robinson's account on page 197.

24 The surrender happened on Saturday, so this was a false rumour, possibly started when the rebels evacuated the GPO on Friday.

25 There is no reliable evidence to show that the rebels possessed any machine guns.

26 Judge Walter Boyd, of 66 Merrion Square, had two daughters, Alice Mary and Ida Jane.

27 Dr Richard Hayes, of 82 Merrion Square, had two sons, Richard and Edward.

'THEY'RE BARMY,' THE SOLDIER SAID. 'THAT'S WOT *THEY* ARE.'

1 *Mister – a Dublin childhood*, Blackstaff Press, Belfast, 1979.

2 See Lady Chance's account, from page 140. No doubt she and her neighbours were some of 'the quality'.

'THE WORK HAD TO BE DONE WHERE FIRING WAS IN PROGRESS'

1 'Irish Rebellion, 1916', in *The Post Office Electrical Engineers' Journal*, Vol. IX, July–September 1916. For more on this little-

tapped source of information, see *GPO Staff in 1916*, by Stephen Ferguson, Mercier Press, 2012.

'THIS LARKINITE & SINN FEIN RISING'

1 NLI Ms 46,626.
2 The county and date were handwritten under the printed address.
3 Joseph Malachy Kavanagh actually survived the inferno that engulfed the Royal Hibernian Academy in Lower Abbey Street. Having been appointed keeper in 1910, Kavanagh lived in the RHA and had his own studio there. The fire destroyed almost everything, and although he got out alive, Kavanagh wasn't able to save any of his own paintings. Consequently, examples of his work are rare.

'WI' THE SINN FEINERS IN DUBLIN'

1 Thanks to the *Ballymena Times* and *Observer*.
2 Wheen = small amount, or few.
3 'M'Keenstoon' was the name M'Keen often used for Ballymena.
4 'Hail Columbia' was often used as a euphemism for 'Hell' around the turn of the nineteenth and twentieth centuries.
5 Thrapple = throat.
6 Here the author is referring to an incident in the Second Boer War, when the town of Ladysmith, besieged by the Boers since November 1899, was relieved by British forces, the first arriving on 28 February 1900.
7 Ayont = beyond.
8 Thole = to put up with, endure.
9 Tile = a stiff hat.

'IT WAS A CREEPY BUSINESS DRIVING THROUGH THE DESERTED STREETS'

1 *Memories: Wise and Otherwise*, Cassell and Company Ltd, London, 1923.
2 Augustine Birrell was Chief Secretary for Ireland, resigning in the aftermath of the rebellion.
3 Sir Matthew Nathan, Under-Secretary for Ireland, who, like Augustine Birrell, resigned in the aftermath of the rebellion.
4 See another description of this incident in Lady Chance's account on pages 152–3.
5 Ivor Guest, 2nd Baron Wimborne, 1st Viscount Wimborne, was Lord Lieutenant of Ireland during the Rising.

'WHEN I SAW HIM HE HAD LESS THAN TWENTY MINUTES TO LIVE'

1 *Betrayal in Ireland: An eye-witness record of the tragic and terrible years of Revolution and Civil War in Ireland 1916–24*, The Northern Whig Ltd, Belfast (there is no date in the book, but it was most likely published in 1968).
2 On 30 July 1915 German forces drove British infantry out of the village of Hooge near Ypres, using flamethrowers to great effect.

'SACKVILLE STREET PRESENTED A BEWILDERING ASPECT'

1 The Dublin Coffee Palace was a temperance hall on Townsend Street, set up by the Dublin Total Abstinence Society.
2 Eustace Malcolm, along with parents and his seven brothers and sisters had already been evacuated from this block – see *The Refugees*, from page 65, for his story of these events.

'THE LOOTERS WERE WORKING WITH FRENZIED ENERGY'

1 Great Brunswick Street – now called Pearse Street.

'THOSE AWFUL DAYS WHEN THE RIOTERS LET LOOSE THEIR VIOLENCE UPON THE CITY'

1   *Britain's Civilian Volunteers: Authorised Story of British Voluntary Aid Detachment Work in the Great War,* Thekla Bowser, F.J.I., Serving Sister of the Order of St John of Jerusalem, Moffat, Yard and Co., New York 1917.

2   Sir John Lumsden, founder of the St John Ambulance Brigade of Ireland.

3   British Red Cross Society.

4   Upper Baggot Street, Dublin.

5   Located in Dun Laoghaire, then called Kingstown.

6   SJAB = St John Ambulance Brigade.

7   Grand Canal Street, Dublin.

'MOST OF THEM WERE STARVED, HUNGRY-LOOKING POOR FELLOWS'

1   Originally published in Robert Hogan & Michael J. O'Neill (eds), *Joseph Holloway's Abbey Theatre: A selection from his unpublished journal, Impressions of a Dublin Playgoer,* Southern Illinois University Press, London and Amsterdam, 1967. Copyright © 1967 by Southern Illinois University Press, reprinted by permission.

2   The Empire Theatre, now the Olympia Theatre, Dame Street.

3   Nally's *The Spancel of Death* was to have been produced on this day, but because of the Rising the performance was cancelled, and it remained unperformed until the 1980s.

4   Possibly Eileen O'Malley, Holloway's niece.

5   No. 25 Northumberland Road, just two doors away, was on the corner of Haddington Road. It was occupied by rebels and fiercely defended, resulting in many casualties.

6   Pacifist Francis Sheehy-Skeffington was later executed without trial by an army officer who was tried for the murder and found

guilty but insane. The author of this section is inconsistent in his hyphenation of the name.

'A GOOD DEAL OF PLAY-ACTING WAS KEPT UP BY THE SINN FEINERS'

1   *An Irish Parish in Changing Days*, Francis Griffiths, London, 1933.

'IT ALWAYS GIVES AN IRISHMAN OF THE LOWER CLASS IMMENSE PLEASURE TO CUT DOWN A TREE THAT DOES NOT BELONG TO HIM'

1   'During the rebellion in Wexford', *Blackwood's Magazine*, NY, June 1916. Higginson's daughter was the well-known author, Molly Keane. Thanks to her granddaughter, Josephine Slater, for giving permission to reproduce this article.
2   Kynoch's Ammunition Factory was in Arklow.
3   'Enniscorthy Emily' was a 15-pounder gun carried on an armoured train.

'CROCODILE TEARS BEING WEPT OVER THE POOR TRAITORS'

1   The w. indicates the Western and Paddington postcode area, also known as the London W postcode area, a group of postcode districts covering part of central and west London, England.
2   NLI Ms 46,627.

'GOD HAS KEEPING OF A GOOD GIRL'S SOUL'

1   NLI Ms 33,020.